Leading People the Black Belt Way

Conquering the Five Core Problems Facing Leaders Today

Timothy H. Warneka

Asogomi Publishing International
Cleveland, Ohio

First printing 2006.

Cover Design by: Patrick J. Warneka
Editor: Cheri Laser

LCCN: 2005903771
ISBN: 0-9768627-1-9

SPECIAL SALES:

Asogomi Publishing International books are available at special bulk purchase discounts to use for sales promotion, premiums, gifts, increasing magazine subscriptions or renewals, and educational purposes. Special books or book excerpts can also be created to fit specific needs. For information, please contact The Black Belt Consulting Group, P.O. Box 20, Cleveland, OH 44092, or email *Patrick@blackbeltconsultants.com.*

Attention readers: If you've had an experience with one of the Five Core Problems of Leadership—either as a leader or a person being led—and you've learned a valuable lesson as a result, share your story and help other people. You could be featured in an upcoming book. To submit your story for inclusion in a future book, please e-mail a copy to Tim Warneka at: leadershipstory@blackbeltconsultants.com or write to:

Leadership Stories
c/o The Black Belt Consulting Group
P. O. Box 20
Cleveland, OH 44092

Special notes to professional consultants & executive coaches: Please help us teach leaders about how to avoid or fix leadership problems. Send your insights to Tim Warneka at: leaderhelp@blackbeltconsultants. com

More International Praise for Leading People

"A well-researched, interesting and informative book that will both equip and inspire readers to become models of leadership for the 21st century. *Leading People* is a thought-provoking experience!"
- **Jim O'Dwyer**, Senior Consultant, Aegis Protective Services, U. K.

"Whether you've been studying Aikido for years or are brand new to it, *Leading People* is a must read!"
- **Pawel Olesiak**, Director, Aiki-Management Consulting, Cracow, Poland

"*Leading People* is a highly original text which draws from a variety of different disciplines. Readers can use Tim Warneka's strategies to improve not only their leadership roles but also their daily life."
- **Robert MacFarland**, Change management consultant, Sussex, England

"This is an excellent book."
- **John C. Kimbrough**, Yoga Teacher, Bangkok, Thailand

"A must read for every health professional, whether they are in a position of leadership or not."
- **Dr. Kirste Carlson**, N.D., CNS, The Cleveland Clinic Foundation

"Drawing wonderfully from Aikido principles, *Leading People* addresses the sorely-neglected issue of emotional satisfaction in the workplace. Tim provides invaluable insight and advice for leaders to lead well in this essential area. A straightforward and *very* important book!"
- **Jamie Zimron**, LPGA Pro/The Golf Sensei

"Leading people is an art and *Leading People* is the science behind that art. Every leader and aspiring leader should read this book."
- **Thomas Chalmers**, Life & Business Coach, Scotland

"*Leading People's* parallels between the disciplines of Aikido and Leadership really heightened my awareness of the need for total commitment—mind, body, and spirit—from all organizational leaders."
- **Jim Smith**, SPHR, President, People, Inc.

"A powerful handbook for leaders."
- **Lynn Williams, Ph.D.**

"Tim Warneka provides the information, insight, and practical tools every leader needs for realizing the full potential of their workforce. *Leading People* is a powerful and engaging book, bringing together a comprehensive scope of resources that bridge the gap between theory and action."
- **Susan Chandler**, President, Chandler Resources

"*Leading People* provides theory and practice for eliciting the best from both leaders and employees."
- **Barbara Cumming**, President, Springboard Consulting

"One does not 'manage' people.
The task is to lead people.
And the goal is to make productive the specific strengths
and knowledge of each individual."
- Peter F. Drucker

* * * * * * * * * * * * * *

"But, you were always a good man of business, Jacob," faltered
Scrooge, who now began to apply this to himself.
"Business!" cried the Ghost, wringing his hands again.
"Mankind was my business. The common welfare was my business;
charity, mercy, forbearance, and benevolence were all my
business. The dealings of my trade were but a drop of water in the
comprehensive ocean of my business!"
From: "A Christmas Carol", by Charles Dickens

* * * * * * * * * * * * * *

"To win without fighting is best."
- Sun Tzu

I dedicate this book to my many teachers (including my clients & students). I bow with deep gratitude to Master Morihei Ueshiba for bringing Aikido into the world. I further dedicate this book to my own children, Christopher & Bridget, and to children everywhere. May we as adults accept the challenge of transforming ourselves so that our children and their descendants may live on an Earth that is more peace-filled and rewarding than our present World.

-T.H.W.

1. Set Your Strategy
A. Lead People with Harmony
B. Use the Four Cornerstones

2. Take Your Stance
A. Leverage Body-Mind Technology
B. Develop Deep Knowledge
C. Use Process to Create Change

4. Assess Your Strategy
A. Many Ways Up the Mountain
B. Every Ending is a Beginning

3. Take Action
A. Seek Balance & Flexibility
B. Double Your Leadership Power
C. Lead Through Conflict

The Black Belt Cycle
of Leading People

TABLE OF CONTENTS

• *Story: The Leader Who Wanted to Know Everything* • *Laying Blame or Finding Solutions?* • *The Five Core Problems Facing Leaders Today* • *New Times, New Rules* • *Strengths & Biases* • *Aikido* • *Leading Out of Flatland* • *Does the World Really Need Another Book on Leadership?* • *You Get Two Books in One*

WHITE BELT
Section 1 – Set Your Strategy

Chapter 1.
• *Story: Understanding Harmony* • *Harmonious Emotional Engagement* • *Harmony–Mastering the Power* • *Emotions–Mastering the Balance* • *Engagement–Mastering the Connection* • *Putting It All Together* • *Commit to Starting Now* • *The Black Belt Cycle of Leading People* • *On Learning Experiments* • *Learning Experiment: Stretching Out, Warming Up* • *Chapter Summary Page*

Chapter 2.
• *Story: "You Can't Move Me!"* • *Why Leaders Fail* • *Pulling People Does Not Work...* • *...And Neither Does Pushing People* • *Beyond Pushing or Pulling: Black Belt Leadership* • *How Harmony in Leadership Creates Success* • *Spotlight: A Leadership Warrior* • *Conclusion* • *Learning Experiment: Are You Pushing or Pulling as a Leader?* • *Chapter Summary Page*

Chapter 3.
• *Story: "My Teacher is the Best!"* • *The Four Cornerstones* • *Cornerstone #1: The Power of Embodied Leadership* • *Cornerstone #2: The Power of Both-And Thinking* • *Cornerstone #3: The Power of Process* • *Cornerstone #4: The Power of Succeeding Through Mistakes & Limitations* • *Ten Tips to Make the Cornerstones Work for You* • *Learning Experiment: Practicing the Four Cornerstones* • *Chapter Summary Page*

YELLOW BELT
Section 2 – Take Your Stance

Acknowledgements

This work has truly been a two-and-a-half year labor of love for me, and I often felt more like an investigative reporter than an author during this time. The deeper I probed into the research, the more empirical support I discovered for the leadership approach I am suggesting here. No author creates from scratch, and I have been profoundly influenced by a vast number of wonderful people over the years, to whom I am enormously grateful.

First and foremost, I would like to thank my wife Beth and my children Christopher & Bridget, without whom this book would not have been possible. The truth is that this work was supported by generous "grants" of time from my children for "daddy's-working-on-his-book-again"; and from the "foundation" of my wife Beth working at her first-grade teaching job and doing more than her fair share of the housework. They all graciously tolerated the tremendous uncertainty, stacks of books, late nights and long days at the computer during the creation of this work. I couldn't have done this without them.

My undying thanks go out to my brother and business partner Patrick J. Warneka for all the late-night conversations and multiple visits (and re-writes) that helped me sharpen the focus of this present work. Patrick's wisdom and encyclopedic knowledge of mainstream leadership and motivational literature helped save this book from becoming a dry academic tome. His humor, flexibility and penetrating insight helped transform a black and white manuscript into the living, breathing work that you hold in your hands. Patrick served as a sounding board for, and co-creator of several sections and key principles in this book. He even had a hand in designing the cover! (Now that the book is done, I am quite certain that Patrick will not miss my calling him at all odd hours of the day and night.)

My deepest thanks go to Cheri Laser, my fearless editor. A consummate professional, as well as an author in her own right, Cheri was able to take my words and make them shine in a way that I never thought possible. She added sparkle to my examples and crispness to my points. Cheri is truly one of the best-kept secrets of the editing world.

In the martial arts tradition, acknowledging your teachers is considered respectful. I have had a number of teachers, both on and off the mat, whose influence touched this book. To Mark Lomasney, who simply listened. To the incredible people at the University of Dayton, including Ray Fitz, S.M.; Fr. Jim Heft, S.M.; Leanne Jablonksi, F.M.I.; Fr. Joseph Lackner, S.M.; Br. Tom Pieper, S.M.; Fr. Tom Schroer, S.M.; Bruce Giffin (now teaching at University of Cincinnati); and Conrad E. L'Heureux. During my graduate work, I was deeply influenced by Carl Rak of Cleveland State University. Each of them taught me about true leadership.

Thanks to my friends & colleagues on the staff of Crossroads Community Mental Health Center in Mentor, Ohio. My deepest thanks especially go out to my long-time mentor and friend Debbie Gurney Manzano, who saw the "diamond in the rough" long before I did, and who taught me the true meaning of systemic thinking. Further acknowledgement goes out to Rev. Annette Dimond, Suzanne Plumb, Patty Smith, Dori Garey and Bill White.

Thank you to all the wonderful teachers at the Gestalt Institute of Cleveland. My experiences were tremendous with Dan Jones, Lalei Gutierrez, Phil Belzunce, Mwalimu Imara, Mark Warren, Mark McConville, Marlene Moss Blumenthal, Michael Clemmens, John Carter, Debbie Dunkle, Mary Ann Kraus, Jim Kepner, Denise Tervo, Herb Stevenson, Arye Bursztyn, Dorothy Siminovitch, Rosanna Zavarella, Gordon Wheeler, Bob Lee, Peter Krembs, Karen Moran, Karen Flemming, Jay Brinegar, and Jody Niinita Telfair (who in many ways is my Aikido grandmother). Special thanks go to Lynne Kweder, a magical woman of unparalleled grace and vitality, who showed me Organizational Development in a new light. And to Jackie Lowe Stevenson, another magical woman, who taught me with her sacred grounds and fire and animals. Words fail me in expressing my appreciation to all of these wonderful teachers.

I hold deep appreciation for all of my fellow students in Gestalt. To Laurie Zuckerman for reminding me of the importance of slowing down and for being such a wonderful friend and teacher. To Ann Carr, for giving me a boost right when I needed it. To Linda Koenig, who taught me even better self-defense through grounding. To Gary Saltus, M.D., who taught me about the importance of re-visioning. Special thanks go to my Gestalt sister and fellow Aikidoka Kirste Carlson, and her wonderful husband, Dennis Dooley. Their warm presence, sharp intellects, and delicious hospitality have helped me more than they'll ever know.

My deepest thanks go out to my Aikido teachers; to the founder of Aikido, Morihei Ueshiba; to the first Doshu, Kisshomaru Ueshiba, who impacted my life significantly through one of his Aikido demonstrations; to Akira Tohei sensei, my first instructor, whose skill continues to teach; to Mary Heiny sensei, whose courage to discover the powerful point of creativity between despair and rage in the face of oppression and hatred has been of inestimable value to me; and to Paul Linden sensei, whose presence, skill, and support kept me connected to Aikido long after I would have given up, while his razor sharp intellect and cutting edge work in somatic process continually keeps me on my toes. I would also like to extend my on-going thanks to the community of instructors and students at the Cleveland Aikikai, especially Jim Klar, Jeff Hadley and Pat Tinkler.

Thank you to the worldwide Aiki Extensions (AE) community, especially Don Levine, whose vision, drive and tenacity helped make AE a reality in the world. In AE I have found a home among people who share a vision of how Aikido can help heal the world.

Thank you to Carol DeSanto, co-creator of *Nervous System Energy Work.* Your gentleness, compassion and discipline have helped me enormously.

Thanks to the teachers who have taught me through their writings (in no particular order), including Ken Wilber, Carl Jung, Daniel Goleman, Richard Boyatzis, Annie McKee, Peter Drucker, John Stevens, Joseph Campbell, Tom Peters, George Leonard, Pema Chodron, Maria-Louise Von Franz, Bill O'Hanlon, Lao Tzu, James Hillman, Thomas Moore, Roger Brooke, Alan Weiss, Peter Senge, Richard Strozzi Heckler, Peter Block, W. Edwards Deming, Burt Hellinger, Peter Drucker, Bessel van der Kolk, Alan Watts, D.T. Suzuki, Adele Westbrook & Oscar Ratti, Thomas Merton, Ashley Montagu and every other author listed in the bibliography.

Thank you to Wendy Palmer sensei, who was kind enough to contribute this book's foreword. Her writings and her compassionate insight helped me improve my work and grow personally. Wendy's presence and grace is a blessing to this world.

All of us are smarter than any one of us, and this book is proof. Thank you to the people who were kind enough to offer comments and observations that made the end product even better (in no particular order): Edwin Nevis, Richard Boyatzis, Riane Eisler, Debbie Gurney, Paul Linden, Kirste Carlson, Victor LaCerva, Ann Carr, Lynn Williams, Mary E. Warneka, James Johnson, Laina Saul, Sherry Greenleaf, Jennifer Druliner, Greg & Kristen Ulm, Thomas H. Warneka, Kate & Gus Cauldwell, Jamie Zimron, Arye Bursztyn, Barbara Cumming, Jan S. Nedin, Jamie Zimron, Donna Nowak, Cheryl McMillan, Meg Selbach, Janis Woodworth, Linda Pannell, Jim Smith, Dagmar Braun Celeste, Susan Chandler, Rick Warger, and Kathy Ray. Thank you to anyone I neglected to mention but should have.

My final thanks go to Johannes Gutenburg; to everyone who had a hand in developing the Internet; and to the creative forces that chose me as vehicle for this book, assisting me in ways that I am only now beginning to understand.

Any errors, omissions and/or slights are unintentional and remain my sole responsibility.

Foreword

By Wendy Palmer, 5th degree Aikido Black Belt

During the many years I have been practicing the Japanese martial art of Aikido, I have often thought of the connection between the challenges Aikido practitioners work with on the mat and the challenges that arise in the world of organizations. Both situations offer an opportunity to learn about and refine how we operate under pressure. Both situations allow us to discover our strengths and our weaknesses. And, if we have the courage, we can use the victories and defeats that we experience to strengthen our commitment and deepen our knowledge.

Leadership is at once obvious and mysterious. Like Aikido, leadership is a mind-body-spirit discipline calling us to create conditions that allow others to contribute effectively and whole-heartedly. From childhood to old age, leadership is a function that touches all of our lives, offering endless opportunities to refine our capacity to lead and be led.

When the phrase "black belt" and leadership are brought together in the same sentence, notions of strength, confidence and focus are conjured up. These are the more obvious aspects of leadership, and in our Aikido practice, we spend time on exercises that develop focus, confidence and strength. Yet the more mysterious sides of martial arts and leadership involve the study of our internal experience, primarily our emotions. Emotions are rarely spoken about or utilized as a comprehensive aspect of the training. As Tim explains, "By…continuing to believe that emotions do not belong in organizations, leaders are allowing a goldmine to slip right though their fingers."

Emotions are a goldmine because emotions are full of energy. As Tim also tells us, "Emotional change must begin with you, the leader," and, "Everyone experiences emotions everyday, and despite this fact, few leaders are formally trained in how to deal with people's emotions." I invite you to use the processes described in this book to inform your understanding of your emotional patterns, which will ultimately empower your capacity as a leader.

In his chapter on *Deep Knowledge*, Tim suggests that the first step for leaders is to "know yourself," and this book offers some highly useful guidelines on how to walk the mysterious path on the way to self-knowledge. Tim brings together more than concepts and exercises. He invites the reader to consider leadership as a holistic approach to life. He affirms that, as leaders travel the path to becoming *better* leaders, they will benefit by having a coach or mentor who can give support along with clear and honest feedback. I have practiced Aikido for more than thirty years, and I know that without my teachers, who were also my coaches, I would not have been able to develop the depth and understanding that I now endeavor to pass on to the students in my school.

This book is full of gems for you to explore, from the wisdom of learning how to handle emotions, to working with conflict and yin power. In this book, Tim leads you through a process of self-inquiry and empowerment. As you read, you will be able to appreciate what you already know while acknowledging aspects of leadership that may not be familiar or part of your strengths yet.

Those of you who like stories are in for a treat, for there is a wonderful collection within this book. Most of these vignettes tell of situations that may have occurred centuries ago, and yet the lessons are still applicable in our daily challenges of leadership.

As I read this book myself, I began to understand how Tim's background in psychology and Aikido lends a depth and grounding to the processes he puts forward. Since leadership covers a wide range of experiences, the capacity for self-knowledge and confidence are keys that unlock the door to a more fulfilling leadership experience. In Tim's words, "Black Belt Leadership is about basic respect, being sincere about who you are, and allowing and encouraging other people to be fully who they are."

Leading People the Black Belt Way gives you an opportunity to find out who you are and how you can contribute to a more fulfilling experience of leadership—both for you and for the people you are leading.

I'm confident you will enjoy the reading experience ahead of you as much as I did.

San Rafael, California
Winter 2005

The Seven Solutions of Black Belt Leadership:

1. Know the Five Core Problems of Leadership.
2. Understand Leadership as a Relational Process.
3. Seek Harmony in Leadership.
4. Lead People Rather than Pushing or Pulling Them.
5. Cultivate Emotional Engagement.
6. Practice Embodied Leadership.
7. Follow *The Black Belt Cycle of Leading People.*

Prelude
Empty Your Cup

Once upon a time, there was an American professor of Asian studies who had always wanted to go to Japan. In due time, he received a grant to go. While he was there, he had the opportunity to meet with a Zen master. During the meeting, the professor began expounding on all that he knew about Zen. While the professor was speaking, the master offered to serve tea. As master began to pour the tea, he continued to pour until the cup was over-flowing, and still he continued to pour. The tea flowed over the rim of the cup and onto the table. "Stop!" cried the professor. "The cup is full! Why do you keep pouring?!?" The Zen master replied, "Like this cup, so too are you full of your own ideas. I cannot teach you about Zen unless you empty yourself."

Asian culture has been studying holistic leadership through the martial arts for several millennia. In Japan, one of the classic guides to strategy is *The Book of Five Rings*, which was written by the great swordsman Miyamoto Musashi over 350 years ago. In China, the Taoist *Tao Te Ching*, one of the most valuable books ever written, was created 2,500 years ago. China also gave us another classic guide to strategy, *The Art of War*, written by the Taoist Sun Tzu around the same time. *Leading People* draws from the sagacity of these great texts as well as the embodied wisdom of the martial arts tradition.

In traditional Japanese martial arts, students begin their studies by walking through the door of the school, or dojo. This may seem obvious, but nothing happens until those first steps are taken through the door. Students start training with a beginning rank (called a "kyu"), signified by a white belt, and then move through the kyu ranks, which are typically organized in descending order. Finally, after many years of study, a student would test for shodan, or first-degree black belt. The chapters of this book have been set up in a similar fashion, following a progression of levels until you reach the end, when you become a Black Belt Leader.

The goal of leading people the Black Belt Way is teaching leaders how to tap into the winning strategy of developing active emotional engagement with those they lead. The Black Belt Way recognizes that, in leadership, an engaged connection pays off—socially, relationally, and financially. This book will help you navigate through the ranks and become a Black Belt Leader.

I invite you to empty your cup and join me in this journey as you learn the truth about *Leading People the Black Belt Way*.

**"Leadership is not domination, but the art of persuading
people to work toward a common goal."**
- Daniel Goleman

*"Wanting to be emotionally engaged
in one's work is a fundamental human need.
Wise leaders tap into this need."*

Story
The Leader Who Wanted to Know Everything

Once upon a time, there was a CEO named Bob who wanted to become the best leader in the entire world. A friend of his told him about a wise old wizard-consultant who was known for having coached some of the best leaders in the world. Perhaps the wizard-consultant could show Bob how to become a great leader.

Bob decided to visit the wizard-consultant, so he set off. When he found the old man, Bob asked him, "Do you really know how to make people become great leaders?"

"Yes, I do." replied the wizard-consultant.

"Could you make me a great leader?" asked Bob.

"Certainly. It's not hard," replied the wizard-consultant. "Take this packet of herbs to the shores of the river north of here. At sunset, build a fire and take three rocks from the river and place them in the fire. Sprinkle the contents of this packet over the rocks. At exactly midnight, pull the stones out of the fire. They'll be cool to the touch. Hold the stones in both hands, and you will become a great leader."

Bob thanked the wizard-consultant and rushed off to the river. He gathered three stones and some firewood, and sat down to wait for sunset. As he sat, he became restless. "This is far too easy!" thought Bob. "That wizard-consultant must have certainly left something out. There must be more to becoming a great leader than this!" Seeing that the sun had not yet set, Bob rushed back to the house of the old man and confronted him angrily. "You haven't told me everything!" shouted Bob.

"You are correct," replied the wizard-consultant calmly, "there is one more thing. It is very important, but you do <u>not</u> want to know it."

"I <u>must</u> know it!" cried Bob. "For there can only be one right way to do this spell."

"No, there isn't," said the wizard-consultant. "There are many ways to do it right."

"It doesn't matter how I do the spell?" said Bob in amazement.

"Yes, it does, it matters very much." said the wizard-consultant.

"You're not making any sense! Please tell me everything about the spell!" shouted Bob.

"Very well," sighed the wizard-consultant. "There is one more thing. When you do as I have told you, be sure not to think of panda bears."

Introduction

Eating the Same Thing Every Day:
The Five Core Problems
Facing Leaders Today

"I think it's dangerous to talk too much... I'd rather listen to your war stories than rehash mine, and you'd rather listen to mine than tell your own... So why don't we call a moratorium on the war stories entirely, and instead talk about how we are going to get out of this mess. How are we going to change our lives? How are we actually going to do it?"

- Terry Dobson

Leaders of today's organizations face enormous challenges. Some of the challenges are perennial while other challenges did not even exist as little as five years ago. Smart leaders already know the challenges exist. Now, to paraphrase Terry Dobson's question, "What are we going to *do* about those challenges?" Like Bob, the CEO in our opening story, some leaders believe that somewhere out there, someone has a magically simple 1-2-3-step plan that will create highly effective leaders. Those same leaders believe that the plan hasn't been discovered yet because we're just not looking hard enough. This is simply not the case. As leaders, we can continue to search for the one "right" way to lead people, but this approach is, as we will see, simply chasing smoke. A better answer lies in leaders using the existing knowledge about leadership in ways that better serve our organizations, the people within them, our society and the world community at large.

Laying Blame or Finding Solutions?

As leaders, we can waste energy assigning blame for the escalating complexities of today's leadership challenges, or we can begin to find solutions. The choice is ours. The issues facing us in our organizations are not Republican or Democratic, feminist or machismo, or management versus line staff. These issues are not caused by Boomers or Generation X or Generation Y, nor do they belong exclusively to either non-profit or for-profit organizations. Like throwing gasoline on a fire, attempting to blame leadership problems on one societal element over another simply makes those problems greater. In the end, we are all responsible for the leadership quagmire in today's organizations.

While leaders have always faced difficulties, contemporary challenges are intensifying due to pressurized factors such as downsizing and global economics. Yet all the research indicates that the solutions to our organizations' most confounding leadership issues are fairly straightforward. Those solutions reside in the *people*—in *us*—in *all* of us. But these solutions must *start* with you, the leader.

A basic fact of leadership is that leaders need to understand people and develop the necessary skills to effectively relate to them. Yet some leaders seem to be willing to face almost any difficulty *except* the challenge of leading people. Often, when faced with a people problem, these leaders freeze and seemingly slip into a state of suspended animation before retreating into their wood-paneled fortresses (otherwise known as executive suites). Like all leaders, those who retreat in such a manner are doing the best they can. They just have not been trained to handle the complexities of leading people. This book helps fill in some of those blanks.

The Five Core Problems Facing Leaders Today

Throughout my years of working with individuals and organizations, and as a result of my two-and-a-half year journey of researching and writing this book, I have discovered the **Five Core Problems** that leaders face today. They are:

1. **Organizations pay an enormous price when leaders ignore emotions.**
2. **Organizations suffer when leaders mistakenly believe there is only one right way to lead people.**
3. **Organizations fail when leaders refuse to believe there are wrong ways to lead people.**
4. **Organizations flounder when leaders think that there are easy answers to leading people.**

5. Organizations lose viability when they follow the old structures that serve people at the top first.

Core Problem #1: Organizations pay an enormous price when leaders ignore emotions. Like using a gun that explodes in your face in order to protect yourself, many of today's leaders are using organizational policies that have devastating consequences. These processes are causing financial damage in ways that are often unseen until the losses are irreparable. In fact, some management policies used in organizations today are eerily similar to those used by totalitarian regimes around the world. While many of these policies are honest attempts to address situations that have occurred in the past, the excessive fear that surrounds these policies creates an unhealthy emotional ripple effect throughout organizations. The ripple effects from these policies include:

- People being required to spend more time navigating the political waters of an organization than completing their tasks.
- People avoiding innovation out of fear of backlash from within the organization.
- People finding their years of service to an organization abruptly terminated with a quick meeting and a security escort out of the building.
- People remaining behind to experience the internal chaos that ensues when colleagues, friends and co-workers are terminated and simply vanish one day, never to be heard from again.

A logical result of these fear-based policies is that many people in organizations are afraid—afraid of speaking up, afraid of offering new ideas, afraid of doing anything at all that might be seen as making waves. Many people have simply given up caring about their jobs, creating a tremendous financial drag on their organizations. For years, these policies have been mistakenly accepted as facts of life in the "hard" reality of organizational life. In the pages that follow, we will debunk the misconceptions around so-called "hard" leadership styles by examining the recent, overwhelming evidence that reveals the high price organizations pay when their leaders use these "tough" approaches to leadership.[1]

The importance of people's emotions in organizations has been understood since 1995 when Daniel Goleman published his groundbreaking book *Emotional Intelligence.* Despite the fact that over 10 years have passed and countless books and enormous amounts of research have been published, a significant percentage of leaders remain unaware of emotional intelligence and emotionally intelligent leadership skills. As a means of comparison, consider the Internet. Most leaders became aware of the Internet in the middle-to-late 1990s, approximately the same time that emotional intelligence was being brought to the attention of leaders. While the existence of the Internet in organizations today is almost universal, the existence of emotionally intelligent leadership practice in these same organizations is still scattered and uneven. In other words, while one rarely finds an organization that does not use e-mail or the Internet, one would also be hard-pressed to find an organization where all of the leaders are fluent in the language and processes of emotional intelligence.

Core Problem #2: Organizations suffer when leaders mistakenly believe there is only one right way to lead people. "Good leadership" is a context-dependent phenomenon, which simply means that in order for leadership to be effective and successful in any given organization, leaders must take into account multiple factors including, but not limited to: organizational culture, type(s) of people being led, strengths and weaknesses of the leader, institutional support, broader cultural perspectives, purpose and mission of the organization, ethics, morality, and adult developmental and educational theory. There is no one single right way to combine all of these factors into a leadership approach that will be effective in every organization. Consequently, every leader must accept the challenge of applying appropriate leadership technology to his or her organization.

Great leadership is a lot like great cooking. What constitutes "great cooking" differs from place to place throughout the world because different people have different expectations about what comprises a "great" meal. Will dinner tonight be spicy or bland, complex or simple? Will we eat meat or only vegetables? The foods we eat and how we cook them are largely learned preferences. While I absolutely love sushi, you could not pay my wife enough money to touch the stuff. The wide variety of ethnic foods found around the world evolved precisely because different people with different requirements in different places had access to different types of food. The same is true with leadership.

Sadly, many leaders today take a "one-size-fits-all" approach to leading people. If you can imagine eating the same thing—boiled oatmeal, for example—at every meal of every day for a year, you get some sense of what I am talking about. "Unappetizing" would be an understatement! But many organizational management teams have been locked in the same leadership rhythm for decades. *We need a change.* We need to throw out the old leadership menu and create a new one, a menu that keeps the best of the old while introducing tasty new dishes in-demand by people today. This way, leadership becomes a creative blend of leaders' approaches and styles best-suited to the needs of unique individuals and specific organizations. [2]

Core Problem #3: Organizations fail when leaders refuse to believe there are wrong ways to lead people. Just because there are many right ways to lead people, that doesn't mean that there aren't any *wrong* ways. Though chicken is cooked differently throughout the world, burning the chicken creates an inedible lump of charcoal in any country. Chicken a lá gasoline served anywhere in the world is a poisonous dish. Again, the same is true of leadership. The factors that impact the roles of leaders vary greatly from organization to organization, just as ingredients and spices change from culture to culture. But across all organizations, there are ways of leading people that are nourishing, and there are other ways that are quite toxic. In general, toxic leadership styles can be classified as either *Pushing Leadership styles* or *Pulling Leadership styles,* two harmful approaches to leading people that we will be discussing throughout this book.

Another way to consider the many wrong approaches to leading people is to think of leadership as a test. Ineffective leaders approach leading people as a true/false test. Because there are few, if any, true/false answers in leadership, approaching leadership from such a concrete perspective invites failure. Mediocre leaders approach leadership as a multiple-choice test. While multiple-choice thinking is better than the black and white thinking of true/false leadership, this approach is simply not effective enough for organizations to survive in today's global economy. *Great* leaders view leading people as an on-going essay test, understanding that there is always more to say and learn about leading people.

Core Problem #4: Organizations flounder when leaders think there are easy answers to leading people. Simply put, there aren't any easy answers to leading people. Every leader must wrestle with his or her problems, seeking individualized solutions that provide a best-fit for each unique organization. Reading sterilized examples from leadership textbooks can unintentionally lull new leaders into believing that leadership issues are easily solved, as if the problems of leading people were as simple and neat as, say, a problem in an Accounting 101 textbook. However, the stark reality is that today's leadership problems are enormously complex. Otherwise, simple answers would have been discovered decades ago.

Easy answers elude leaders because a paradox lies at the heart of leadership. On one hand, each of us is a leader to the extent that we influence and direct the behaviors of those around us. At the same time, some of us are "more" leaders than others by virtue of the power invested in us by our organizations. While every person is responsible for the problems of leadership as they exist today, our ability to impact those problems lies in direct proportion to how much power we have in the systems in which we work. The CEO of a company has far greater impact than the janitor who sweeps the floor at night. What some leaders fail to see is that greater leadership power comes with equally greater responsibility to use that power in a way that safeguards the leader and other people, both inside and outside of the organization.

While responsibility for today's leadership quagmires can be directly correlated to the amount of power a person holds in an organization, everyone else is not let off the hook. People who hold little power within an organization still carry responsibility, for *there can be no tyrannical leaders without followers.* There is a pull deep within every human being that invites us to turn over our responsibility to any leader we believe might hold easy answers to our problems. People with little power in organizations often give up their responsibility and perpetuate the problem by seeking a leader who will ride to their rescue and solve all of their problems—and such a leader does not exist. People with little power within organizations also avoid their responsibility when they demonize the leader while holding themselves blameless. None of us is blameless. To quote Pogo, "We have met the enemy and they is us."

Core Problem #5: Organizations lose viability when they follow the old structures that serve people at the top first. Initially, being served first might strike leaders as a good thing. In truth, being served first *is* a good thing—as long as you avoid looking under the surface. This is because most of today's organizations are made up of pyramid-shaped infrastructures with lots of room at the bottom and little room at the top. The closer leaders get to the top of these organizations, the less room there is. No matter how many talented and promising leaders exist in any given organization, there is generally only one position at the very top.

Having less and less room at the top breeds unhealthy forms of competition. Our present organizational infrastructures create a zero-sum game—someone wins and someone loses. The game is rigged from the start. While leadership failures are often viewed as personal failings, this is not necessarily so. Today's leadership problems are not anyone's fault, including the person occupying the uppermost position. This zero-sum perspective is hard-wired into today's organizations and has an enormous negative impact both *within* organizations as well as *between* organizations.

The damage that today's organizational structure causes *within* an organization is epitomized in the selection process for the highest spot in every organization. If, for example, both you and I are in line for the CEO position, then we are in a serious bind. Someone is going to win and someone is going to lose. If I help you reach your potential by becoming a CEO, then I lose, and vice versa. Or worse, the board of directors brings in someone from outside the organization to become the new CEO, and we both lose. This win-lose dynamic occurs in almost every organization, even those non-profit organizations whose explicit mission is to support people who have been marginalized. In fact, this dynamic stands out *especially* in non-profits, because the contrast of the support given to people *outside* of the organization stands in sharp relief to the organization's very infrastructure that continues to marginalize people *within* the organization. Regardless of the mission or tax status of an organization, this type of win-lose dynamic has repercussions throughout all levels of the organization.

To understand the damage that today's organizational structure creates *between* organizations, consider Dr. I. Eat Sweets, a dentist who owns a practice in a mid-sized town. Dr. Sweets is both an excellent dentist and a wonderful teacher, and he freely passes along his knowledge to Sam, Pat, and Sally, young dentists who work for him. Soon, Sam, Pat and Sally decide to leave Dr. Sweets' office in order to open up their own practices. Now there are *four* dentists in town. As with their mentor, Sam, Pat and Sally value the sharing of knowledge. So they each hire three young dentists, who, after "interning" open up three more individual practices. Now there are *thirteen* dentists in town. Soon these dentists, who initially placed a high value on collaboration, are going to feel the pressure of too many dentists and too few customers. As each dentist struggles to have a practice that simply survives, he or she is going to be less willing to share information with any other dentist.

New Times, New Rules

The rules in today's organizational structures have served us in the past, but those rules no longer work. As we saw above, a fundamental rule in most of today's organizational structures is: "I have to step on others in order to help myself." If you do not believe this, imagine that you have to make a choice between cutting either your job or that of a person under your direct report. Whose job gets axed?

These are new times, and new times call for new organizational structures. Unfortunately, the answer is not as easy as simply inverting the pyramid, or even turning the organization's infrastructure into a circle or square. The problem with all of these organizational shapes is that they remain flat, two dimensional structures. Because they are two-dimensional, these structures remain in what I like to refer to as *flatland*. (We'll talk about flatland more in a minute.)

New times call for new rules for leaders. We are living in an era of amazing changes, and no one knows for certain just what new organizational structures will look like. But one rule of the new leadership approach appears to be, "I have to help others in order to help myself."

Addressing the Five Core Problems calls for the creation of even healthier organizations, a process which requires personal development on the part of every leader. In fact, one important measure of the health of an organization is the amount of focus the organization places on employee personal development, *especially* that of the leaders. [3] Healthy leaders create healthy organizational structures. Healthy structures create healthy organizations. Healthy organizations create healthy people.

The Five Core Problems can be resolved as long as leaders understand that "helping myself" is *not* the same as "being greedy." Seeking a comfortable lifestyle for ourselves and our loved ones is not wrong. As with the oxygen masks in airplanes, leaders have to take care of themselves before they can take care of anyone else. If, for my example, my children are starving and I have just been evicted from my home, I am in no position to help anyone. When I earn enough money to meet the needs of my family, then I am in a much better position to help other people.

Strengths & Biases

Discovering solutions to these Five Core Problems of leadership is what this book is all about and will save you time and energy because you will learn about Black Belt Leadership. This approach is based upon cutting-edge leadership technology as well as the principles of the Japanese martial art of Aikido, without requiring the extensive commitment of time and resources demanded by either traditional Aikido practice or graduate-level business schools.

As we begin, I want to introduce the strengths and blind spots which I bring to this book. I am an independent executive coach, consultant, clinical counselor and martial artist. I am a father and husband, of Irish/German/Polish descent, living outside of Cleveland, Ohio. In the past several years, some of the most exciting part of my work has been combining the principles from the martial art of Aikido with cutting-edge approaches to leadership. The clients and workshop participants with whom I work have successfully incorporated these principles into their own lives, often with astounding results. For years, my clients have told me that I should be sharing my theories in a book. Here, at last, is that book.

Aikido

I have been studying the Japanese martial art of Aikido since 1989. One of the most modern of martial arts, Aikido was developed by Morihei Ueshiba (c. 1883-1968)—arguably the greatest martial artist who ever lived.[4] Aikido is a revolutionary, non-aggressive martial art that seeks the resolution of conflict. Often called "The Way of the Spirit of Harmony," Aikido is the physical embodiment of the Win/Win strategy.[5] My many years on the Aikido mat led me to the central idea of this book: **that pushing and/or pulling people is always less effective than truly leading people.** These words are easy to say, but difficult to actually put into action because humans are biologically hard-wired to either push or pull. However, leaders can learn to reprogram their impulses to push or pull others, and to learn, instead, how to authentically lead people. Leaders who master this process can then have the power to channel other people's energy into practices and methods that generate success for entire organizations.

Aikido is a very difficult art that demands an enormous investment of time and effort. Earning a black belt in Aikido typically takes anywhere from five to ten years of intensive practice several times each week. While the results are well worth the effort, not everyone can make such an enormous commitment. In order to help you become an even more effective leader, I have distilled some of the principles of Aikido into the practices of The Black Belt Way.

Understanding Aikido principles is essential for leaders because these principles offer a sophisticated method for studying engagement that is unlike any other.[6] In learning the principles of Aikido through this book, you will gain a deeper understanding of how to successfully create emotional engagement in the people you lead. This book will challenge you to examine, at multiple levels, how you engage with the people you lead. Those levels include the:

- Verbal
- Emotional
- Mental
- Ethical
- Spiritual
- Physical

Leading Out of Flatland

I draw the terms "integral" and "flatland" from the work of American philosopher Ken Wilber, whose work is both groundbreaking and breathtaking. An integral approach to leadership is an approach that coherently organizes the greatest number of truths out of the greatest number of valid leadership sources. Wilber's four-quadrant model recognizes the subjective (intentional – Upper Left), objective (behavioral – Upper Right), intersubjective (cultural – Lower Left), and interobjective (social – Lower Right) dimensions of being.[7] One of the fundamental causes of the Five Core Problems is that organizational structures have reduced people/workers/human resources into what Wilber would describe as "flatland."

> "[The] belief that *only the Right-Hand world is real*—the world of matter/energy, empirically investigated by the human senses and their extensions (telescopes, microscopes, photographic plates, etc.). All of the interior worlds are reduced to, or explained by, objective/exterior terms."[8]

Not only does a flatland perspective hurt the people who work within organizations, but **current data suggests that this flatland perspective hurts an organization's bottom line.** The way out of flatland is to create a three-dimensional, "second tier" organizational structure, and these organizational patterns are only beginning to emerge. While there are no second tier organizations in existence yet, the need for an integral model of leadership (and by extension, organizations) is tremendously important for creating organizational success in today's global economy.[9] This, then, is the main premise of the book when looked at through the lens of Wilber's theory.[10]

Does the World Really Need Another Book on Leadership?

No—and yes. There are many books out there that offer leadership model after leadership model. The world does not need *another* leadership model, and I do not offer one. What I am presenting here is different. I am presenting an "un-model," if you will, an approach to leadership that brings the art out of flatland. **This book is not just about leadership, but rather about leading people—and there is a difference.** Most leadership approaches turn people into objects and demand, "Do what I want!" Leading people, on the other hand, respects and honors people while seeking to co-create conditions that benefit the individual and the organization collectively.

Learning to lead people authentically requires a commitment to self-development by the leader. Just as every master chef completes years of in-depth study in the preparation and presentations of a variety of foods, herbs and spices, so too do effective leaders become masters of their art by practicing the discipline of self-development. In the pages that follow, I will show you the rewards that self-development holds for you in your own leadership role—information you can use immediately. I make no claims to have discovered something new, and I have little interest in discovering the "truth" about leadership so I can mount a plaque on a wall. Nor do I claim that Black Belt Leadership is the one and only approach. Today's organizations are at a dangerous crossroads, and we need new kinds of leadership to move us successfully beyond this challenge. What I have done is to integrate leadership technology in ways that my clients have told me is both exciting and effective. Both individuals and organizations I have worked with have found this new integration beneficial. I offer these insights as my contribution to the dialogue about new leadership that is taking place in all parts of the world today.[11]

About the material in this book

Many concepts about leadership were researched for this book, and in deciding which to include, I tried to maintain a pre-established level of rigor. In order to be considered for inclusion, every concept had to meet three specific criteria:

1. **There had to be support for the concept from at least two independent sources in the existing leadership research.** This allowed me to rule out theories and practices that were too individualized or one-sided in their approaches.
2. **The concept had to pass the test of effectiveness in my own life and work.** I have no interest in offering ideas and advice to others that I am unwilling to try myself.
3. **The concept had to pass the test of effectiveness in the lives and work of other people.** In the two-plus years I spent writing this book, I field-tested these concepts with a variety of individuals and organizations, and those that showed merit were then included.

A Word about Language… and "Leader"…

Like so many other writers, I struggled with the "he/she" difficulties of our language. I believe that "s/he" is awkward, so I use "he" and "she" randomly when referring to leaders. Despite the often misogynistic, patriarchal roots of the martial art world, my deeply held experience is that both men and women can be strong leaders, effective martial artists, and explorers along the path of emotional growth—with some wonderful people even doing all three!

In this book, I chose to use the word *leader* to describe anyone who influences other people's behavior. Using this definition, *everyone* leads at different times in his or her life, for one cannot be alive and not lead. I stayed away from words like "manager" or "supervisor" because these titles only apply to certain job positions. Since the fundamentals of leadership are the same for all people and professions, the information contained in this book is applicable to everyone in a position of leadership—whether you are a foreman on a shop floor, an officer in the armed services, a CEO of a Fortune 500 company, an educator, a parent, an ordained clergy, an entrepreneur, a small business owner or a supervisor in a non-profit organization. Leadership is not limited to organizational structures, nor does everyone who leads within organizations carry the designation of leader. Neither is leadership limited by age. I have watched my six-year old daughter share leadership responsibilities with her same-age playmate as they led their energetic gaggle of friends off into a fantastic world of teen-age-wizards-meet-child-spies-while-riding-on-ponies, as only six-year-olds can create. I have been humbled while watching a 78-year-old matriarch lead her family through the healing and recovery following the devastation and horror of discovering that a child in the family was being sexually abused. Yes, *everyone* will lead at some point in life, and I believe that everyone can benefit from the material contained in this book.

Writing about leadership poses the dilemma of providing clear and specific details regarding individuals and organizations in order to illuminate the concepts I am trying to convey. At the same time, I need to protect the privacy and confidentiality of the individuals and organizations involved. I have tried to balance both demands by altering the specifics in order to disguise the identity of those involved, without changing the essential dynamics. Some examples that I provide are composite pictures of interactions that I have experienced frequently in my coaching or consulting work, and any dialogue is not verbatim.

You Get Two Books in One

What you are holding in your hands is really two books in one—the book as a stand-alone piece, and the book along with the extensive endnotes. I designed the work in this manner in order to meet the needs of leaders, and to blend with different leadership learning styles. Leaders today need to understand both the "Big Picture" of leadership, the view from 50,000 feet as well the "nuts-and-bolts" approach for working elbow-to-elbow with people in the trenches. This book provides both views. Read the book as a standalone for the aerial, 50,000-foot approach. Then, when you are ready, go back and re-read the book along with the endnotes for a deeper, more extensive view.

I also wrote this book in a manner designed to appeal to different leadership learning styles. If you are a leader who is just learning the fundamentals of leadership, or if you find endnotes distracting, please feel free to ignore the endnotes. The book will stand up quite well without them. On the other hand, if you are a leader who enjoys details, or one who is familiar with the existing leadership literature and ready to go deeper, then feel free to read the book along with the endnotes, cutting away to the annotations sequentially as they appear in the text. Most importantly, whichever way you read the book, please do so in a way that best fits your learning style.

Finally, please do not accept anything as true or valid simply because the words are written on these pages. I invite you to carefully consider what I have said in light of your own experiences, exploring those things that you find beneficial and then incorporating them into your own leadership style as you see fit.

*"Leading people
demands active participation.
The skill cannot be learned by watching
from the sidelines."*

WHITE BELT
Section I
Set Your Strategy

"Until one is committed, there is hesitancy, the chance to draw back, always ineffectiveness, concerning all acts of initiative and creation.
Whatever you can do or dream you can begin it.
Boldness has genius, power and magic in it.
Begin it now."
Goethe

Story
Understanding Harmony

Once upon a time in ancient Japan, a young man was studying martial arts under a famous teacher. Every day the young man would practice in a courtyard along with the other students. One day, as the master watched, he could see that the other students were consistently interfering with the young man's technique.

Sensing the student's frustration, the master approached the student and tapped him on the shoulder.

"What is wrong?" inquired the teacher.

"I cannot execute my technique and I do not understand why," replied the student.

"This is because you do not understand harmony. Please follow me," said the master.

Leaving the practice hall, the master and student walked a short distance into the woods until they came upon a stream.

After standing silently beside the streambed for a few minutes, the master spoke. "Look at the water," he instructed. "It does not slam into the rocks and stop out of frustration, but instead flows around them and continues down the stream. Become like the water and you will understand harmony."

Soon, the student learned to move and flow like the stream, and none of the other students could keep him from executing his techniques.

Chapter 1
Walking through the Door: What Leaders Are Missing
"Export anything American to a friendly country, except American management."
-W. Edwards Deming

As a leader, do you ever wish you could read other people's minds? Let's grant your wish—just for a minute. Join me as we drop in on a management meeting already in progress. Since your wish came true, you can hear what people in the meeting are thinking. You see a group of well-dressed professionals seated around a beautiful mahogany conference table strewn with loose papers and cups of coffee. Through the high windows that surround the conference room, the skyline of a modern city spreads off into the distance. Rick, the CEO of this multinational manufacturing company, is listening to one of his lieutenants present a strategic plan for the up-coming fiscal year. Bored by the lukewarm presentation, Donna, the director of Accounting, stifles a yawn and thinks about the date she went on last night. The lieutenant, Ricardo, is sweating, unable to guess what Rick might be thinking about the strategy being articulated. Dave, the director of Marketing, scarcely dares to breathe, wondering when Rick is going to explode into one of his trademark tirades. Dale from Legal shifts in his chair, worried about his young daughter who went to daycare sick this morning. Rick is frustrated, wondering why nobody in the room seems excited about what they're hearing. Temper rising, he slams his fist down on the table and shouts, "I've had enough!" The tirade begins.

There are a myriad of things wrong with this picture, but topping the list is Rick's heated invective. This sort of outburst goes well beyond a managerial faux pas, and today's organizations can no longer afford such egregious mistakes. In the past several decades, organizations have downsized, re-engineered, and streamlined. Organizations have gone through the lengthy and sometimes painful process of inserting technology into their very heart and soul. We have new software systems that track, support, and inform our business processes from accounting to manufacturing. Due to the technological advances of the past 50 years, the pace in our organizations has picked up exponentially. And yet, something is still missing. Our organizations are neither as profitable nor as productive as they could be.

The solution to organizational success resides within the people populating your organization. This book will show the mission-critical importance of leaders learning approaches that respect, honor and acknowledge those people—in mind, body and spirit. This method of leading people is one I've dubbed *Black Belt Leadership*, a set of techniques that is not only humane and courteous, but also embodies **smart business**. Leaders who want to be successful must learn effective ways of dealing with emotions (both their own and those of whom they lead) because of the negative impact that emotionally *un*skilled leadership has on the bottom line.

Are people in organizations struggling? Yes they are. Consider these facts:

- In one survey, nearly 40% of workers described their office environment as "most like a real-life survivor program."[12]
- In a recent Gallup Poll, 80% of workers feel stress on the job; nearly half say they need help in learning how to manage stress; and 42% say their coworkers need such help.[13]
- Between 70% and 80% of people within organizations are not working anywhere near their peak capacity because they are not emotionally committed to their work.[14]
- In another recent survey, one-fourth of employees view their jobs as the number one stressor in their lives.[15]

Should leaders care? Absolutely. Consider *these* facts:

- Employee stress costs businesses $300 billion per year in absenteeism, health costs, and programs to reduce stress.[16] Much of the workers' stress and lack of emotional commitment emanates from the very leaders who are supposed to be managing them.[17]
- Increasing your employees' emotional connection to their jobs can save your organization over $3,000 for every $10,000 spent on salary.[18]
- Employee feelings toward a company account for 20% to 30% of business performance.[19]

- Providing appropriately emotionally skilled leadership could impact the U.S. economy to the tune of an additional $254 to $363 billion in profits annually.[20]
- Creating emotionally satisfying working environments is critical to retaining qualified people in your organization. Experts are predicting a labor shortage within a few short years, so retaining skilled workers is critical for success.[21]
- In their best-selling book *Follow this Path*, authors Coffman & Gonzalez-Molina identified three levels of employee engagement: 1) engaged, 2) not-engaged, and 3) disengaged. Noting that "…disengaged employees cost companies hundreds of million of dollars annually," they discovered that as many as 75% of people in organizations are not emotionally engaged in their tasks. [22]

As you can see from the data, there is a serious problem with leadership in our organizations. In the past, when things were less complicated and profit margins were greater, organizations could tolerate the temper tantrums and ignorance of behavioral science that passed as leadership. Today's global economy and tighter profit margins means that your organization can no longer afford these "luxuries." Are you willing to accept the fact that three-fourths of the people in your organization are emotionally disconnected from their tasks? If not, there is a way to rectify the situation, as you will see.

Compounding the problem set forth thus far is the litany of leadership approaches bombarding all levels of management today. While many of these approaches are helpful to some small degree, most of them consistently make one giant mistake:

They completely overlook people's bodies, seeming to believe that people are nothing more than heads floating in space.

This, then, is the core principle of Black Belt Leadership: *Great leadership begins with the body.* As a leader in your organization, fully understanding these words will enable you to increase the level of human productivity in your workforce without the added expense of hiring a single additional employee. If you could learn how to increase your employees' commitment and passion toward your organization, while at the same time reducing their job-related stress, would you be interested? This book will show you how to do just that—but not by teaching you another leadership system. Instead, these pages will teach you about The Black Belt Way, an exciting approach that allows you to harness the emotional power of people in your organization in a manner that creates even greater success. You will also learn the critical importance of recognizing that there are multiple ways to lead effectively, not just one, and the impact of emotions and relationships on the success of your organization. In short, you will develop simple and effective practices for leading that incorporate the wisdom of your body, tools which I call *embodied leadership skills.*

Harmonious Emotional Engagement

Harmonious Emotional Engagement is the tool that allows leaders to take full advantage of these three simple but profound principles:

People respond emotionally to every situation that occurs in an organization.
People's negative emotions reduce their performance in an organization.
People's positive emotions enhance their performance in an organization.

This is so simple. Yet today's leaders rarely take these seemingly straightforward principles into account, even though putting these principles to work could have a tremendous impact on their success. We hope to change that.

So what does *Harmonious Emotional Engagement* mean? Let's take a closer look at each of the three parts of this phrase—"harmony," "emotional," and "engagement," beginning with harmony.

❋ ❋ ❋

"Common wisdom, of course, holds that employees who feel upbeat will likely go the extra mile to please customers and therefore improve the bottom line. But there's actually a logarithm that predicts the relationship: For every 1 percent improvement in the service climate, there's a 2 percent increase in revenue."
Goleman, Boyatzis, & McKee

❋ ❋ ❋

Harmony—Mastering the Power

When learning how to lead people successfully, an understanding of harmony is vital because only harmony addresses the quality of the fit between the leader (and their leadership style) and the environment in which the leader works (which includes the other people with whom the leader works). There is no one-size-fits-all approach to leadership.

For our purposes here, **harmony is defined as the process of being integrally in tune with those around us.** By integrally, I mean in ways that are all-encompassing and holistic—ways that incorporate mind, body, and spirit. The more integrally we lead, the better leaders we become, because we constantly enrich and enliven our leadership abilities with other life experiences. An example is relevant here. In the book *Being Human at Work*, consultant Peter Luzmore describes working with a senior vice president named Pete. Luzmore describes Pete as impatient, overly demanding and given to bouts of shouting that left his staff demoralized. After Luzmore used an integral approach in his coaching of Pete, Luzmore gathered feedback from Pete's executive team. The team reported that Pete had changed tremendously, that he was now patient, better focused and more effective as a leader.[23] Harmony's importance becomes clear when the concepts of *relationship* and *context* are recognized. Let's learn about relationship and context by considering musical notes.

A musical note cannot be said to be harmonious in isolation. A note is only harmonious in relationship to—or in context with—the other notes in the musical score. A note that is perfectly harmonious in a given section of *Somewhere over the Rainbow* sounds jarring to the ears when heard in a section of *Jailhouse Rock*. The concept of relationship recognizes that *Somewhere over the Rainbow* and *Jailhouse Rock* cannot be accurately qualified as "right" or "wrong" just because a particular note cannot be played in both songs. In fact, even talking about whether a song is "right" or "wrong" doesn't make any sense. This is an important point to which we will return later.

Leadership styles fail to be harmonious (and successful) when they fail to take into account these concepts of *relationship* and *context*. These concepts assume even greater importance when one realizes that the most productive styles of leadership are typically those that are flexible, present-centered and aware of changing circumstances. Leaders who spend time talking about "right" or "wrong" styles of leadership, without addressing the relationships and contexts within their leadership environments, are simply wasting their energy. In order to be a successful leader, you need to do the difficult work of developing a leadership style that *fits the needs of the people in your organization.*

Remember that when I speak about harmony, I am *not* speaking of the false harmony that exists wherever people are afraid, intimidated, or bullied by leaders. People are very skilled at being externally compliant. But external compliance is not harmony. Nor does harmony exist in situations where team members avoid conflict by refusing to name obvious but unspoken truths that are apparent to everyone but may cause strife if mentioned. Rather than being harmonious, these are forms of dissonance (the opposite of harmony), which are disguised in silence and masquerade grotesquely as harmony.

While you will learn more in the pages that follow about the central role that harmony plays in leadership, I want to take a moment and answer a question that I often hear in my coaching practice, which is: "How do I know when harmony is present?" The answer is fairly simple and straightforward. A leader experiences harmony as a sense of balance that pervades the organization—an easy sense of flow between the mind, body and emotions.

This brings us to the important topic of *emotions in leadership.*

❋ ❋ ❋

"In recent years, both neuroscience and cognitive neuroscience have finally endorsed emotion… Moreover, the presumed opposition between emotion and reason is no longer accepted without question."
Antonio Damasio, M.D.

❋ ❋ ❋

Emotions—Mastering the Balance

Do emotions affect people's performance in an organization? Unquestionably. Recent research provides clear support for the pivotal role that emotions play in organizations. There should be no question in a leader's mind that emotions play a key role in the success or failure of an organization. Understanding the profound impact that emotions have on the workplace is to recognize the wisdom of the adage (also supported by current research): "People don't leave jobs, they leave people."

A basic requirement for leading people is having a fundamental understanding of emotional intelligence—which is a leader's ability to manage his or her emotions in relationships with others. Increasing your emotional intelligence means expanding your capacity to understand and leverage the emotional component of leadership. Just as a five-pound sack is inadequate for fifty pounds of sugar, a limited capacity to tolerate and contain emotional experiences restricts your growth and development as a leader—as well as that of the people within your organization. Expanding your emotional capacity entails every dimension of your human experience—mind, body, and spirit.

❋ ❋ ❋

A Key to Leading People:
Wanting to be emotionally engaged in one's work
is a fundamental human need.
Wise leaders will tap into this need for the benefit
of their organizations.

❋ ❋ ❋

Engagement—Mastering the Connection

To learn more about emotions, we must also consider the concept of engagement. For our present purposes, I'll define engagement as **the connection that occurs between one person and another person, group, organization, or entity.** A person can be engaged to marry another (which is, hopefully, entering into a deep emotional relationship with another person), or she can be engaged in a hobby or sports, or even be engaged with an enemy. Engagement is fundamentally about the quality and type of connection and contact that occurs between people. Engagement involves all levels of a person—mental, physical, spiritual and emotional. For our purpose at hand, we will consider emotional engagement to be *positive*, and emotional disengagement and/or not-engaged to be *negative*.

Engaging Emotions

Type of Engagement	Impact on Organization
Emotional	EngagementPositive
Not-Engaged	Negative
Disengaged	Negative

Many leaders ignore emotions, resulting in millions of dollars in lost revenues when up to 75% of people in organizations have no emotional connection to what they are doing. This trend is not irrevocable, however. Whether we consider professionals working for a Fortune 500 company or volunteers at the local hospital, the same rule holds true: People in every organization want to be actively engaged—to be emotionally connected—with their role(s). Sadly, many organizational cultures actively prevent people from becoming so engaged. I have had countless discussions with people in a wide range of industries who share this same idea: They want to care about their work, but find they cannot care and still do their jobs effectively. Many people faced with this dilemma choose to leave their jobs, which increases costs due to lost productivity, new-hire training, and a lack of cohesiveness that disrupts projects throughout the organization. Other people faced with this same dilemma simply stay at their present job and become disengaged workers, which also hurts the bottom line of the organization, usually in hidden ways that do not readily appear on the company's books. Either way, your organization loses.

Ignoring the relational and emotional realities of people in your organization is a lose/lose situation. Organizations lose money, they lose employees, or worse, they lose both. Employees lose quality of life. Customers lose consistency when employees move on and need to be replaced with less experienced, less familiar workers. When relational and emotional realities are ignored, everyone loses.

Creating emotional engagement in the people within your organization is not something that happens automatically or overnight. Instead, the process is like building up a bank account. Rather than walking into a brand new bank and immediately demanding to make a withdrawal, one must first make an investment. Whether dealing with money in the bank or people's emotional engagement, the same rule holds true:

To maintain a positive balance, you have to make deposits in order to make withdrawals.

Leaders need to make emotional deposits with the people they lead so that when the time comes to make withdrawals, leaders do not overdraw their account with these same people.

Putting It All Together

As a leader, you want to win.

Even as you read this sentence, negative emotions are making a tremendous impact on your organization. The choice for leaders like you is clear. Either you effectively lead people and their emotions in your organization, or you risk undermining your organization's success, as harmful emotions eat away at your bottom line. The choice belongs to you. Which force of influence will affect the success or failure of your organization—*you*, or the negative emotions that run unmanaged throughout your organization?

Putting the concepts of harmony, emotions, and engagement together, we get a very powerful leadership tool. Simply stated, Harmonious Emotional Engagement is both a decision and a process. When leaders make the choice to lead others with Harmonious Emotional Engagement, they are making a commitment to create, develop, and maintain positive emotional connections in ways that benefit both the individuals involved as well as the entire organization. **Harmonious Emotional Engagement allows everyone to win.** Leaders who harness the power of Harmonious Emotional Engagement are well on their way to becoming *extraordinary* leaders.

✻ ✻ ✻

A Key to Leading People:
Do not wait for conditions to be perfect to become a better leader.
Conditions will <u>never</u> be perfect. Begin today.

✻ ✻ ✻

Commit to Starting Now

The famous Taoist Lao Tzu said, "The journey of a thousand miles begins with the first step." In the same way, you begin the journey of becoming a Black Belt Leader by taking your first step. I invite you to begin your journey today. *Now* is the right time. *Here* is the right place. What are you waiting for? What have you got to lose?

The Black Belt Cycle of Leading People

The Black Belt Cycle of Leading People forms the foundation of this book. This cycle provides leaders with a quick, easy and effective roadmap

through the process of leadership. Here are the steps that take us through
The Black Belt Cycle of Leading People:

1. **Set Your Strategy.**
2. **Take Your Stance.**
3. **Take Action.**
4. **Assess Your Strategy.**

1. Set Your Strategy. You can only become an excellent leader when
you are completely engaged in your leadership role. Like diving into a cool
pool of water on a hot summer day, developing excellence in leadership
demands that you jump in with both feet, allowing your leadership role
to surround you, enfold you and support you. Becoming a superior leader
demands that you become aware of, and intimately familiar with, the
cutting-edge strategies of leadership. How aware of technique are you
when you lead others? Can you tell the difference between *push* and *pull* in
your own management style? In the pages that follow, we will examine the
differences and contrast them with more effective leadership strategies.

2. Take Your Stance. A solid fundamental stance is as crucial in
leadership as in tennis, golf and the martial arts. In these pages, you will
learn the basics of The Stance of Black Belt Leadership. Together we will
examine cutting-edge leadership research around what I call *embodied
leadership*, which is the importance of recognizing and leveraging the innate
knowledge contained in our bodies for increased leadership effectiveness.
The Stance of Black Belt Leadership will show you three simple, powerful
disciplines for engaging yourself more fully in your leadership role.

Leading people involves understanding how to be in relationship with
people emotionally. When you lead, how emotionally aware are you? How
high is your own emotional involvement in your work? Leading people
in a way that improves the bottom line requires that you understand the
concept of *Deep Knowledge*, a key to understanding leadership, emotions
and relationships. This book will show you how to best work with Deep
Knowledge by teaching you the *Law of Emotionally Successful Leadership*.

Many leaders believe that emotions should be handled like facts. This is
wrong for the simple reason that emotions change while facts do not. You
will learn straightforward, effective strategies for harnessing the ever-changing
nature of emotions. In these pages, you will discover effective leadership

strategies for managing change with *The Four Rules of Change for Leaders*. You will also learn the importance of tapping into the power of process.

3. Take Action. There are five essential principles within this step: i) Emotional flexibility; ii) Seeking harmony; iii) The importance of yielding; iv) Valuing working relationships; and v) Managing conflict appropriately. When these essential principles work together, like the five fingers of our hands, they are remarkable tools. In the same way, integrating these five principles into a leader creates a superior leader who succeeds through his ability to be fully present physically, spiritually, intellectually and emotionally.

Effective leadership is fundamentally about the appropriate and ethical use of power. Understanding harmony allows you to wield leadership power in a way that is vastly different—and incredibly more commanding—than ordinary approaches to leadership. In the pages that follow, by learning quick and effective ways of integrating harmony into your leadership style, you will discover the secret to doubling your effectiveness as a leader. Since managing conflict and leadership go hand-in-hand, you will also identify the necessary action steps for successfully resolving conflict.

4. Assess Your Strategy. This step will allow you to demonstrate an understanding of the many creative ways there are to solve any particular problem. We'll wrap up our journey along the Black Belt Way by recognizing that every leadership ending is really only a beginning. You will envision a time when you will have achieved harmony in your leadership style—when you will have stopped pushing or pulling—as you step forward into an exciting new level of leadership success, that of Black Belt Leadership.

On Learning Experiments

Reading a book is a one-way process. I write and you read the words that I have written. That has only limited value. Leadership, however, is a two-way street. You will benefit greatly as a leader if you do more than read words. Throughout the book, I provide you with Learning Experiments at the end of each chapter. These experiments will give you a deeper understanding of the material that I have presented in this book. **Remember: the return on your investment in this book increases significantly when you are able to empty your cup and practice these experiments.**

Please understand that there is no right or wrong way to do these experiments. The experiments are about learning, *not* about being right. This distinction is key. Feel free to change, add to, modify, or subtract from these experiments in whatever way(s) you believe will most effectively support your learning.[24]

As most people do not learn well under excessive pressure, please do not force yourself into believing that you *must* do the experiments in this book. You are in control of your own learning here, so please do what works best for you. At the same time, I invite you to challenge yourself by trying the experiments. Most people find that moving from thinking and reading to actually doing something can be a rather uncomfortable experience. Thinking and reading involve little risk. Actually doing something, on the other hand, inherently involves at least some level of risk. Gaining the wisdom to know when to move into action is crucial to your ability to become a better leader.

Learning Experiment
Stretching Out, Warming Up

Every martial arts practice begins with a period of stretching in order to warm up. I invite you to complete this exercise as a way of warming up at the beginning of this journey:

There is value in exploring our thoughts. Let's explore some of those you've had while learning about Black Belt Leadership thus far. By recognizing that your thoughts impact your behavior, you are taking the first steps of your journey along the Black Belt Way.

To begin stretching your mind, take a few minutes to complete this exercise.

Feel free to use additional paper if necessary.

Thoughts that catch my curiosity:
Some concepts about Black Belt Leadership that have peaked my attention are:

Co-workers & Colleagues:
What are two concepts of Black Belt Leadership in which my co-workers and colleagues might be interested?

Emptying my Cup:
Recalling the story at the beginning of this chapter, what else might I need to do (or not do) to "empty my cup" before I read more about Black Belt Leadership?

Chapter Summary
Congratulations!

By recognizing what leaders are missing in organizations, you have taken your first step—walking through the door—toward becoming a Black Belt Leader! Throughout the book, these Chapter Summaries will be used to: (1) Highlight the points in the chapter you have just read; (2) Suggest further reading about the topics covered in each chapter (full citations are listed in the bibliography); (3) Tell you what's ahead in the next chapter; and (4) Provide a space for notes that you'd like to keep.

Chapter Summary:
We began with the story of a martial arts master using water to teach his student about the importance of harmony. In this chapter, you learned about how people are struggling within their organizations and why leaders should care. You were briefly introduced to one of the main themes of this book, the concept that "Great leadership begins with the body." You learned about *Harmonious Emotional Engagement*, as well as gaining an overview of *The Black Belt Cycle of Leading People*, two important strategies for leaders who want to become even more successful.

Suggested further reading:
Primal Leadership by Daniel Goleman, Richard Boyatzis & Annie McKee
Follow This Path by Curt Coffman & Gabriel Gonzalez-Molina
The Randori Principles by David Baum & Jim Hassinger

Looking Ahead:
In the next chapter, we will explore the differences between pushing, pulling and actually leading people.

"People follow emotions, not force."

Story
"You Can't Move Me!"

Once upon a time there was a famous Zen monk who was also a renowned martial artist. One day while the monk was giving a public lecture, an enormous man strode up to the raised platform where the monk was speaking.

"Hey there!" shouted the large man. "I hear that you are a famous martial artist. I don't think you look so tough! I don't think you could even move me, let alone defeat me in a fight!"

The Zen monk sat quietly for a moment, then told the man that if he wanted to be moved, he should step up onto the platform. The large man jumped up onto the platform and folded his arms with a satisfied grin on his face. The Zen monk stood next to the man, and looked down at where the man was standing on the platform.

"I think," began the monk, pointing at the opposite end of the platform, "that it would be better if you stand over there."
The man moved to the other side of the platform.

"No," said the monk, "a little further back," indicating a spot several steps behind where the large man was standing. With an annoyed look on his face, the large man complied.

"There," said the monk, "You asked me to move you, and I have moved you. Now please sit down so I can finish my lecture."

Chapter 2

Leadership Styles: Are You Pushing, Pulling, or Actually Leading?

"No one is going to change as a result of our desires...
People resist coercion much more strenuously than they resist change."
- Peter Block

Why Leaders Fail

In many organizations, leading and leadership are seen as something that leaders do *to* other people. This commonly held view of leadership is fundamentally flawed and can quickly leads to problems. Human nature actively resists anything being done to us without our consent. True leadership is about being in relationship *with* people.

Leadership can be understood in two sentences:
1. Harmonious leadership styles deliver success.
2. Dissonant leadership styles deliver failure.

In *Primal Leadership*, leadership experts Goleman, Boyatzis, & McKee identify several forms of ineffective leadership styles, such as Pacesetting, Commanding, and the SOB, which they refer to as dissonant styles. These all discourage people from becoming emotionally engaged in their work, exactly the opposite effect sought by effective leaders. Dissonant leadership styles typically operate out of one of two modes: *Pushing* or *Pulling*. While I acknowledge that there may be times for leaders to either push or pull, both experience and research show that the times and places for effectively using either of these two modes of leadership occur much less frequently than most leaders realize, and that caution and care should be exercised whenever these two styles are used.[25]

❋ ❋ ❋

**"Dissonant leaders sometimes may seem effective in the short run...
but the toxicity they leave behind belies their apparent success."
Goleman, Boyatzis, & McKee**

❋ ❋ ❋

Pulling People Does Not Work...

Pulling as a leadership style involves a particular kind of coercion. The leader who pulls believes that "People won't....unless I...." For example, a Pulling Leader says, "People won't work at this job unless we offer bonuses." Pulling Leaders believe that people are like the proverbial donkey with the carrot needing to be motivated by external factors. So the leaders then bribe people with rewards to pull whatever cart the leaders want them to pull. Pulling Leaders try to *drag* people, and people resist being dragged anywhere. Like a tug of war, when a Pulling Leader pulls, people pull back... even harder.

With a *Pulling* style of leadership, the leader is the one who expends the most energy—and when the leader stops pulling, employees stop moving. Pulling Leaders create conditions in their organizations that continuously pull people with rewards such as employee of the month parking places and paper certificates for "perfect attendance." Pulling Leaders usually complain that their employees lack "internal motivation," when, in fact, the employees are actually showing a high degree of intelligence by adapting to their organizational culture of constant external rewards.[26]

A *Pulling Leader* is evident in the narcissistic "it's-all-about-me" style of leading. These types of leaders egocentrically demand that they alone make every important decision. Working with a Pulling Leader is like watching one person trying to play every position on a basketball team at the same time. A Pulling Leader is a ball-hog and not effective.

A Pulling Leader focuses on "I" and "me." In his book *Good to Great*, author Jim Collins offers a perfect example of a Pulling Leader. Collins describes Stanley Gault, who led Rubbermaid for a period of time. Collins and his research team examined 312 articles collected on Rubbermaid and reported that Gault came across in these articles as "a hard-driving, egocentric executive."[27] Collins recalls an article where Gault described his ability to affect change, and notes Gault used the word "I" forty-four times, while the word "we" appeared only sixteen times.[28]

…And Neither Does Pushing People

Pushing Leaders focus on external punishments, with the "push" being more coercive and often accompanied by threats or actual use of force. Pushing Leaders frequently have a very dim view of human nature (themselves excluded, thank you very much). Just like Pulling Leaders, Pushing Leaders also believe, "People won't…unless I…," but with a slightly different twist. Pushing Leaders focus more on punishments. Examples of phrases I have heard Pushing Leaders use include: "People won't do their job unless I stand over them," and, "This training needs to be mandatory for everyone, or else no one will attend." While the Pulling Leader overuses external rewards as in, "Do *this* and you'll get *that*," the Pushing Leader overdoes external punishments through statements such as, "Do *this* and *that* won't happen to you."

Like the Pulling Leader, the style of a Pushing Leader also requires the leader to generate all the energy. A Pushing Leader tries to move employees in a direction that the leader has chosen. But without the employees' emotional commitment to that direction, all of the momentum and energy has to come from the leader. Just as with pulling, people do not like to be pushed. When a Pushing Leader pushes, people push back… even harder. The moment a Pushing Leader stops pushing, people stop moving.[29]

Another example from the book *Good to Great* has author Jim Collins decribing a Pushing Leader named Al Dunlap, the former CEO of Scott Paper. "[He] loudly beat on his own chest, telling anyone who would listen (and many who would prefer not to) about what he had accomplished."

Collins goes on to describe Dunlap's leadership approach:

> …Dunlap personally accrued $100 million for 603 days of work at Scott Paper (that's $165,000 per day), largely by slashing the workforce, cutting the R & D budget in half, and putting the company on growth steroids in preparation for sale. After selling off the company and pocketing his quick millions, Dunlap wrote a book about himself, in which he trumpeted his nickname Rambo in Pinstripes."[30]

An isolated case? Not in my experience—or in yours, most likely.[31]

❋ ❋ ❋

A Key to Leading People:
Black Belt Leadership is an exciting new approach to leading people
that lets leaders maintain the power of their role, while at the same
time allowing leaders to be more positively
connected to those around them.

❋ ❋ ❋

Beyond Pushing or Pulling: Black Belt Leadership

Leaders who rely primarily on either *Pushing* or *Pulling* styles of leadership are not true leaders. These two styles of leadership are ineffective because both styles cost your organization money. Fortunately, there is another way: Leading People with Harmony.[32]

Successful leadership is about leading people in ways that are mutually rewarding for the individuals as well as the organization as a whole. Rather than trying to push or pull people in a certain direction, Black Belt Leadership involves a sensitive joining with, and an orchestration of, the *momentum* of people in an organization, in order for them to move in the direction you want them to go. This redirection may either be large and vigorous or small and gentle, because, being practical, successful leaders lead harmoniously by focusing on working with "what is" rather than trying to create "what is not."

Consider the example of employee training. Offering ways for the employees in your organization to improve their skills is very cost-effective, as generally only about 20% of employees will take advantage of the opportunity. These 20% will be the employees who are ready and willing to learn new skills in order to move up in your organization. Providing leadership by recognizing and supporting the interest that already exists (that is, the 20% of the people who are ready to learn at any given time), you create less work and less cost for your organization than if you had selected the employees to attend training via some managerial mandate (*pushing*). As an added bonus, you increase the pool of trained talent within your organization.

The Black Belt Way, like other harmonious leadership approaches, can work for all people in all professions, at every level of every organization.

From gentle one-on-one management within a small partnership to the energetic implementation of strategic initiatives throughout an international organization, harmonious leadership is a very powerful and effective way to lead people.

❊ ❊ ❊

"Act when it is beneficial, desist if it is not. Anger can revert to joy, wrath can revert to delight, but a nation destroyed cannot be restored to existence, and the dead cannot be restored to life."
Sun Tzu
❊ ❊ ❊

How Harmony in Leadership Creates Success

The concept of harmony can be easily misunderstood. As we saw in Chapter 1, harmony occurs when individual elements work together to produce results exponentially greater than the sum of the individual elements. Many leaders incorrectly believe that harmony is a spineless concept that offers little power and has no place in the hard-nosed environment of business and leadership. In fact, claims of success for these so-called "hard-nosed" and "tough-minded" leadership approaches simply do not hold water in the face of a vast amount of research on leadership. Here is a brief sampling of that research, which shows how flawed those "tough" approaches to leadership actually are:

- Jeffrey Pfeffer, the Thomas D. Dee II Professor of Organizational Behavior at Stanford University's Graduate School of Business and author of *The Human Equation: Building Profits by Putting People First*, shares: "[L]ittle evidence exists that being a mean or 'tough' boss is necessarily associated with business success."[33]
- Over 2,500 years ago, Sun Tzu recognized the folly of "tough" leadership approaches when he wrote: "To be violent at first and wind up fearing one's people is the epitome of ineptitude."
- In their book *Follow This Path*, authors Coffman & Gonzalez-Molina argue that "a productive workplace is one in which people feel safe enough to experiment, to make mistakes, to challenge, to share information, and to support each other."

- Finally, consider this quote from the National Institute for Occupational Safety and Health: "Recent studies of so-called healthy organizations suggest that policies benefiting worker health also benefit the bottom line."[34]

Most of the great religions and philosophies of the world have long held the importance of harmony as a powerful leadership tool. There is enough data available now to suggest that modern-day leaders would do well to come to similar conclusions. One of the best ways for leaders to comprehensively understand harmony is by examining leadership through the lens of the Japanese martial art of Aikido.

Aikido, the martial art created by Morihei Ueshiba, is often translated as "the Way of Harmony." Aikido teaches leaders that rather than using force against people, leaders will be more successful when they blend harmoniously with people. Master Ueshiba was not talking about harmony just because the idea sounded good and made people feel warm and fuzzy inside. He spoke of harmony from the pragmatic perspective of the martial arts: Harmony *works* better. While he was alive, Master Ueshiba repeatedly proved that harmony leads to success, and he did so in the most practical terms. In Asia, if you create a martial art and call that art effective, people are going to come and test your art. They do this by trying to kill you. Nothing personal. You simply have to put your money where your mouth is. As the founder of Aikido, Master Ueshiba walked his talk. Many different fighters from all walks of the world challenged Master Ueshiba, and he was never defeated. Furthermore, he rarely even injured anyone who challenged him. The lesson here for leaders is this:

The simple truth is that harmony is the most effective method of interpersonal interaction. Harmony leads to success.[35]

Research consistently shows that when groups of people interact in truly harmonious ways, these groups are always—*always*—smarter than any single person.

This is true because of a term called "multiple perspectives," which simply means that every person will observe any given situation from a slightly different angle because of the unique life experiences they bring to the present moment. Since every person in your organization is unique, each person brings his or her own particular mix of thoughts, emotions and beliefs into every situation that occurs within your organization.[36] Ineffective leaders see multiple perspectives as a threat, and they try to get everyone thinking, seeing and doing things in exactly the same way, a goal virtually impossible to achieve. Superior leaders, on the other hand, recognize the value of multiple perspectives, and they leverage that value to move their organization toward greatness.

Leaders need to understand that valuing multiple perspectives, as well as the accumulated knowledge and wisdom in a group led by a harmonious leader, will always provide greater return than the same group led by coercive styles of leadership. For example, take the story of the eight blind men and the elephant. Each blind man experienced a different part of the elephant, and consequently each man drew different conclusions about the elephant's qualities. Individually, each man had only part of the picture. Together, they had a much clearer picture of the elephant. The key to an effectively operating group is the simple (yet sometimes difficult to achieve) factor of harmony.

Spotlight: A Leadership Warrior

Harmony is powerful, and Richard Strozzi-Heckler, Ph.D., will tell you so.

Dr. Strozzi-Heckler is an internationally known authority on leadership and mastery. He has authored five books, including In Search of the Warrior Spirit, in which he chronicled the leadership program that he developed for the United States Army Special Forces. Dr. Strozzi-Heckler holds a 6th-degree black belt in Aikido, and he also holds ranks in judo, jujitsu, and capoeria (a Brazilian martial art). For over 30 years, Dr. Strozzi-Heckler has been working with a variety of organizations in a leadership training process that he calls the Leadership Dojo™, which emphasizes leaders attending to the wisdom of their bodies.

I caught up with Dr. Strozzi-Heckler and asked him about harmony and the value of somatic, or embodied, practices.

"Somatic practices," Dr. Strozzi-Heckler proceeded to tell me, "connect moral imperative with a physical presence that makes harmony a pragmatic way of being in the world. Without these practices, harmony remains simply a 'good idea' instead of an action to be lived. Harmony is a virtue that has been celebrated and emphasized in all the great religions and philosophies of the world. If you ask almost anyone, they will tell you the importance of an inner har

mony and a harmony between people."
When asked where the problem is based, Dr. Strozzi-Heckler responded, "When we look around we see so little harmony. What's missing are the practices that make harmony an embodied way of being in the world."

Identifying those practices is what this book is all about.

❋ ❋ ❋
A Key to Leading People:
"Simply put, ineffective leadership, in the form of
either Pushing or Pulling,
does not pay—ethically, financially or any other way.
True leaders seek harmony when they lead people."
❋ ❋ ❋

Conclusion

Power is inherent in every leader's position, and leaders bears the responsibility for using that power ethically, humanely and effectively. Misusing power as a leader takes very little effort. After all, where's the challenge in pushing and pulling people around? A leader's misuse of power only results in the loss of both people and money. On the other hand, leading in a powerful, balanced, and harmonious way is an effective means of creating an emotionally engaged group of people within your organization in ways that will improve the bottom line.

Fundamentally, there are only two ways to lead people: harmoniously or coercively. The choice is yours. You can choose to be a leader who pushes others, or you can choose to be a leader who pulls others. But these coercive methods of leadership are destined for failure because people do not *like* to be pushed or pulled. To become an even more successful leader, make the choice, instead, to lead people with the power of harmony.

Learning Experiment

Are You Pushing or Pulling as a Leader?

Are you a leader who pushes, pulls or actually leads? Remembering that pushing and pulling are hardwired biologically into humans, you as a leader need to understand your own tendency toward either approach. This awareness will help you identify what you need to do in order to become a leader who practices Harmonious Emotional Engagement.

Answer questions 1 and 2 right now. Then, as you lead people over the next few weeks, observe whether you tend to push or pull. Don't try to change yourself or do anything differently. Just take this time to become more aware of your style. Take notes as you go through the week, and at the end of the week, answer questions 3 and 4.

1. Some ways that I find myself **pushing** others when I lead include:

2. Some ways that I find myself **pulling** others when I lead include:

3. After watching myself for the past week, I notice that I usually tend to:
   [ ] Push   [ ] Pull

4. One thing that I might do differently in order to practice Harmonious Emotional Engagement would be:

Chapter Summary
Congratulations!

By recognizing the differences between pushing, pulling, and actually leading people, you have taken your next step toward becoming a Black Belt Leader!

Chapter Summary:

We began with the story of a Japanese monk who was able to move an "enormous man" with only his voice—and with harmony. Then we delineated the Black Belt Leadership style of *Harmony* from the more commonly used styles of *Pushing* and *Pulling*. We recognized that *Pushing* and *Pulling* usually take more energy and achieve less desirable results. Similar to all leadership approaches that focus on harmony, Black Belt Leadership is more about joining *with* those we are leading rather than doing something *to* them.

Suggested further reading:

Intentional Revolutions: A Seven-Point Strategy for Transforming Organizations by Edwin Nevis, Joan Lancourt & Helen G. Vassallo
Aikido in Everyday Life: Giving In to Get Your Way by Terry Dobson & Victor Miller
Stewardship by Peter Block

Looking Ahead:

In the next chapter, we will explore the Four Cornerstones of Black Belt Leadership, and you will learn how to incorporate them into your leadership style.

"Smart leaders recognize the critical roles both logic <u>and</u> emotions play in leadership."

Story
"My teacher is best!"

*A martial arts student was bragging about his sensei (teacher)
to a student from another martial arts school.*

*"My sensei is so great," began the first student, "She can defeat 100 people
with one hand tied behind her back. She can cut through 10 trees
with a single sword cut."*

"Can she?" asked the other student.

"Yes, she can! What can your master do?" asked the first student.

*"My sensei is so great," began the second student, "When he holds the sword,
he holds the sword. When he eats, he eats, and when he sleeps, he sleeps."*

The first student bowed low in acknowledgement of a true master.

Chapter 3
The Four Cornerstones of Black Belt Leadership

*"Part of the problem is that you cannot solve the problem
by using the same management strategies that created the problem."*
- Peter Block

The Four Cornerstones

Fundamentals. Basics. Cornerstones. Call them what you will—every successful martial artist begins and ends with them. Every successful leader does the same. Successful leadership is fundamentally about one thing—relationships. Period. Not flashy techniques or skills. Not the number of books you have read or where you earned your degree, but relationships. Focusing on relationships makes you better able to lead people through the upheavals that invariably occur within organizations, without getting defensive or yelling, without jumping in prematurely to make the problem disappear or attempting to manage (i.e., *fix*) other people.

The Four Cornerstones of Black Belt Leadership are powerful processes that lie at the very heart of the Black Belt Way. They are:

1. The Power of Embodied Leadership
2. The Power of *Both-And* Thinking
3. The Power of Process
4. The Power of Succeeding through Mistakes & Limitations

Cornerstone #1: The Power of Embodied Leadership

Great leadership begins with the body.

To understand this important point, consider the martial arts, which come out of a tradition of life and death experiences. If you were an ancient warrior engaging in hand-to-hand combat, the martial capabilities that you developed in your training would have a direct impact on whether you lived or died on the battlefield. Consequently, the martial arts were grounded in seeking the most effective approaches. To a warrior of old, "most effective" meant, very literally, "best chance of surviving." With their very lives on the line, ancient warriors sought to develop the most comprehensive ways of training possible. These warriors recognized a fundamental pearl of wisdom that is so often overlooked by modern leaders: **People are embodied beings, and therefore leaders need to lead from embodied experience.**

Embodied leadership is important because our bodies are the instruments through which we express ourselves as leaders. The most important form of expression for leaders lies in the emotional arena—expression captured by the concept of emotional intelligence. There is an overwhelming amount of research that demonstrates how vital an understanding of emotional intelligence is for successful leaders. While much of the research on emotional intelligence focuses on the recent incredible advances made in the study of the emotional centers of our brain, we must remember that, as holistic beings, emotions exist throughout our entire bodies.

Organizations can succeed or fail, expand internationally or close their doors forever, and the difference lies in the actions of the leaders. Leaders who want to lead successful organizations would do well to follow the wisdom laid out by thousands of years of martial arts experts. You have the potential to develop a highly effective, hard-working leadership tool that is literally at your fingertips every moment. This tool is more commonly known as your body. Inside your physical structures lies an innate wisdom that can tremendously increase your capacity for leading people, but only when you learn to practice embodied leadership.

A computer is a collection of parts that work together as a whole. The central processing unit (CPU) serves little purpose sitting alone on a table. But when teamed up with other components, i.e., a printer, modem, keyboard and monitor, the CPU becomes part of a machine powerful enough to tap into a cyberspace that connects the world in a blink of an eye. The same is true with people. As majestic as our brains are, they can do little on their own because they require our bodies to carry out instructions. Our bodies provide the interface between our brains and the environment. Without the constant stream of information that our bodies provide our brains, our brains would quickly atrophy and die.

Taking this idea a step further, we need to recognize that our bodies are not merely fiber optic telephone lines along which environmental information pours. Our bodies also have an intelligence in their own right. The wisdom held in our bodies is often referred to as *somatic intelligence*, a core component of intelligence as a whole. In my coaching and consulting practice, I instruct leaders on increasing their somatic intelligence in order to become even better leaders. The results are often dramatic. Consider Dave, an executive in a large Midwestern corporation. Dave initially came to me because of issues he was having in controlling his temper. Dave's anger had become such a problem that his wife was threatening to leave him and he was in trouble with his board of directors. He and I worked on his anger problem, and I taught him the principles of embodied leadership. Initially, Dave was skeptical of what he called my "touchy-feely" approach. After a short time, though, he was seeing the results of embodied leadership in action—and he was sold. By the end of our work together, Dave's relationship with his board of directors was back on solid ground, and so was his marriage.

Embodied leadership goes far beyond a holistic understanding of the fact that we are unified beings, and that our mind, body, and spirit function as an integrated whole. Embodied leadership *lives* that truth. The difference between understanding and embodying a fact is the difference between understanding the lottery and actually winning the lottery. The more embodied we become as leaders, the better leaders we are. This is true because tapping into the wisdom of our bodies provides us with even greater leadership resources to draw upon. Leading people from an embodied perspective enriches your abilities by allowing what happens in one area of your life to impact all other areas of your life. All of the experiences in your life can then act as a fertilizer that nourishes the people in the organization you lead. Great leaders know that this cross-fertilization of life experience creates tremendous value, while ineffective leaders hang onto the outdated belief that work should remain separate from every other area of their lives.

Leaders who fail to lead from an embodied place create stagnation and decay in their organizations, a rather undesirable outcome for a leader, to say the least. This happens because these leaders are closed-off, feeding on only their own experiences and thoughts. Think about placing a candle in a sealed jar. Without fresh oxygen, the candle soon goes out. The same is true with leadership. Leaders need embodied leadership approaches in order to stay fresh and vital, and with a combined focus on both emotional and somatic intelligence, embodied leadership is so important that I focused the next two chapters on the subject.

❋ ❋ ❋

"Economy is the basis of society. When the economy is stable, society develops. The ideal economy combines the spiritual and the material, and the best commodities to trade in are sincerity and love."
Master Ueshiba

❋ ❋ ❋

Cornerstone #2: The Power of *Both-And* Thinking

Becoming a successful leader calls for *both-and* thinking. In their book *Built to Last,* James Collins and Jerry Porras praise *both-and* thinking, dubbing the concept "the Genius of the AND." The business world of today calls for a much greater ability to think in terms of *both-and* rather than *either-or,* the former recognizing that both ends of opposing arguments have some validity. A sensitive balance between the two arguments is usually required, based upon the conditions in which the decision is being made. In other words, the *right* decision made in one organization would not always be the *right* decision in another organization. Or, as one executive I coached said, "Deciding between a *right* and a *wrong* is easy. The tough part comes when I have to decide between a *right* and a *right.*"

❋ ❋ ❋

A Key to Leading People:
Exchanging *either-or* thinking for *both-and*
thinking will speed your transformation into a superior leader.

❋ ❋ ❋

As an example, consider the overused phrase "thinking outside of the box." Instead of thinking outside or inside the box for any given situation, The Black Belt Way teaches that thinking inside *and* outside the box can be right when done at the right time. Knowing the right action to take at the right time is a complex decision. Ultimately, the right action for leaders is all about making appropriate decisions in the face of incredible complexities. This calls for leaders who are willing to go beyond set models of leadership, for no model is going to account for every situation that leaders face. Superior leaders are willing to take the journey far beyond the ordinary cookie-cutter approaches to leadership, using the power of *both-and* thinking.[37]

Playing with Knives… and Sticks… and Fists…….

Martial artists train to expect the unexpected. The same should be true for leaders. For example, Aikido practitioners do more than just practice techniques against unarmed partners. In Aikido, we practice techniques where our partner attacks us with knives (*tanto*), sticks (*jo*), and swords (*bokken*). We also practice against multiple attackers. *Either-or* thinking would be, "I will only practice with a person attacking me with their hands," or, "I will only practice against a person attacking me with a knife." Clearly, you never know what you will encounter in this world, so to *only* practice against one type of attack would be naïve indeed.

But sadly, *either-or* thinking is still quite prevalent in today's organizations. A case in point involves an executive I coached recently named Sharon. Early in our work together, Sharon came to one of our sessions quite upset. She had just come from a meeting at work that, in her words, had "blown up in my face." Sharon recounted that she began the meeting with her direct reports by presenting a strategy she had created to move her department forward. Her team began to critique Sharon's plan, offering suggestions as well as possible pitfalls. The more the pitfalls were discussed, the more the team grew concerned about the viability of the plan. Sharon then concluded the meeting by informing her team that her plan would be implemented next week. The team responded to Sharon with anger and frustration. "I think they are just being resistant to change," Sharon told me at the start of our session.

Sharon and I then created an embodied experiment that opened her eyes to the fact that she had fallen into *either-or* thinking. She discovered that she had stumbled because she believed that she had to *either* implement her plan *or* listen to the concerns of her team. With another embodied experiment, Sharon realized that she had alienated her team by asking for their input and then effectively ignoring everything they said. "I became intimidated when they began to critique my plan," she confided as she described her emotional response. "So I just decided that it was my way or the highway! I realize now that this was the wrong decision to make."

As another example of *either-or* thinking, consider most leaders' views on the subject of emotions. Many have long believed that a choice must be made between emotions or logic. These leaders typically hold logic and reasoning in high esteem, while viewing emotions as weak and even childish. Today this picture is changing dramatically, with scientists from many disciplines coming to understand the importance of emotions and the way they actually *support* and *underlie* logic and reasoning. Leadership should not be a question of choosing between emotions *or* logic, but rather about tapping into the "genius of the AND" and recognizing the importance of both emotions *and* logic in leadership. [38]

Cornerstone #3: The Power of Process

Great leaders understand the difference between process and content, and they value the power of process. Process is very important in emotional interactions because every emotional interaction has a process. By "process" I mean *a series of actions, changes, or functions that take place in order to bring about a result.* Understanding the importance of process, and learning effective ways to attend to *leadership* processes are both crucial to becoming a better leader. As a result, leaders need a language that describes process. Otherwise, processes remain in the shadows and wreak havoc. The power of process in leadership is so important that Chapter Seven addresses the subject exclusively.

Content is what is generally understood to be knowledge. Content is the "what" of any conversation or event. The assets of a company, the details behind writing a business plan, or the marketing of a widget—these are all content areas. In today's environment, any one of these content elements can change with lightning speed. Attending to process—the "how" in something getting done—will assist you in creating a positive engagement with members of your team. A leader can provide information to his troops using only content and create an emotionally disengaged team of people. Or, a leader can pitch his project or task with the *how's* of process, thereby increasing people's positive emotional engagement. Both methods of leading will have an impact on the bottom line—the former resulting in shrinkage, the latter in improvement.

As we mentioned earlier, the subject of *process* will be covered in much greater depth in Chapter 7.

❋ ❋ ❋
**"Freedom is not worth having if it does not include
the freedom to make mistakes."
Mahatma Gandhi**
❋ ❋ ❋

Cornerstone #4: The Power of Succeeding through Mistakes & Limitations

We are all human. We all make mistakes and have limitations.

We become effective leaders by learning from our mistakes and limitations. We do not become effective leaders by pretending that we do not make mistakes or have limitations. In his book *Zen in the Martial Arts*, author Joe Hyams talks about being trained by the great martial artist, Bruce Lee. Hyams recalls a discussion with Lee in which Lee revealed that Lee's right leg was one inch shorter than his left, and he was also very near-sighted. Lee went on to tell Hyams that he never allowed these limitations to prevent him from becoming a martial artist. In fact, by learning to adapt to those limitations, Bruce Lee went on to become one of the most successful and well-known martial artists of the 20th century.

Becoming a great leader requires development, both on your part and that of your organization. Developing even stronger leadership skills without making mistakes is simply impossible, for development and mistakes are two sides of the same coin. When a child first learns to walk, falling down is inevitable. If your intention is to develop your leadership abilities, then making mistakes will be a natural part of your learning curve. Mistakes cannot be avoided, because growth is impossible without them. Thus, embarking on a path to develop your emotional leadership skills requires having the heart, discipline, and courage of a Warrior.[39] There are no easy answers. Trial and error, mistakes and limitations are all inevitable for every successful leader. Whether you are learning to become a better leader or learning a martial art, you will find one very important aspect in common: **You will not succeed if you are not willing to make mistakes…again and again.**

Some leadership methods mistakenly tout leaders as having so many positive qualities that they begin to sound like minor deities. No human can live up to the standards that these leadership methods hold for leaders, and no leader is immune from mistakes. Regarding vulnerability, Richard Strozzi Heckler, in his book *In Search of the Warrior Spirit*, offers a definition of a warrior: "Believing you can be perfect is the fatal imperfection. Believing you're invulnerable is the ultimate vulnerability. Being a warrior doesn't mean winning or even succeeding. It means risking and failing and risking again, as long as you live."[40]

Making true, honest mistakes is one thing. Making excuses and expressing a constant victim mentality are quite another. Understanding that mistakes and limitations occur is no justification for lackluster performance or unethical decisions as a leader. Set your leadership standards as high as possible for your given situation. Leaders should expect and look for excellence, *not* perfection. At the same time, you should consider honest mistakes as valuable teachers because of the lessons they carry, both for you and the people you lead.[41]

Later on in this book, you will learn about how leaders can impact the emotional engagement levels of the people in their organizations. In order to become emotionally engaged, people require an environment in which mistakes can be tolerated. If you cannot tolerate mistakes in yourself, you will never truly be able to tolerate mistakes that others make. As you move along the path of leadership mastery, give yourself and others the permission to make honest mistakes.[42]

❋ ❋ ❋

**"If you're not failing every now and again,
it's a sign you're not doing anything very innovative."
Woody Allen**

❋ ❋ ❋

Ten Tips to Make the Cornerstones Work for You

The Four Cornerstones are fundamental building blocks to every successful leadership strategy. These cornerstones can easily be integrated into your existing approach to leadership. The Four Cornerstones can help you lead with confidence, make fewer leadership mistakes and help you readily fix whatever leadership mistakes you do make.

A fundamental requirement of the Four Cornerstones of Black Belt Leadership is that leaders change the patterns of their emotional interactions with all the people in their lives, not just a select few at work. The path of emotional mastery for leaders is more all-encompassing than other areas of business such as Finance or IT, for example. An accountant can be effective at work and still remain emotionally dysfunctional. But an emotionally dysfunctional leader can *never* be effective. If you try to pretend you're an emotionally engaged leader at work during the day and then go home at night and scream at your children, ignore your partner, and kick your dog, then you are an imposter—and as an imposter, you cannot move forward on the path toward leadership mastery.

Here are ten tips that will help you make the Four Cornerstones work for you:

1. Drop it.

The next time you find yourself on the opposing side of an argument, drop your need to be right for a moment. See if you can fully understand the other person's point without letting go of your own.

2. Go easy on yourself.

The next time you make a mistake, rather than letting your internal critic run you over, do something different. Take a breather and give yourself a break.

3. Go easy on others.

When someone else in your life makes an honest mistake, practice compassionate leadership. Remember, nobody's perfect.

4. Hold on to the big picture.

Keep focusing on the details, but never forget the importance of the larger picture. Holding onto the larger picture is one of the vital roles of every leader.

5. Watch the *how*.

The more our emotions get stirred up, the more likely we are to forget the *how* of the process, and instead focus in on the *what* of content. Do not let this happen to you. Always keep an eye on the *how* of process.

6. Trust yourself.

You are everything that you need to be right at this moment. Trust in your skills and ability to be successful.

7. Expand yourself.

Remember the importance of increasing your emotional capacity. Find a coach, mentor or a peer group who can assist and challenge you to expand your emotional capacity.

8. Drop the "But."

Make the conscious choice for a day to replace the word "but" in your vocabulary with the word "and." See how this simple word substitution can change your day—and also change how people respond to you as a leader.

9. Embody gratitude.

Recognize your interdependence with others, and find at least one small way each day to let those who support you know that you appreciate them. A word or small gift can go far toward building engaged relationships.

10. Seek hidden talents.

This week, try to find one new talent in each of the people who you lead as well as the people in departments that you work with and depend upon. You will be pleasantly surprised about all of the talent and goodwill waiting to be discovered within your organization when you approach people harmoniously.

Learning Experiment

Practicing the Four Cornerstones

Here are four easy ways to begin incorporating the **Four Cornerstones** into your on-going leadership style this week:

1. The Power of Embodied Leadership

At least once each day, pay attention to the physical sensations you are having when you are leading people. Do not judge the sensations as right or wrong, and do not try to change these sensations. Just notice "what is."

2. The Power of *Both-And* Thinking

At least once each day, make a conscious decision to replace the word "but" with the word "and" when you are leading people.

3. The Power of Process

During at least one meeting this week, pay attention to the *process* of the meeting by asking yourself, "How is this meeting being run?" See what patterns you notice about the process of the meeting.

4. The Power of Succeeding through Mistakes & Limitations

At least once a day, pay attention to how you respond when you or someone else makes a mistake. Discover what you might want to say or do in order to be easier on yourself and others.

Chapter Summary
Congratulations!

By understanding the cornerstones of Black Belt Leadership, you have taken your next step toward becoming a Black Belt Leader! You are now ready to advance to blue belt!

Chapter Summary:

We began with a story of two novice martial artists arguing about who had the greater teacher. We saw that being able to fully attend to the fundamental basics of life can make us very powerful. In this chapter, we learned about the Four Cornerstones of Black Belt Leadership:

1. The Power of Embodied Leadership

All great leadership begins with the body.

2. The Power of *Both-And* Thinking

Replace the more limited *either-or* thinking with the more expansive *both-and* thinking… and discover the possibilities.

3. The Power of Process

Successful leaders pay greater attention to the *process* (how something occurs) than the *content* (what is being said).

4. The Power of Succeeding through Mistakes & Limitations

Trial and error, mistakes and limitations, are all inevitable (and on-going) for every successful leader.

Suggested further reading:

The Answer to How is Yes by Peter Block
In Search of the Warrior Spirit by Richard Strozzi-Heckler
Leadership Aikido by John O'Neil

Looking Ahead

In the next chapter, we will examine how you can incorporate mind-body technology into your leadership strategies in ways that will make you an even better leader.

BLUE BELT
Section II –
Take Your Stance

"The softest thing in the universe
overcomes the hardest thing in the universe."
- Lao Tzu

"Great leadership starts with the body."

Story
Heavy Rocks

In ancient times, Asian martial artists trained in physical techniques as well as philosophy and meditation. Once, a student went to demonstrate his knowledge to his master.

"Sensei (teacher)," the youth began, "I have meditated as you have taught me and I have transcended time, space, and physical existence. I understand the unreality of existence. I now know that everything is a thought."

The master looked at the student, and then glanced out at a formation of rocks that were sitting in a nearby garden.

"How about those rocks?" the teacher asked. "Are they too thoughts in your mind?"

"Absolutely." replied the student confidently, "Everything is a thought."

"Your head," the teacher said quietly, "must be very heavy from carrying all of those rocks."

Chapter 4
Embodied Leadership Technology

*"Whatever happens to the body also happens to the mind. The sanity of the
body is the sanity of the mind; the violation of the body
is the violation of the mind."*
-Thich Nhat Hanh

On the very first page of their best-selling book *Primal Leadership*, Daniel Goleman, Richard Boyatzis, and Annie McKee point out that "Great leadership works through the emotions." This is an important, groundbreaking idea. If we carry this idea out to its logical conclusion, then we have just arrived at the core principle of Black Belt Leadership:

Great leadership starts with the body

Leadership that begins with the body is what I refer to as *embodied leadership*. While you have already been introduced to embodied leadership as the First Cornerstone of Black Belt Leadership, this chapter will serve to deepen your understanding of this important concept. I hope to help you understand how practicing the technology of embodied leadership can create even greater success in your life. To begin, consider these two important facts:

1. 100% of the people you lead have bodies.
2. 100% of leaders have bodies.

A basic, albeit often overlooked fact of leadership is that we all exist in the physical realm. Each of us comes into this life with a body. We live and die in our bodies. What happens to us either before our births or after our deaths is the subject for philosophies and religions. The fact remains that, while we walk the Earth, everything that happens to us is an *embodied* experience. Though obvious, this truth has been completely ignored by most leadership strategies. Instead, those strategies have focused almost exclusively on thoughts and ideas, as if people were simply heads floating around in space.

As a key component of my coaching and consulting practice, I teach clients how to improve their leadership skills by increasing their *somatic intelligence,* a core component of embodied leadership technology. Somatic intelligence is the wisdom that is contained within our bodies, down to the core of our very bones—a level of intelligence that most leaders fail to leverage, to the detriment of themselves as well as their organizations. Conversely, leaders who learn to leverage the full implications of somatic intelligence experience dramatically increased levels of success over those who do not.

✳ ✳ ✳
"Training the body in this sense doesn't mean losing weight, building big biceps, having a flat stomach, or developing the ability to hit a golf ball a long way; it means training the self to be an effective and ethical leader."
Richard Strozzi-Heckler
✳ ✳ ✳

Mind & Body: Two Sides of the Same Coin

People are living, organic beings, and medical research is increasingly recognizing the truth that mind and body are, in fact, one.[43] While we often speak about *mind* and *body* as separate entities, great leaders understand that mind and body are, in reality, two sides of the same coin. Superior leaders recognize further that an awareness of their own physical selves is a critical component of their success. In a very real way, our toes, stomachs, and shoulders are on equal footing (pardon the pun) with our thoughts and ideas.[44] As with any other tool, however, leaders must be trained to use embodied leadership technology appropriately and effectively. This chapter will introduce you to three specific ways you can use embodied leadership technology to assist you in becoming a better leader.[45]

Embodied Leadership & the Rapture of Leadership

Wise leaders know that people learn from experience. Research shows that the best kind of learning for adults is experiential. The more senses we involve in our learning experiences, the better the results—and our physical selves can teach us a tremendous amount about emotions and the emotional realm.

A gentleman by the name of Joseph Campbell (1904-1987) was an American scholar of mythology and comparative religion who gained fame with such works as *The Hero with a Thousand Faces* (1948), *The Masks of God* (1959-1968), and the multi-volume *Historical Atlas of World Mythology* (1968). Campbell's theories were made popular through a series of Public Broadcasting System television interviews with Bill Moyers, which were ultimately published as a book that became a best-seller. In one of those interviews, Campbell shared the following regarding *experience*:

> "People say that what we're all seeking is a meaning for life. I don't think that's what we're really seeking. I think that what we're seeking is an experience of being alive...so that we actually feel the rapture of being alive. That's what it's all finally about..."

Embodied leaders value experience and experiential learning, and they use embodied leadership technology to act at the correct moment, which in turn gets others to act with greater emotional engagement. Today's leaders would do well to leverage an important lesson from the warrior tradition. Ancient warriors did not simply *talk* about something—they *acted*. Warrior leaders of old were very invested in creating learning experiences in order to simulate actual conditions of the combat battlefield as closely as possible. What they did was create a *dojo*—a place of practice. The *dojo* is a working laboratory of sorts where people can experiment with various methods of attacking and defending, leading and following, without losing their lives. From the earliest days, warriors of old discovered the methodology of embodied learning to be one of the most effective ways for humans to acquire new skills.

Embodied Leadership: The Black Belt Leadership Stance

People increasingly recognize the importance of our physical selves in our daily lives. More and more, they are turning in record numbers to ancient physical practices like Yoga, Aikido and T'ai Chi. Yet there are martial arts practitioners today who have been practicing 20, 30, or even 40 years and who still consider themselves mere beginners. For example, in Aikido, you might practice anywhere from five to ten years before you earn a black belt. Understanding that you might not have the time or energy to commit to this extended period of practice, I have distilled the principles of Aikido into the three disciplines of embodied leadership, which you will learn about in a moment.

But first, embodied leadership combines the twin qualities of ethical principles and effective practice. Master Ueshiba, the founder of Aikido, was already recognized in Japan as a great martial artist when he became disillusioned with the competitive, hurtful face of the martial art world where ethical principles and effective practice materialized as separate disciplines. A deeply spiritual man, Master Ueshiba sought to *combine* ethical principles with effective martial arts practice. He developed the art of Aikido as a way to bridge the gap he saw between these two realms, and he even went so far as to state that, "In true *budo* [martial arts], there are no enemies. True *budo* is a function of love... Aikido is the manifestation of love."[46]

❊ ❊ ❊

A Key to Leading People:
Becoming a better leader is less about
learning new techniques and more about
reconnecting with the wisdom in your body.

❊ ❊ ❊

Master Ueshiba's words are strikingly familiar to Martin Luther King, Jr.'s Nobel Prize acceptance speech, in Stockholm, Sweden, on December 11, 1964 in which Dr. King said, "Nonviolence is the answer to the crucial political and moral questions of our time: the need for man to overcome oppression and violence without resorting to oppression and violence... The foundation of such a method is love." Leaders who aspire to follow the spiritual insights of Martin Luther King, Jr., Mahatma Gandhi, the Dalai Lama, Dorothy Day and Mother Theresa would do well to study the principles of embodied leadership.

Master Ueshiba saw the martial arts as an activity that played a crucial role in the development of personal character. This fact is often lost on the Western world. In the West, we are enamored with the heroes who appear on our theater screens—characters who are able to defeat multitudes of enemies and walk away unscathed. Many people have fallen under the siren song of unlimited power that Hollywood spins around martial arts. In reality, in Asia, the martial arts have been viewed historically as a way of refining character.

In his work, Master Ueshiba drew from the Asian religions and philosophies of Zen Buddhism, Shinto, and Taoism. In fact, people often refer to Aikido as "Zen in motion." Achieving a calm state in the quiet of the meditation room is all well and good, but how well does that translate into your day-to-day life? One of the goals of The Black Belt Way is striving to maintain a relaxed and supple calmness in the midst of increasingly conflictual situations—a perfect fit for leaders, don't you think?

Embodied Leadership: The Three Disciplines

When you begin learning a martial art, or even a sport such as golf or tennis, one of the very first techniques you address is the proper stance. By standing in a particular way—the way your feet are positioned, the way you hold your legs—you become more firmly connected to the ground, and consequently better able to perform the task at hand. Since martial arts are a matter of life and death, the stance of any particular martial art could be considered the root of life. In fact, the technique is so important that high-level martial artists can often tell the skill of another martial artist simply from watching their stance.

In leadership, as in the martial arts, your stance is critical to your success. If you have a weak stance, then every way you lead will be fundamentally flawed. For example, if you have a weak stance in your emotional life, then you will have significant difficulties when you attempt to lead other people relationally. Recalling that we are embodied beings, I do not mean the word *stance* to be understood only metaphorically. I am also using the word *stance* in the literal sense, in terms of how leaders actually carry themselves physically when they lead others. In a moment, I will teach you an effective leadership stance that can aid your transformation into a superior leader. Learning this embodied stance will deepen your capacity for experiencing your own emotions, and better equip you to cope with the emotions of others, from the lighthearted to the highly conflicted. Your stance, you will learn, has a very literal, not to mention enormous impact on your ultimate success as a leader.

❋ ❋ ❋
A Key to Leading People:
Develop your embodied leadership skills by using
The Stance of Black Belt Leadership
in your leadership interactions.
❋ ❋ ❋

The Stance of Black Belt Leadership involves three disciplines that incorporate mind-body technology, which anyone in almost any physical condition can practice.[47] Those three disciplines are:

1. **Relaxing and Opening**
2. **Grounding**
3. **Centering**

While you will be introduced to several tips for each discipline, there is one very important thread that connects all three: **PRACTICE**. As in any other art/science form, practice in leadership makes the difference between those who succeed in leadership and those who fail. One of the best ways to learn embodied leadership technology is to work with a coach, mentor or consultant who has expertise in that area. While the individual disciplines described below are important, remember that leadership is always done *in relationship.* So having a coach or mentor actually teach you embodied leadership technology in a one-on-one setting can provide you with a significant return on investment.

❋ ❋ ❋
"Without openness, it is generally impossible to break down the
game-playing that is deeply embedded in most organizations."
Peter Senge
❋ ❋ ❋

Discipline #1: Relaxing and Opening

Try this simple exercise suggested by Buddhist master Thich Nhat Hanh:
Breathing in,
I am aware of my heart.
Breathing out,
I smile to my heart.

I vow to eat, drink,
and work in ways
that preserve my health and well-being.

The genius of Aikido teaches us that being open and relaxed is the safest and most effective way to be a leader. Verbal, mental and emotional leadership challenges can be dealt with more effectively when we can remain relaxed and open. Because we are hard-wired to resist against force, embodying the quality of openness is counter-intuitive for many leaders. "Be open" is very easy to say, yet, very difficult to actually do. For most leaders, staying open requires continual practice. On the Aikido mat, attacks come in the form of strikes, punches, grabs, and even weapons. When someone is coming to punch me, I notice a tightening of my muscles, and a strong desire to either hide my head in my arms or hit the person back. Thankfully, most leadership challenges do not come in the same physical form as on the Aikido mat, but the effect on our bodies is the same. How many meetings have you been in where you felt your muscles tighten and you had a strong desire to either run and hide or leap forward and attack? By practicing the discipline of relaxing and opening, you can re-program yourself to perform more effectively under those types of pressures.

Relaxation, as described here, does not mean a limp or weakened condition. Instead, relaxation means flexibility and a muscular looseness that enables you to respond in any number of directions—and this state of relaxation can be extremely powerful. If you have ever had a baby grab onto your finger, you have some sense of what I mean. The baby does not grip with muscular tension, and yet the relaxed grip can be very tenacious.

In order to be relaxed, however, we must be open to receiving whatever information is in our environment. Great leaders understand that all information is important information, and that staying open to the receipt of information puts them in a much safer and more powerful position. If you have ever watched an animal in the wild, you have some sense of what I mean. For animals in the wild, being open to new information—things like sounds, scents, even silence—is a matter of survival. Ignoring or denying such information only means that the animal will become lunch for the next predator. The same premise holds true for leaders in organizational environments. Leaders who shut out important information—whether out of arrogance, complacency or fear—will soon discover that someone else has eaten their lunch.

Five Tips for Practicing Relaxing & Opening:

1. Develop Greater Awareness of Your Breath.

Proper breathing is vital for leaders who seek to practice relaxing and opening. When they encounter problems, most leaders' breathing typically becomes quite shallow, decreasing the amount of oxygen they're taking in. But breathing more fully increases the oxygen in our bodies and thus helps us become more aware and alert. Conscious breathing can be practiced through meditation, breathing exercises, swimming, Aikido, and other physical activities.

2. Practice Guided Meditation.

You can practice relaxation and openness by periodically following a guided meditation that alternates tension with relaxation. Find a quiet room, put on some soft music, and practice alternating between tightening various muscles in your body and then relaxing them. Pay attention to how you experience both the tensing and the relaxing.

3. Listen To Others.

People use their ears to gather (or keep out) information. Rather than assuming that you already know what people are trying to tell you, take time to actually listen to them. The skill of being an open listener is so critical that we will address the subject again in Chapter Twelve.

4. Do One Thing Differently.

Being open and relaxed includes being receptive to new experiences. Just for today, decide to do one thing differently. Stop at a different coffee shop on the way to work. Drive home a different way. Be open to doing *something* different from your normal habits and routine, and then see what happens.

5. Take a Break.

Treat yourself to the gift of a massage or other form of bodywork. A massage can be a wonderful way to relax… and maybe even to discover something new about embodied leadership technology.

Discipline #2: Grounding

Effective leaders are well grounded. In the martial arts and other somatic training systems, grounding is identified as a way of being in touch with and connected to the earth. In life, we often speak of "standing our ground" when an issue comes up that we firmly believe in. If I am not grounded, any passing person, thought, or desire will easily sway me.

Developing a deeper experience of being grounded creates more success for leaders by:

- Increasing leaders' abilities to move forward.
- Decreasing leaders' stress.
- Providing leaders with clearer knowledge about what their next step should be.

Being grounded involves our relationship with the physical structures that support us, which include our muscles and bones, the buildings we inhabit, and even the planet Earth itself.

Leaders are generally well rewarded for thinking, and therefore many of us have only developed ourselves from the neck upwards. Becoming more physically grounded is an effective way for you to tap into the wisdom of your body.

❋ ❋ ❋
**"Great ideas have an immediate
physical impact on your body."
Scott Adams[48]**
❋ ❋ ❋

Five Tips for Practicing Grounding:

1. Take Up a Physical Practice.

Yoga, Aikido, T'ai Chi, and other body-oriented disciplines can go a long way to helping you physically ground yourself. Consider enrolling in a physical discipline class in your community.

2. Take a Walk.

Most of us have been blessed enough to be able to use our own two feet. Whenever you can, take a walk and pay attention to how your feet connect with the earth. Take a friend along and practice together. Walking on uneven terrain (such as woods, mountains and/or streams) can be even better because nature invites us to practice grounding ourselves even more fully as we walk on irregular surfaces.

3. Take a Breath.

As with being Relaxed and Open, proper breathing is also very important for grounding yourself. Most people breathe only with the upper-third of their lungs. Take several deep breaths, allowing your lungs and stomach to expand. Imagine drawing the breath down deep into the pit of your stomach. Breathing deeper increases the flow of oxygen into your system and keeps you more grounded so you can better face the problems that inevitably arise throughout your day as a leader.

4. Take a Moment.

Take a short break right now. Take note of where you are sitting right now, and pay attention to how you are physically supported in your chair. Be curious. See if you can discover how you allow (or do not allow) the chair to support your physical self. Notice how your feet make (or do not make) contact with the ground.

5. Take What Works.

As you try any of the above tips, experiment with different ways of connecting to the ground, and pay attention to what works for you. See if you can discover ways to bring these grounding techniques into your work setting. For example, I often encourage my clients to ground themselves simply by pressing their toes into the floor. You can easily ground yourself by pressing your toes into the floor during meetings, and no one in the room will be any the wiser.[49]

❋ ❋ ❋

"The greatest gift that you can give someone is to get yourself together."
Wendy Palmer

❋ ❋ ❋

Discipline #3: Centering

With their strong over-emphasis on thoughts and ideas, most leaders consider the center of the person as being in the middle of the forehead. In the Asian traditions, the center of the person is considered to be located in the physical center of a person's body. This area, generally about one fist below your navel, which is called *hara* in Japanese and *seika tanden* in Chinese, is the physical center of the human body.

After learning their stance, martial arts beginners are then taught the difference between head and hara. This is not simply a philosophical, conceptual difference. Leading from our hara—our physical center— produces quantitative and qualitative differences in our leadership outcomes. Moving from a centered place allows me to make decisions and interact with others from the core of my being, which then allows me to be more authentic. People who lead from their centers are better leaders, and within organizations, those who practice embodied leadership are better able to stay emotionally connected with others while more effectively deal with whatever problems arise.

Tips for Practicing Centering:

1. Center on the Truth.

Telling the truth and being honest—both with ourselves and others— are two very important ways that we can help ourselves stay centered. As you go through your day, pay attention to giving people responses that are sincere and honest.

2. Center your Full Self on Any Leadership Decision.

When most leaders are asked a question, they typically respond with the first thought that pops into their minds, impulsively thinking that they must come up with an immediate answer. Fast answers can sometimes get leaders into hot water. Don't be afraid to *pause*, and pay attention to the wisdom of your body. Don't worry—you are not crazy if you listen to what your stomach (or your heart, or your shoulders) might be telling you about the words you're considering or the important decision you're on the verge of making. Your embodied wisdom can often provide you with the additional data you need to make just the right decision.

3. Breathe to Center.

Once again, breathing is important. Many leaders use shallow breathing as a way of disconnecting from their physical selves, which ends up diminishing the impact of their leadership interventions. Consciously deepening your breathing is a valuable way to help you become a more centered, effective leader.

4. Center Your Attention on Your Body.

If you are hungry, sleepy, or otherwise in physical need, then you are more easily moved off center. Be in tune with what your body is requiring, and take a little time to satisfy those needs. Don't skip lunch, for example. The extra 20 minutes you allow for that sandwich will buy you a couple of energetic hours later on in the day. Even more important, regulate your sleep. Taking better care of yourself physically will bring you many rewards, and will most assuredly equip you with a greater sense of center as a leader.

5. Center on Expansion.

Expand your ability to contain emotions by staying aware of any emotion(s) arise within you during the course of leading people. Rather than moving away from the emotion(s) or closing yourself off in denial as many leaders typically do, train yourself to stay aware of the emotion(s) for as long as possible. Encourage yourself to remain positively engaged in a debate or emotionally heated discussion for a few moments longer than you would normally feel comfortable. Work with a coach or mentor to help you expand even further. Over time, investing in this additional effort will pay off as you strengthen your ability to contain emotions and increase your emotional intelligence.

Embodied Learning Experiments

Up to this point, I have ended each chapter with a *Learning Experiment.* Since great leadership starts with the body, from this point on, each chapter will end with an *Embodied Learning Experiment* designed to support the leadership skills and strategies you've begun to learn in these pages. Of course, you are free to skip these exercises, but I would strongly suggest that you give them a try. As a leader, you will be well-served to remember the vast difference between *thinking* about something and actually *doing* that same thing. Participating in these embodied experiments will increase the return on your investment in this book, as well as help you reach your leadership goals more quickly.

Embodied Learning Experiment #1
Emotions & Leaders' Bodies

Every emotion is an embodied emotion—that is, every emotion exists in your body. Developing increased awareness of your body—your physical self—requires increasing your capacity for emotional awareness and regulation. This is one instance when focusing more on *being* than on *doing* will help you get you where you want to be as a leader. Understanding the techniques of leadership is important. Even more important, however, is discovering ways to truly embody these techniques in order to discover even greater success as a leader.

Here's an experiment to help you understand the embodiment of emotions. Read the directions, and then give the experiment a try.

Step #1

Take a moment and put yourself in a comfortable position. Imagine you are with a person, or performing an activity, that you very much despise or feel animosity toward. Don't just imagine the person or activity as an intellectual experiment. Take time to truly *experience* the negative emotions that you would feel toward that person or activity. Become aware of the negativity streaming throughout your entire body. Concentrate on those feelings.

Now, holding on to that emotional state, get up and walk across the room, and through your house (or whatever building you may be in). Pay attention to how you feel physically. Write down a few things that you notice, i.e., chest tightening, stomach churning, and so forth.

Step #2

Now do the same experiment again. This time, however, imagine you are with a person you love or that you're performing an activity you deeply enjoy. Take your time to truly embody those feelings. Once you have a sense of your embodied state, walk around, and pay attention to your body. Again, write down a few things that you notice to be different about your physical self.

Now, turn the page and consider the Discussion Questions.

Discussion

Welcome back!

Here are some questions to consider:

- For each experiment—animosity and love—what did you notice physically? (Be specific.)
- What were you most aware of physically each time?
- When you were experiencing animosity, were you more aware of your internal state or of the external world around you?
- How about when you were experiencing love?
- What were the biggest physical differences between the *love/hate* experiences for you?

Please remember that there are no right way or wrong answers to this experiment. There are commonalities among people's reactions, however. When I have performed this experiment with groups and individuals, these are some of the responses that I frequently hear:

- Many people experience a contraction inward and a tightening when they experience hateful feelings.
- Many people experience an outward expansion and softening when they experience love.
- Many people find that they are more focused on their internal state when they experience anger.
- Many people find that they are more focused on the world around them when they experience love.

If your experience fits these descriptions, that's fine. If your experience is different, that's also fine. Increasing our emotional capacity is about fully experiencing who we are in relationship with the world (and people) around us.

One of the purposes of this experiment is to increase your awareness of the important role of intentionality in emotions. Being a successful leader is about being your authentic self. In order to become an even more effective leader, your intention must be to bring yourself fully to every interaction you have with others. False, denied, or closed intentions all serve to move us out of the realm of emotionally skilled, embodied leadership.[50]

Chapter Summary
Congratulations!

By incorporating the Black Belt Leadership Stance as a basic component of your leadership repertoire, you have taken your next step toward becoming an even more successful leader!

Chapter Summary:
We began with a story about a young man who mistakenly believed that his thoughts were the basis of life. Fortunately, his teacher knew better. In this chapter, you learned that great leadership begins with the body, because mind and body are two sides of the same coin. You learned how embodied leadership is critical to successful leadership, and you learned the three disciplines from the stance of Black Belt Leadership, which include:

- Staying Relaxed and Open
- Staying Grounded
- Staying Centered

Suggested further reading:
Being Human at Work: Bringing Somatic Intelligence into Your Professional Life by Richard Strozzi Heckler
The Intuitive Body: Aikido as a Clairsentient Practice by Wendy Palmer
The Life We Are Given: A Long-Term Program for Realizing the Potential of Body, Mind, Heart, and Soul by George Leonard & Michael Murphy

Looking Ahead:
In the next chapter, we'll be exploring the answers to a very important question: What leaders do not know about the rocks and weeds in their organizations.

*"Black Belt Leaders engage
the emotional power of people."*

Story
Eyes on the Sword

Long ago in Japan, a young man was an eager student of the sword. He roamed the land seeking instruction from any master who would teach him. As he traveled, he heard rumors about a great sword teacher who had grown weary of fighting and had retired to the mountains to meditate. After months of searching, the young man finally discovered the teacher's hut high in the mountains. Finding the teacher at home, the young man begged him to instruct him in the Way of the sword. The teacher agreed to take the young man on as a student.

"How long will it take for me to master the sword?" the young man inquired.

"Five years," the teacher replied.

"Five years!" exclaimed the young man. "That is FAR too long! I promise to practice every day as hard as I can. How long will it take me then?"

"Ten years," said the master.

"Ten years!" exclaimed the young man, "what if I agree to study and practice night and day — how long then?"

"Fifteen years," said the old man softly.

"I do not understand!" said the young man. "Why is it that the harder I say I will work, the longer you say it will take me to master the sword?"

"Because," the wise teacher responded, "the more you seek to master the sword, the less I will be able to teach you. I cannot teach you to have two eyes on the sword if you have one eye on your goal."

With that, the young man bowed deeply.

Chapter 5
Emotional Intelligence: Deep Knowledge for Leaders

"There is no such thing as a "resource" until people find a use for something in nature and thus endow it with economic value. Until then, every plant is a weed and every mineral just another rock."
- Peter Drucker

The history of business is filled with stories about untapped resources viewed as worthless until some intuitive leader looked beyond the obvious to uncover value. Today, emotions are the untapped resources of every organization. Most leaders treat emotions as the rocks and weeds of the organization. Smart leaders, on the other hand, understand the value of emotions and therefore develop *Deep Knowledge* of their own emotional lives. Before you can understand Deep Knowledge (which you will learn about in a moment), I want to repeat this one very important fact:

Emotions are the untapped resources of every organization.

Emotions provide the third leg of a three-legged stool for your organization. The first leg is the physical part of the company. The second leg is your technological infrastructure. The third leg is the emotional drive of the people within your organization. Only by incorporating all three legs of the stool can your organization truly be successful.

Despite the enormous success of books about the importance of understanding emotions—such as the international best seller *Emotional Intelligence* by Daniel Goleman and *Primal Leadership* by Goleman, Boyatzis, and McKee, both of which we've already referenced—many leaders continue to think of emotions as rocks and weeds having no value in the marketplace. These leaders are locked into this mindset mainly because they've never experienced the truth about emotions. Their view of both leadership and the people in their organization has narrowed for many of them, and consequently that view blocks even the slightest awareness of the value emotions can bring to the table. Unfortunately, this way of looking at the world—called a worldview, which we will discuss further in the next chapter—is leading to lost revenues. Current research conclusively shows that organizations prosper when people are led in emotionally intelligent, sensitive ways. Based on the evidence, leaders would do well to remember that emotions are the untapped resource hidden within every organization.

The Tomato Effect & Lost Revenues

For far too long, emotions have not only been ignored as a factor in organizational success, they have been blatantly discouraged, overlooked, and undervalued. By believing emotions are worthless, leaders fall victim to a simple fallacy—the *Tomato Effect*. The Tomato Effect is what happens when people believe that something is harmful to them and should be avoided, when in reality, just the opposite is true.[51]

Consider the history of the lowly tomato. Originally discovered in Peru, the red succulent was exported back to Europe. By 1560, the tomato was being widely consumed across Europe. In America, however, the story was different. People in America "knew" that tomatoes were poisonous because the tomato plant is related to another plant called the nightshade (which *is* a poisonous plant). As a result, tomatoes were avoided in America until 1820, when a farmer named Robert Gibbon Johnson stood in front of a crowd on the steps of the courthouse in Salem, New Jersey and ate a tomato—and lived to tell the tale.[52]

In less than 200 years, Americans have gone from eating *no* tomatoes to consuming a whopping 4.8 billion pounds of them per year.[53] This is approximately 17.8 pounds per American, making the tomato our fourth most popular vegetable, which translates roughly into annual gross sales of $6.6 billion dollars.[54] Not bad for a product once thought to be lethal.

Regrettably, the Tomato Effect is alive and well in today's organizations. Leaders who continue to believe that emotions have no place in their organizations are allowing a goldmine to slip right through their fingers. Great leaders understand the importance of emotions, and they harness the emotional power of the people they lead.

A Key to Leading People:
Recognize that the power of emotions is the driving force behind
most decisions of commerce—from the boardrooms of Fortune 500
companies to the aisles of your neighborhood Wal-Marts.

Two Different Hats… But the Same Person

As a leader, becoming aware of the emotional component of leadership is just the beginning, because the world is already a step ahead of you. Emotions have been playing a huge part in your organization for a long time due to this simple truth: Your employees are someone else's customers. For better or for worse, the past two generations have been raised as consumers—*sophisticated* consumers. People have become very savvy and have developed fine-tuned sales pitch detectors that differentiate between an emotionally insincere approach and one that is honest. This skill isn't the product of formal education or specific to any particular demographic, but rather one of living in a consumer culture.

According to Standard & Poors, businesses worldwide recently spent $471 billion dollars on marketing and researching the emotional impact of colors, logos, brand names, music, and everything else that helps sell a product. These factors are all about creating an emotional experience in order to create an emotional engagement between consumers and the products businesses want them to buy.

For example, if you were feeling depressed and went to your doctor for medication, which options for medication sound more appealing: *Fluoxetine Hydrochloride* and *Sertraline Hydrochloride,* or Prozac and Zoloft?[55] The latter two are the respective brand names for the former medicines. Most people would probably choose the latter, even if they knew the choices were the identical drugs, because the technical names for medications can be intimidating. Furthermore, if you believe that the commercial names for medicines are chosen for any *medical* reason, think again. Creating a commercial name for a drug is done strictly for marketing purposes. Drug brand names are routinely chosen by marketing departments based on the emotional impact of the names.[56]

Consumers are inundated with marketing messages that appeal to them emotionally everywhere they turn—at work, at home and at play.

These consumers also happen to be your employees—they are the *exact* same group of people. Leaders who expect their employees to check their emotions at the office door are making a costly error in judgment by trying to fight a billion dollar industry that is actively promoting emotional engagement in those same employees. Worse, the leaders frequently do not even know that they are fighting this battle, simply because they insist on holding onto the outdated notion that emotions do not belong in the workplace.

Organizations where the emotional components of leadership are ignored are drastically underperforming because the people within the organization are underperforming—and most of the time, leaders have not made the connection. Locking themselves into an "emotions are wrong" approach to leadership are sorely lacking in vision. While they invite, and even encourage, emotional responses in the consumers they target for their companies' products and services, they refuse to acknowledge, much less foster, the same emotional responses in their employees. This is crazy. Wise leaders have moved beyond this schizophrenic leadership style and are reaping the benefits of emotional engagement, knowing that the core of employee job satisfaction, motivation and emotional engagement is the degree of emotional safety that the leaders establish.

❋ ❋ ❋
**"Self-awareness—often overlooked in business settings—
is the foundation for the rest. Without recognizing
our own emotions, we will be poor at managing them,
and less able to understand them in others."
Goleman, Boyatzis, & McKee**
❋ ❋ ❋

Emotions & the Bottom Line

Let's look at the numbers. In their groundbreaking book *Follow this Path*, authors Coffman and Gonzalez-Molina offer an incredibly vast body of empirical support for the importance of emotions in the workplace. Coffman and Gonzalez-Molina base their conclusions on a staggeringly large pool of data from Gallup Poll research.[57] They discuss how the success of an organization depends upon both employees and customers being emotionally engaged with a company (and, conversely, how costly the results can be when employees and/or customers are *not* emotionally engaged). Disturbingly, Coffman & Gonzalez-Molina identify that, in the average organization, only about 20%-30% of people are emotionally engaged in their work; 54% are not-engaged; and about 12%-18% are actively disengaged.

These numbers are staggering. **This means that approximately 75% of people—almost three out of four people—have no emotional engagement with the organization where they work.** Imagine 75% of the goods your company produces being defective, and you will have some idea of the order of magnitude of this problem. This level of active disengagement is creating a tremendous drag on our economy. Coffman and Gonzalez-Molina report that disengaged employees cost companies hundreds of million of dollars each year."[58]

Characteristics of Emotional Engagement

Coffman and Gonzalez-Molina identified that an engaged person has the following characteristics:[59]
- Uses their talent everyday.
- Has a consistently high level of performance.
- Has natural innovation and a drive for efficiency.
- Participates in intentional building of supportive relationships.
- Is clear about the desired outcomes of their role.
- Is emotionally committed to what they do.
- Can challenge purpose to achieve their goals.
- Has high levels of energy and enthusiasm.
- Never runs out of things to do, and creates positive things to act upon.
- Broadens what they do and builds upon progress.
- Is committed to the company, their work group, and their role.

Coffman and Gonzalez-Molina describe a not-engaged person has having the following profile:[60]
- Meets only the basics.
- Is often confused or unable to act with confidence.
- Uses low-risk responses and commitment.
- Often has no real sense of achievement.

- Holds a possible commitment to their organization, but not always to their role or work group.
- Will speak frankly about negative views.

Coffman and Gonzalez-Molina describe the actively disengaged person[61] as:
- Typically reacting with resistance.
- Having low trust.
- Believing "I'm okay, everyone else is not."
- Having an inability to move from the problem to the solution.
- Having low commitment to company, work group, and role.
- Often feeling isolated.
- Usually unwilling to speak frankly about negative views, but will act out their frustration, either overtly or covertly.

❊ ❊ ❊
"When dollars and cents are tallied, the cost of disengagement is severe."
Coffman & Gonzalez-Molina
❊ ❊ ❊

The Costs of Employee Disengagement

People not emotionally committed to an organization are more likely to leave that organization. In *Follow this Path*, Coffman & Gonzalez-Molina cite statistics published by The Corporate Leadership Council of the Corporate Executive Board. Those statistics show the cost of turnover for corporations as being equal to:

- **Front-line employees turnover costs = 0.41 x salary**
- **Professional associates turnover costs = 1.77 x salary**
- **Managers turnover cost = 2.44 x salary**

From these numbers, we easily see the enormous amounts of revenue that can be saved when leaders are committed to creating an emotionally engaged workforce. The impact of emotions on an organization's bottom line is astonishing.

❋ ❋ ❋
A Key to Leading People:
Leaders who seek to become the best learn from the best.
❋ ❋ ❋

Developing Deep Knowledge for Leaders

Smart leaders understand that emotional engagement begins and ends with them.

Positively engaging your employees requires a special kind of knowledge I call *Deep Knowledge*, which also begins with you. Working with Deep Knowledge is, to paraphrase Gandhi, "*becoming* the emotional change that you want to see."

More specifically, Deep Knowledge is:

- A way for leaders to access their full wisdom, experience and knowledge in mind, body, and spirit.
- The place from which true wisdom—and true leadership—come.
- A way of being in relationship with people that involves much more of ourselves than just cognition and thinking.

Deep Knowledge is what we see when we watch high-level martial artists subdue multiple opponents in a manner that appears magical; or professional dancers move their bodies in intricate positions in time to a musical rhythm in ways that seem effortless; or computer programmers create magical programs instantly with simple lines of code. [62]

Deep Knowledge can be found in anyone who fully embodies his or her craft. Consequently, Deep Knowledge can be found in leaders just as easily as in the martial artist, dancer, and computer programmer. If you've ever had the experience of being led by a master leader, you know what I mean.

In the same way, just as experienced martial artists make their art look easy, those farther along the path of emotional leadership mastery can also make leading people look easy. Don't be fooled by the appearance of simplicity, however. There are years and years of practice behind anyone who is skilled in the realm of emotionally intelligent leadership. But do not despair. Every emotionally skilled leader had to begin their journey somewhere. Hopefully, your journey is now underway.

Deep Knowledge is essentially about knowing yourself integrally—in mind, body and spirit. Improving your effectiveness as a leader through Deep Knowledge is not something that can be simply taught in "ten easy lessons." First you must be willing to take the risk to grow as a leader. Only *you* can decide that the process begins with you. If you cannot manage your own emotional life, you will not be very effective in developing sound relationships with the people you lead. Rather than looking to change someone else, first seek to change yourself. Again, you can change by developing Deep Knowledge of yourself—in mind, body, and spirit.

Developing Deep Knowledge requires practice, and practice requires paying our dues. In *Make Your Own Luck*, author Peter Kash, co-founder of Paramount Capital, Inc., tells the story of a woman who approached the great artist Pablo Picasso and asked for a small drawing. Mr. Picasso complied, and when she offered to pay him, he requested $30,000.

"But it only took you a minute!" exclaimed the woman.

To which Picasso replied, "Madam, you are not paying me for the minute it took me to do that drawing. You are paying me for the forty years it took me to be able to make such a drawing in a minute." Picasso clearly recognized that he had paid his dues and developed Deep Knowledge. [63]

❀ ❀ ❀
A Key to Leading People:
Leaders who develop Deep Knowledge increase the
amount of emotional engagement within their organization.
❀ ❀ ❀

Ten Ways to Cultivate Deep Knowledge

1. Know Yourself. Deep Knowledge can only be gained through self-awareness. Find a good coach or mentor to help you increase your Deep Knowledge. Leaders need people outside of their organization who provide them with honest feedback for their own development and learning. No athlete ever reached the Olympics without a coach. No martial artist ever became great without a teacher. No leader can expect to become a superior leader without coaches and mentors.

2. Stay Open. Recall the quality of Openness that we discussed in the Black Belt Leadership Stance. One of the best ways to identify a great leader is by his or her ability to be open. In order to make the best decision, a leader needs to be open to all information—both good and bad—that permeates every level of their organization.

3. Always a Student, Never a Master. No single person ever fully masters any subject area, the emotional realm included. Even Morihei Ueshiba, the undefeated master of Aikido, considered himself a beginning student to the very end of his life. Each of us is human, and therefore fallible and limited by our own perspectives. Leaders simply cannot know everything about any given subject. Still, this does not stop superior leaders from always striving to develop themselves further. They proceed in their quest for Deep Knowledge with humility and recognition of their status as life-long students.

4. Expect the Unexpected. Myths, dreams, and stories can be powerful tools for developing yourself as a great leader. A common theme in myths and stories is that the main character unexpectedly stumbles into the adventure, like Alice falling down the rabbit hole, or Neo being found in "The Matrix." Alice would never have found the rabbit hole if she had searched using only her rational mind. Instead, she allowed her Deep Knowledge to carry her into an adventure of growth. When you seek to develop Deep Knowledge as a leader, you can expect the unexpected.

5. Cultivate Patience. A typical question that comes up early in coaching & consulting sessions is "How long will this take?" There is no magical pill for emotional growth, which is organic and takes time. Think about your emotional development as a garden. If a gardener impatiently tried to make his plants grow faster by going out into the garden and impatiently over-watering them, the only thing he would have to show for his work would be a garden full of dead plants. Cultivate patience in your emotional growth as a leader. The results are well worth the effort.

6. Get Support. You cannot develop Deep Knowledge in isolation. Surround yourself with people who will support your emotional growth as a leader. Every leader needs support, feedback, and challenges from friends and colleagues, coaches and mentors alike.

7. Life Is a Two-Way Street. Recognize that while leaders impact those they lead, those who are led also impact leaders. Emotional life is *always* a two-way street.

8. Practice. Professionals who seek to cultivate Deep Knowledge practice constantly. Follow their lead. Rather than simply putting in time at work, treat every day as a practice session. Pick a skill out of this book and practice—for a day, a week, or even longer. Then pick another skill and do the same thing. You'll soon find yourself living Deep Knowledge.

9. Begin Where You Are. The famous Taoist master Lao tzu said, "The journey of a thousand miles begins with the first step." You must begin every journey where you are, with what you have. Be patient. No matter who you are—young, old, rich or poor—or *where* you are, do your best, and do not let excuses interfere. Every leader has the capacity to cultivate Deep Knowledge, regardless of the path followed to date.

10. Look Around. As you become more aware of emotions in your own life, you will discover that you're becoming more aware of the emotional life of others around you. You can learn something from everyone. Pay attention to the emotional qualities that you like in other people and try to emulate them. Give consideration to the emotional qualities that don't seem to work for other people, and attempt to rid yourself of those same qualities.

Embodied Learning Experiment #2
Building Deep Knowledge

Your embodied learning experiment for this chapter is designed to increase your awareness of the emotions in your life. Because leaders are at different stages of emotional growth, I've provided you with basic, intermediate, and advanced embodied experiments that center around emotions. Begin with the one that feels most comfortable to you, and then challenge yourself to complete them all.

Basic

This week, take a few moments throughout each day and write down whatever emotions you are currently feeling. At the end of one week, review your list. What surprises you the most about your list? Are there emotions that repeat themselves? Are there emotions not on the list that you would like to experience?

Intermediate

This week, take a few moments throughout each day and write down whatever emotions you are currently feeling. After each emotion, rank in order the intensity of that emotion from 1 to 10. For example, if you find yourself becoming very angry with someone at work, you might write down "anger" and assign a rating of "8." At the end of one week, review your list. What surprises you the most about your list? Which emotions do you consistently experience most intensely? Which emotions do you consistently experience least intensely?

Advanced

This week, take a few moments throughout each day to document and rank whatever emotions you experience in that moment. See if you can identify the physical sensations that go along with each emotion. For example, many people find that when they get angry, their shoulders become tighter. Write down the physical sensations that you've identified next to each emotion. At the end of one week, review your list. What surprises you the most about your list? Which emotions produced the most easily identifiable physical sensations for you? Which emotions were more difficult?

Chapter Summary
Congratulations!

By recognizing the value and importance of emotions in the workplace, and by understanding emotions as a process, you have taken your next step toward Black Belt Leadership.

Chapter Summary:

We began with a story about a young man who was so focused on his goal that he almost missed his journey—and his mastery. You learned that emotions are the untapped resources of every organization and how important emotional engagement is to every organization. We reviewed the data on the enormous financial drag that lack of emotional engagement creates on our organizations. By now, you should understand how creating emotional engagement is the mission critical task of ever leader. We discussed the relationship between Deep Knowledge and emotional engagement, and I suggested ten ways for you to cultivate Deep Knowledge.

Suggested further reading:

Emotional Intelligence by Daniel Goleman
Integral Psychology by Ken Wilber
Authentic Happiness by Martin Seligman

Looking Ahead:

In the next chapter, you will explore in greater depth your understanding of emotions by learning about the process of leading people through the Law of Successful Leadership.

*"Skilled Leaders know and follow
the rules of Emotional Logic."*

Story
Chop Wood, Carry Water, Keep Practicing

A long time ago in Asia, a high-level martial arts master owned a school. After teaching students for a number of years, he promoted one of his students to black belt status and announced that the student had achieved an advanced stage of enlightenment, an announcement the teacher rarely made. Naturally, this caused quite a stir in the school. The other students went to talk to the new black belt.

"The sensei said that you were enlightened. Is that true?" they asked him.

"It is," the student replied.

"How do you feel?" the other students wanted to know.

"Not much different," the black belt replied.

When the other students expressed disappointment at such a reply, the black belt said, "Many people believe that enlightenment comes with supreme calmness, absolute peace, and complete understanding, but this is not so. With each level of enlightenment we must still chop wood, carry water, and keep practicing our martial art. Our practice never ceases."

Chapter 6
The Law of Successful Leadership

"If you know others and know yourself,
you will not be imperiled in a hundred battles;
if you do not know others but know yourself, you win one and lose one;
if you do not know others and do not know yourself,
you will be imperiled in every single battle."

-Sun Tzu

George, a mid-level manager for a multi-national corporation, came to me for specific coaching around emotional intelligence issues. He came of his own volition because he knew he was having difficulty recognizing emotions in the people he led. During one session, George was struggling with a particularly difficult emotional interaction he'd encountered recently. "Tim," George exclaimed in frustration, "emotions are not just different *things*—they are a different *world!*"

George could not have been more correct, and he was onto something. Emotions *do* exist in a different world. For leaders who believe that the world is completely rational, working with emotions is like visiting a foreign country. This emotional world, like any other foreign place, has different rules—not right or wrong, just different.

Throughout the coaching process, George learned that, contrary to his previous belief, understanding emotions didn't mean he would no longer have to *experience* emotions. He was using his ability to think as a way of moving farther away from his emotions, rather than closer. In the same way, when leaders attempt to apply the laws of rational logic to the logic of emotions, they only create headaches for themselves and those around them.

Everyone experiences emotions every day. Despite this fact, few leaders are formally trained in how to relate to those emotions skillfully, as they are with other areas like technology. If you're having problems with a computer, you can always shut down and reboot. But there is no switch you can push to reboot a person. You have to *deal* with that person. As such, there is no magic bullet or ten-easy-steps list for effective emotional interactions with people.

In order to help you become an even better leader, I created the **Law of Successful Leadership**. Before you understand this law, however, you must first understand three areas of emotions: 1) Emotional Worldviews, 2) Emotional Logic, and 3) Emotional Traditions.

Emotional Worldviews

All worldviews are emotional worldviews. A *worldview* is the combination of how we view the world and the beliefs we hold about how that world operates. Since most of the significant elements in life, such as birth and death, for example, have yet to reveal their secrets, we are left on our own to fill in the blanks in order to understand life. In doing so, we all create our own *worldviews*. Leaders are no exception, and like everyone else's, their worldviews are unique to the individual person while, at the same time, part of the collective culture in which they live. Furthermore, every worldview is emotional, because both emotion and reason play a role in helping us build the lens through which we view the world around us. Reason contributes the view's various parts, and emotions cement those parts together.[64]

Leaders need to be keenly aware of their own worldviews because those views are part of what creates an organization's unique culture. This inward understanding is only the beginning, and can frankly become a slippery slope. Problems arise when leaders begin to believe that the way they look at the world is the *only* way to understand the world, and that anyone who does not share their view is wrong. Leaders make this mistake because they fail to understand the emotional component that makes up every worldview.[65]

The emotional component of worldviews is based upon two factors: 1) emotional logic, and 2) emotional traditions. Let's examine each in turn.

❀ ❀ ❀
A Key to Leading People:
Wise leaders keep in mind this ancient martial art maxim:
"If your mind is correct, then your technique will be correct."
❀ ❀ ❀

The Six Rules of Emotional Logic

As bewildering as emotions often seem to leaders, they actually have a logic, consistency, and coherence to them. When I refer to *Emotional Logic*, I'm speaking about the reasoning and patterns under which emotions operate. Attending to *Emotional Logic* as a leader makes good interpersonal interactions even better, and better interpersonal interactions excellent.

The Six Rules of Emotional Logic:[66]
1. **People Are Fragile.**
2. **The Emotional Realm has Different Rules than the Rational Realm.**
3. **Know Yourself.**
4. **Not All Emotional States Can Be Easily Put Into Words.**
5. **Every Emotion Needs To Be Honored and Respected.**
6. **Slowing Down Will Get You There Faster.**

Emotional Logic Rule #1: People Are Fragile. When people first consider stepping onto the Aikido mat to begin their training, their initial question is often, "How long will it take until I get good?" Implied in this question is the deeper question, "How long will it be until I can hurt someone?" My standard answer is: "Not very long." The human body is actually a very fragile organism. Relative to other creatures, we humans require a narrow range of environmental conditions simply in order to exist. Our bodies are physically fragile as well. There isn't much pressure required to cause significant injury to a wrist, elbow or other joint. As anyone knows who has ever gotten whiplash in a minor car accident, there doesn't need to be a great deal of force involved for serious, long-term physical damage to occur.

People are holistic beings, so our emotional aspects are as fragile as our physical aspects. We are all wounded—*all* of us. Far too many leadership perspectives presuppose that a "tough" stance is the best stance for a leader to take. Since Chapter One, I have been presenting data that argues against such "tough" leadership stances because they consistently fail. They fail because "tough" leadership approaches ignore the all-too-real fragility of humans. This fragility is nothing to be ashamed or embarrassed about. Instead, acknowledging this fragility is simply being realistic and pragmatic about "what is."

Having shortcomings, weaknesses and emotional wounds are all part of being human. Denying these basic human conditions is not effective leadership, but rather a pathological sickness. In the behavioral health sciences, one of the most serious emotional disorders that a person can have is a personality disorder, and one of the most serious, difficult-to-treat personality disorders is the Narcissistic Personality Disorder, or narcissism. People who suffer from narcissism have an inability to admit that they are wrong or have any shortcomings. In short, with a narcissist, everything is always someone else's fault.

Spurred on by popular leadership approaches, many leaders act as if they have no frailties or shortcomings, whereas wise leaders always take the full human condition into account, keeping in mind that there is not a single person in their organization who does not have an emotional sore spot. Everyone is insecure about something—this is the normal human condition. Remember *both/and* thinking. Leadership is not simply about directing people, but also about nourishing people in ways that support their growth. Leadership is not only about the "power of positive thinking," but also about being willing to walk with people as they examine their doubts and fears. All of these elements are essential to successful leadership.

Superior leaders nourish the people they lead, and in order to do so, they need to attend to their own need for nourishment first. As I have pointed out before, leaders need to take care of themselves, and then take care of others. In the introduction to Core Problems of Leadership, we talked about leaders who either focus on blaming everyone else or who remain fixated on nourishing themselves to the exclusion of others. Sometimes they do both, but neither approach works when trying to create a successful organization.

Recognizing that people are fragile does not mean that leaders should behave in a demeaning, co-dependent fashion, avoiding conflict in order to keep from hurting people's feelings. Leaders still need to set limits and establish productivity goals. But acknowledging the fragility of the human condition *does* mean recognizing people's strengths and weaknesses, dreams and fears—all with compassion and the realization that, as a member of the human race, you share those same characteristics.

Emotional Logic Rule #2: The Emotional Realm has Different Rules than the Rational Realm. Emotional logic follows a different set of rules from rational logic, and some leaders make the mistake of trying to apply the wrong rules to the wrong situation. Attempting to understand the logic of people's emotions through rational logic is like speaking English where none is spoken. Any conversation will inevitably end in frustration and misunderstanding.

Because people's emotions can range from being as fragile as spun glass and as torrential as a downpour, becoming a Black Belt Leader requires openness to emotional experience and the ability to follow the rules of emotional logic. Emotions cannot be measured or quantified. One cannot have five pounds of happiness, or three gallons of anger. Rather, emotions can only be experienced, communicated, and dealt with in dialogue.

This is not at all to discount the importance of the rational realm. Leaders clearly need to have a strong grasp of logical thinking. The main point here is that a successful leader cannot just have a grasp of logical thinking, but needs to also be fluent in both the logic of the rational realm *and* the logic of the emotional realm. Think of them as different tools. Just as you wouldn't use a hammer when you needed a saw, neither should you use rational logic when emotional logic is needed.

❀ ❀ ❀
"The glue that holds people together in a team, and what commits people to an organization, are the emotions they feel."
Goleman, Boyatzis, & McKee
❀ ❀ ❀

Emotional Logic Rule #3: Know Yourself. Emotional change in your organization must begin with you, the leader. A basic principle that behavioral scientists have known about for years is that **you cannot change other people—you can only change yourself.** You cannot force or mandate change. You can only force compliance with external measurements. True change—the kind of change that unleashes a tremendous potential for success through both embodiment and emotional engagement—can only come from within each one of us.

Some leaders waste all of their energy trying to get *other* people to change. These executives drag their subordinates to consultants and coaches, demanding that the employees emerge changed (a.k.a., fixed). People drag their spouses to therapy, demanding that the therapist change the errant spouse. Parents drag their children to see their rabbi, minister or priest, expecting the child to change as a result. Change rarely follows in any of these cases. Hopefully, you have already identified these scenarios as simply being more examples of the harmful *Pushing* and *Pulling* types of leadership that we discussed in Chapter Two.

Trying to change someone else without his or her commitment and involvement is futile. The effort rarely works. Worse, when we focus our energies on trying to change someone else, we are more likely to avoid our own responsibility for the challenge at hand. Strong leaders accept appropriate levels of responsibility for the co-creation of the difficulty facing them, and work with other people to rectify the situation.

As Peter Block says in his book, *The Answer to How is Yes*, "To move away from the spirit of coercion, we replace the question, 'How do we get them to change?' with 'What is the transformation in me that is required?' or 'What courage is required of me right now?'"[67] The willingness to discover the courage required of you as a leader in any given situation is part and parcel of what will move you toward becoming a superior leader.

Some leaders waste time focusing on changing others. Great leaders focus on changing themselves.

Emotional Logic Rule #4: Not All Emotional States Can Be Easily Put Into Words.

"I can't find the right words!" Ask anyone newly in love or conversely, someone who is infuriated by the response of a clueless manager, to describe their experiences. You will most likely find that neither can completely put their experience into words. This is quite normal. Emotional experiences— gentle and strong, sacred and profane—are often as difficult to put into words as they are fleeting.

Culturally, because we do not value our physical selves as important sources of information, we do not have a readily available set of words and phrases to describe the physical sensations associated with a particular emotion. As a result, we tend to stumble whenever we try and articulate what we are feeling. Yet this is nothing new.

Thousands of years ago, Lao Tzu wrote, "The Tao which can be told is not the Tao." With this seemingly simple sentence, Lao Tzu pointed to the perennial difficulty of not being able to fully describe our human experience. Our physical experience is ultimately beyond words.

Our on-going struggle to fully name our emotions is evident in our continuous rush to measure and quantify emotional experiences. In actuality, measurements and quantification are best left to engineers building bridges, rather than to those daring to focus on emotions. Instead of measuring them, we need to give emotions a voice. But rather than trying to do so through the lens of science, we need to reach for the poet within each one of us, since poets are those who come closest to giving voice to our emotions.[68]

In short, go easy on yourself. Even people who are experienced in the language and realm of emotions often find themselves at a loss for words. Rest assured that the more that you practice giving voice to your emotions, the easier the experience will become.

❋ ❋ ❋
A Key to Leading People:
Acknowledging an honest mistake openly unleashes
greater power than is gained from hiding those same mistakes.
❋ ❋ ❋

Emotional Logic Rule #5: Every Emotion Needs To Be Honored and Respected. Emotions are powerful things. Sometimes they can be highly in sync with what's going on in our lives—the bliss of receiving a promotion that you've wanted or the horror of being laid off. At other times, they can be highly out-of-sync. We might experience moments of bliss inside of intense difficulties, or longing in the midst of joy, or some other mood—good or bad—that can seemingly come out of nowhere and take over our day. However we experience them, emotions can be very overwhelming—and the fact that they are not always in tune with our lives is a key indicator that emotions march to the beat of a different drummer than the world of rational logic.

Whether experienced in a whisper or a rage, emotions need to be respected and honored as messengers with information. Just as when we communicate with a stranger who speaks another language, we may not always know what message(s) our emotions are carrying. But these messages are *always* important. If leaders learn to listen to their emotions and not rush to cut them off, then powerful leadership lessons can be learned.

Effective leaders know that little is to be gained by telling themselves they "should" be feeling this way or that. In the emotional realm, considering the "should" of a situation is about as effective as going outside and shouting to the skies that rain should not be pouring down. Great leaders focus on the present moment, respecting and honoring whatever emotion is present at the time, both in themselves and in other people.

A few caveats are in order here. Respecting emotions does not mean delaying decisions until everyone feels exactly the same way about the decision at hand. I have seen individuals hold entire groups hostage simply by insisting that the decision being contemplated by the group did not "feel right." Complete emotional consensus is rare among groups of people, and none of us get our way all of the time. Nor does honoring emotions mean that the emotional "rightness" of a situation is the sole criteria for decision-making purposes. For example, the task of re-evaluating and restructuring a team that is no longer producing may not always be emotionally satisfying. But the effort is the right thing to do for the health of the organization. Finally, "honoring and respecting" emotions is never a reason to excuse abusive or hurtful behavior. Even in the emotional realm, people are still accountable to act appropriately and with civility toward one another.

❀ ❀ ❀
"It does not matter how slowly you go so long as you do not stop."
Confucius
❀ ❀ ❀

Emotional Logic Rule #6: Slowing Down Will Get You There Faster. Human nature causes us to rush through events that we believe are unimportant. Ineffective leaders look at the subject of emotions in the same way—highly unimportant. Since those leaders place little value in emotions, they want to "get through" the situation whenever emotions inevitably arise in organizations, believing the objective is to "put everything behind us" as quickly as possible. In contrast, great leaders know that the objective is to slow down when confronted with emotions, because they understand that slowing down paradoxically helps them reach their goal more quickly.

The paradoxical power of slowing down was discovered by martial artists thousands of years ago. Perhaps you have seen people in a park practicing T'ai Chi, a slow-moving, graceful martial art. The full name of the martial art is T'ai Chi Ch'uan, which means "Supreme Ultimate Fist."

The brilliance of T'ai Chi, discovered long ago by the Chinese masters, is that moving slowly actually makes you faster and more effective in combat. The same is true for leading people in emotional matters.

These ancient insights from the martial arts world are supported by modern science. Recent neurological research proves that the brain's limbic system—the center of the brain that oversees emotions—is a much slower learner in comparison to the neocortex, the part of the brain that oversees analytical modes of thinking. Retraining the limbic system, which means learning how to deal with emotions more effectively, requires repetition and practice. While this retraining takes time, the benefit of the limbic system's slow learning curve is that anything learned is retained for longer periods of time.[69]

In my coaching, I once worked with Marcia, a small business owner who came to me because she was experiencing overwhelming amounts of stress in her job and with her employees. When I first began meeting with Marcia, she related a number of stories about her company in a rapid, almost breathless fashion. She told these stories so fast that I had difficulty getting a word in edgewise. Previously unaware of this high-speed speech pattern, Marcia eventually acknowledged that she had more than likely been using this same style of interaction with her direct reports.[70] Her leadership style was having such disastrous consequences on her organization that together we conservatively calculated the cost to be more than $50,000 annually. Over the next year, I worked with Marcia to help her develop a more effective leadership approach. Gradually, she began to discover for herself the benefits of slowing down and attending to her physical sensations as a way of becoming an even better leader.

Superior leaders draw a page from both traditional martial arts and modern neurological science and, paradoxically, they achieve more results in less time when they slow down.

Emotional Traditions

Emotional traditions are the unwritten ways of acting and feeling that are present in every organization, and that are central to every organizational culture. An organization with positive, healthy, and productive emotional traditions will have a record of success. Conversely, an organization with unhealthy and destructive emotional traditions is destined for failure.

In *Who Says Elephants Can't Dance*, retired IBM CEO Louis Gerstner, the man who masterminded IBM's historic turnaround in the 1990's, underscores the importance of organizational culture by writing:

> Until I came to IBM, I probably would have told you that culture was just one among several important elements in any organization's makeup and success—along with vision, strategy, marketing, financials and the like...**I came to see, in my time at IBM, that culture isn't just one aspect of the game – it *is* the game.** In the end, an organization is nothing more than the collective capacity of its people to create value.[71]

At first glance, many organizational cultures may appear similar. Most organizations present their culture using similar phrases like "outstanding customer service," "excellence," "leader in the field," "teamwork," and so on. But the reality is that no two organizations are alike. Just as each and every fingerprint is unique, so too does every organization have a uniquely different culture. The key to understanding your organizational culture is to understand the unwritten rules that exist in your organization, which combine to create a unique emotional tradition.

❋ ❋ ❋

A Key to Leading People:
Emotional traditions are unwritten, agreed-upon ways of behavior
present in every organization.

❋ ❋ ❋

The Law of Successful Leadership

"It's the relationship, dummy!"

Great leaders know that relationships are the keys to their success. They understand that if you want to lead a group of people who are emotionally engaged in what they do, you must first and foremost build trusting relationships with them. Trust is the critical component to all successful working relationships. Always walk your talk. The fastest way to destroy trust is to say one thing and then do another.

When I suggest you focus on the relationship, I want to be clear that I am **not** suggesting that leaders avoid conflict or let those they lead do whatever they want. Leadership always involves a level of limit setting. However, limit setting is best done in an atmosphere of caring and concern for the well being of the person being led. This is especially true on the extreme ends of limit setting, such as staff layoffs. Building appropriate relationships and the investment of trust over time with your employees can go a long way toward keeping the relationship amiable and avoiding vendettas (legal or otherwise).

Over time, the content of your business will change, the problems of your business will change, but the relationships you have with people will always be present. Keep the relationships primary.

This brings us to the Law of Successful Leadership, which is:

To be a successful leader, focus on "we" and not just "me."

Modern leaders erroneously place far too much value on independence. Our compulsive focus on independence is reflected in movie heroes such as John Wayne, Rambo, Arnold Schwarzenegger, and Steven Seagal, who independently save the day. The proclamation that "I did it *all by myself!*" is completely appropriate...for a three-year old child. Any adult who seriously believes that they obtained success solely on their own merit is quite naïve. A different perspective is to acknowledge and value our *inter*dependence, recognizing that we are able to achieve what we accomplish only through the hard work, support, and emotional relationships of others.

Peter Kash, in his book *Make Your Own Luck*, describes this very principle:

> One of the principles that the Japanese cultivate is the recognition that success is achieved through cooperation and joint efforts, rather than the work of any single individual. The Japanese symbol for people is shaped like a teepee, with two lines converging at the apex. If either line is removed, the other line falls. The image symbolizes our interdependence with each other for survival and success. This is especially true in business. Business works best—that is, more people experience success and personal fulfillment—when we maintain certain values that are mutually supportive.[72]

Some leaders incorrectly believe that needing other people is a sign of immaturity and weakness. Nothing can be more damaging to your organization than misunderstanding the importance of interdependence. The fact of the matter is that we all need other people. None of us can survive alone. The Law of Successful Leadership acknowledges our interdependence with others.[73]

This is not to deny the existence of independence. For leaders, acknowledging and understanding people's need for both independence and interdependence is vital to creating a successful organization. Using *both-and* thinking allows us to focus on both independence and interdependence and to move freely between the two. Recognizing people's need for both independence and interdependence means recognizing both sides of this equation in ourselves, as well. Leading people competently involves not only acting independently in our roles but also knowing how to find and accept guidance and assistance when necessary. No one can lead people effectively in isolation or in a vacuum.

The Law of Successful Leadership underscores the fact that emotions happen in relationship with other people. While ineffective leaders easily become enchanted with the idea of "me" and "mine," effective leaders focus on "we" and "ours." For example, Kash, a successful venture capitalist, extends his belief in interdependence to the bottom line. He shares the financial benefits of success with everyone who works with him, in the belief that "We will all succeed together, or we will fail together."[74]

✳ ✳ ✳

"We cannot change others, we can only learn about ourselves. Even when we are responsible for employees and children, we surrender our freedom and capacity to construct the world we inhabit when we focus on their change."
Peter Block

✳ ✳ ✳

Five Tips for Following the Law of Successful Leadership:

1. When in Doubt, Ask.

I once coached Dave, a mid-level manager in a large organization who became very upset when his staff would not use the paperwork forms he so carefully created for them. When he and I investigated the process together, we identified the problem. He would leave staff meetings and create forms that he thought would address the problems raised in the meeting. The problem became clear, however, when Dave acknowledged that he launched the new forms without ever asking his team for feedback or input ahead of time. As a result, the forms frequently did not solve the problems they were designed to solve, and consequently, the team members would not use them. After I coached Dave on the importance of getting team input *before* he designed the forms, his work matched the team's requirements to a much higher degree—and everyone was satisfied.

2. Don't Assume. Listen.

Besides neglecting to gather input on his form design, Dave made another very common leadership mistake: He assumed that he knew what his direct reports wanted. Uninformed assumptions made by leaders are very dangerous things that can wreak havoc throughout any organization. Confirming assumptions with the people involved in any given project is far more time- and cost-effective than simply moving forward as if your assumptions were true, only to discover the need to re-do all of your work that was based upon your erroneous assumptions.

3. Change Your View.

Many leaders only give lip service to "we." As we have seen, people in organizations are already savvy consumers who are highly skilled at tuning out condescending lip service. Successful leaders embody the importance of "we." As you go through your day, take time to consider all of the people who contribute to your effectiveness. The security guard at the door, your personal assistant, and even the person who dry-cleans your suits are all people who contribute to your success. Make sure you recognize and acknowledge them— even if only in some small way.

4. Trust Yourselves... and Others.

"Independent thinkers wanted." Many organizations claim to seek independent thinkers, hire them, and then proceed to implement lock-step rules and guidelines that make thinking independently almost impossible. Superior leaders know that they have hired good people and then trust them to get their jobs done.

5. "Not-How-I-Would-Do-It" Does Not Mean "The-Wrong-Way-to-Do-It."

Different people accomplish tasks in different ways. Hire good people and trust them. Great leaders avoid the impulse to micro-manage. Unless an employee's direction is clearly out of bounds (illegal or unethical), let that person take the lead, even if your decision means completing a project differently from the way you originally envisioned.

※ ※ ※
"Bilbo used to say there was only one Road; that it was like a great river:
its springs were at every doorstep, and every path was its tributary.
"It's a dangerous business, Frodo, going out of your door,"
he used to say. "You step into the Road, and if you don't keep your
feet, there's no knowing where you might be swept off to."
Frodo Baggins
※ ※ ※

Upgrading Worldview: The Power of Experience

When I was a twenty-three year old graduate student, I got up early one cold November weekend to drive across Chicago. As I navigated the empty Sunday morning streets, I thought to myself, "What am I doing? I should be home in bed." I found the place that I was looking for, and parked my car. The building I was seeking was a short walk away, and I passed only a few people on my way there. I walked through a door and climbed up a flight of stairs.

The contrast between the early Sunday morning quiet of the city streets and the activity in the room hit me like a splash of cold water on my face. The large room was filled with people dressed in the white uniform and flowing black skirts of Aikido practitioners. The room was warm and a blur of motion, with people throwing people throwing people. The white and black of the uniforms blended together as those same people turned, pivoted, and shifted on the mat in ways that seemed both puzzling and logical.

I took a seat on the side of the mat and observed, absolutely captivated but having little idea of what I was watching. After several minutes of activity, the teacher clapped his hands, and everyone scrambled to the edge of the mat where they sat in silence. A feeling of palpable anticipation fell across the room.

I leaned over to the middle-aged gentleman sitting next to me and whispered to him, "Excuse me, but what's going on?"

"We're waiting for the Doshu—the son of the founder of the Aikido—to come and give an Aikido demonstration."

We waited several more minutes, and then suddenly the downstairs door opened up, revealing a frail, elderly gentleman who was accompanied up the stairs by a group of people. The elderly gentleman held onto the arm of one in the group as he came up the stairs.

"Come on. This guy is so old he needs an entourage to take care of him," I thought.

The gentleman sitting next to me must have seen the look of skepticism on my face. As if he knew what I was thinking, he grinned at me and said, "Just wait."

The old man slowly made his way up the stairs. Everyone on the mat bowed low. The old man smiled and, addressing the class instructor in Japanese, told him to continue class while he changed.

Class continued for a short period of time. Then Doshu walked out onto the mat, and class stopped. What I saw changed my life.

Beginning his demonstration, Doshu called out four very large men. The men began attacking him, single and en mass.

No longer a frail old man leaning on another's arm for support, Doshu seemed to have grown three feet taller. He moved with an overwhelming masculine power and astonishing feminine grace (or was it an overwhelming feminine power and astonishing masculine grace?). His attackers rushed at him, striking and grabbing, and Doshu moved these huge men without any effort. He threw a few of the men through the air to land on the mat some distance away from him. Others he immobilized with pins neatly at his feet. He seemed to be everywhere and nowhere all at the same time.

Stunned, I had no words for what I had just witnessed.

The man sitting next to me must have seen my jaw hit the floor in amazement. With a warm friendly smile on his face, he leaned over, chuckled, and said, "Still think he's a frail old man?"

I decided then and there that I wanted to learn Aikido.

That decision changed my life.

❈ ❈ ❈

"The question, 'What is my contribution to the problem I am concerned with?' is an antidote to our helplessness. It affirms that we have had a role in creating the world we live in…If we decide to choose freedom, we surrender innocence and exchange it for guilt."
- Peter Block

❈ ❈ ❈

Upgrading Worldviews for Leaders

The Aikido school (dojo) where I train is located on a well-traveled road, and we receive our share of drop-in visitors who come and watch the class. Many of them seem to be desperately searching for something.

During one evening session, a young, athletic man came into our dojo. I stepped off the mat and welcomed him. He introduced himself as Mark and told me that he'd heard about Aikido and wanted to learn more. I explained our dojo to him and invited him to take a seat and observe the class. After watching for some period of time, he began to lecture me about how Aikido would never, in his opinion, work "in real life." He watched for a while longer and then left the dojo. I never saw him again.

From experience, I know that a highly trained eye is required to watch Aikido and understand what is going on. For many people who watch for the first time, Aikido can look "fake" or "made up." Having had the opportunity to study with, and be thrown by, several high-ranking Aikido teachers, I can personally attest to the effectiveness of Aikido. Furthermore, I'm convinced that I got up off the mat only through the good graces of those teachers. Yet people are often quick to judge Aikido because the view of conflict resolution the art offers the world does not fit with their preconceptions of what a martial art "should" be. Like many others, Mark could not see "what is" because his worldview got in the way. Unless he is careful, his rigid worldview will prevent him from growing and changing in a world of opportunity and possibility. He may need to upgrade his worldview in order to be successful in life.

The same is true for leaders, who often have difficulty upgrading their own worldviews. There is something deep within all of us that struggles against change—that fights against taking in any information threatening to contradict or alter our worldview. Although critical analysis is an important skill for leaders, many tend to challenge and disregard new and uncomfortable data that doesn't fit in with their old way of seeing things. When personal computers first made their appearance on the global scene, leaders at IBM—whose bread-and-butter had been large, mainframe systems—simply did not believe that there was a market for this technology, especially in the home. That decision had critical, negative ramifications a few years later when the PC market for home users exploded exponentially, and, for the first time in their corporate history, IBMers found themselves suddenly playing catch-up.

Many leaders balk at the prospect of upgrading their worldview for the plain and simple fact that such a step requires work. Despite the level of work involved, however, upgrading a worldview is a mission critical task for every successful leader. Just as no sane leader would argue that all computers in his organization should be running on software designed ten years ago, so too should every leader work constantly to upgrade his or her worldviews in order to leverage any and all newly emerging data that will have a profound impact on their organization's bottom line.

✳ ✳ ✳

A Key to Leading People:
Great leaders benefit from continuously upgrading their worldview.

✳ ✳ ✳

Knowing When to Upgrade Your Worldview

Worldviews, like technology, should be upgraded when they become obsolete. Like most other advanced technology, the life cycle of a worldview these days is fairly short. You will know when your worldview is becoming obsolete when you discover your views being challenged more and more frequently. Many of the concepts that are presented in this book will most likely challenge all or part of your current worldview. Rather than swallowing my words unquestioningly, I invite you to test my words in your day-to-day life and upgrade your worldview accordingly. As a tool to assist your upgrade, here are the three signs that you may be holding onto an outdated worldview:

1. **You refuse to accept multiple data points that support a position contrary to the position you currently hold.**
2. **You persist in holding onto the belief that whatever has worked in the past will continue to work in the future.**
3. **You feel the rise of anger and irritation when you are supportively challenged about an outdated worldview.**

Let's explore each sign:

1. Refusal to accept multiple data points that support a position contrary to the position currently held.

Humans do not want to believe anything that doesn't fit into their worldview. In the wonderful book *The Experts Speak*, authors Christopher Cerf and Victor Navasky have compiled an entire collection of all the misstatements made by so-called "experts" throughout history (such as the guy at the patent office in 1880 who wanted to shut the office down because he believed that everything had already been invented). Cerf and Navasky demonstrate dramatically the incredibly poor ability of humans to predict the future with much accuracy.

Cerf and Navasky give the example of Brigadier General Billy Mitchell, who, in order to raise support for what would become the U.S. Air Force, proposed to sink a battleship by dropping bombs from airplanes. He was met with utter scorn and contempt. Even after he proved his idea by sinking a captured German battleship, people (including Theodore Roosevelt, Jr., who was then the Assistant Secretary of the U.S. Navy) refused to give his ideas the credit they deserved.

2. Persisting in holding onto the belief that whatever has worked in the past will continue to work in the future.

The basic leadership operative here is that if "what works" has served us well to this point, the same will continue to work indefinitely. This belief is flawed, because organizations must be open to change to avoid falling behind the competition. Advances in new technology and the global economy require leaders to move beyond "business as usual," because "business as usual" simply creates more opportunities for your competition to eat your lunch.

3. Anger and irritation rise up when an outdated worldview is supportively challenged.

Letting go of old worldviews in favor of newer, better-functioning worldviews can be difficult for most leaders. They often respond to this difficulty by becoming angry, irate, and lashing out at others, but nothing is gained from this response. While angry outbursts may feel good at the time, they are wholly unproductive—and you are still stuck with your outdated worldview.

I want to be clear that responding with anger based on fear is different from being passionate about your beliefs and knowledge. There is nothing wrong with passion and intensity, often mistaken for anger. But there *is* something wrong when ineffective leaders lose control and blow up in anger at the slightest deviation from a rigid path. The road to business success is littered with the carcasses of failed organizations whose leader(s) used anger to avoid the difficult work of upgrading their own worldviews.

Embodied Learning Experiment #3
Increasing Your Emotional Logic Performance

Remember The Six Rules of Emotional Logic:
1. People Are Fragile.
2. The Emotional Realm has Different Rules than the Rational Realm.
3. Know Yourself.
4. Not All Emotional States Can Be Easily Put Into Words.
5. Every Emotion Needs To Be Honored and Respected.
6. Slowing Down Will Get You There Faster.

Now here's a brief experiment for you to try:
1. Write down four emotions that you felt today.

2. Rank in order each emotion based on the difficulty you had recalling the emotion. "0" is barely being able to recall, and "10" is being able to recall very well.

3. Choose one difficult situation for you at work right now. List the emotions you experience around this situation. Rank in order the intensity of the emotions from 0 (no intensity) to 10 (very intense). Record one physical experience you had when the emotion occurred.

4. Complete this exercise each day for a week.

For now, do not try to change your emotions. Simply notice them in the same way that you notice the weather in the morning.

Chapter Summary
Congratulations!

By learning the Law of Successful Leadership, you have taken the next step toward becoming a Black Belt Leader.

Chapter Summary:
We began with a story about a leader who understood the value of practice. We continued our discussion with the importance of leading people emotionally. We then learned about emotional worldviews, emotional logic, emotional traditions, and the important role that each plays in leadership. We covered the six rules of emotional logic, as well as the Law of Successful Leadership.

Suggested further reading:
Primal Leadership by Goleman, Boyatzis & McKee
The Practice of Freedom: Aikido Principles as a Spiritual Guide by Wendy Palmer
The Fifth Discipline by Peter Senge

Looking Ahead:
In the next chapter, you will learn about the value leaders find in unlocking the power of process.

"Wise leaders create successful organizations by unlocking the power of process."

Story
Is That So?

The most beautiful young woman in the small Japanese village was pregnant.

Dismayed and angry, her parents demanded to know the identity of the father. Initially, the young woman refused to name him. Finally, after intense pressure from her parents, she named the famous martial arts sensei who lived in the same village. The sensei was famous for teaching about and leading a pure life.

When the outraged parents confronted the sensei, he simply said, "Is that so?"

When the child was born, the parents brought her to the sensei, who was now seen as a disgrace by the entire village. The parents demanded that the sensei care for the child.

"Is that so?" is all the sensei would say, as he took the child in his arms.

The sensei took good care of the child for many months, until her mother could no longer live with the lie she had told. She confessed to her parents that the baby's real father was a young man from the next village. Horrified, the parents immediately went to the sensei to see if the sensei would return the child. With many, many apologies the parents explained what had happened.

The sensei simply said, "Is that so?"
and gently returned the child to the mother.

Chapter 7
Unlocking the Power of Process

"Each situation has two elements: The technical/business problem that has to be resolved and the way people are interacting around that problem."
- Peter Block

Some leaders make the mistake of thinking that emotions are something fixed in concrete. In reality, nothing could be further from the truth. Great leaders understand that emotions are always in process. Emotions are like a kaleidoscope—constantly shimmering, changing, and evolving into something else. Rather than naming and dismissing an emotion as some leaders do, successful leaders know that simply identifying an emotion is very similar to grabbing onto a wet bar of soap. Just when you think you have control, the emotion pops off in a different direction.

Since emotions are always in process, you need to develop a *process perspective* in order to become a Black Belt Leader. Recall our discussion in Chapter Three about Black Belt Cornerstone #2, the Power of Process where we defined process as a *series of actions, changes, or functions that take place in order to bring about a result.* In short, process is the *how* of what is happening.

Three Keys That Unlock the Power of Process

Key #1: Realize that Creativity Follows Technique.
Key #2: Understand Creative Adjustments.
Key #3: Use The Gestalt Cycle of Experience.

Key #1: Realize that Creativity Follows Technique

Developing a process perspective can't be accomplished by learning new techniques any more than a black belt can be achieved just by reading books on the martial arts. Some leaders don't understand this, so they learn a series of techniques and then consider themselves experts in process. Top-notch leaders don't stop with the techniques, but move well beyond them into the realm of creativity. Great leaders also understand that gaining a creative leadership edge requires continual practice.

The martial arts are called "arts" because they, like every other art form, are all about going beyond techniques into creativity. In order for martial artists to walk the path of mastery, the art must be deep within their bones. Likewise, great leaders learn technique in order to move beyond technique, seeking to embody their leadership principles until those principles inform and impact every move and decision the leader makes.

Key #2: Understand Creative Adjustments

To lead people through process relationally, great leaders understand that emotions should not be judged, because judgment is best reserved for the realm of cognitive, logical thinking. As we learned in Chapter Six, emotional logic is different than rational logic. To be a leader who does not judge other people's emotions requires a great deal of effort, skill, and training, and is what makes a leader superior.

Leaders can adopt one of two different perspectives regarding emotions: 1) The Success/Failure Trap, or 2) The Way of Creative Adjustments.

The Success/Failure Trap

Falling into the success/failure trap forces leaders into *either-or* thinking and sets people up to fail. Success and failure are judgments, and people do not like to have their emotional responses judged. Thinking about people's emotional responses as personal shortcomings is very unproductive for leaders. In doing so, they establish an unhealthy blame/shame dynamic within their organization, turning people into problems, and focusing on weaknesses rather than strengths. None of these actions is the hallmark of an effective leader.[75]

Falling into the success/failure trap is easy to do, even for the experts. For example, in the book *Primal Leadership*, authors Goleman, Boyatzis, & McKee fall into the success/failure trap at least once. They offer a story about Jack, who is the "head of a marketing division in a global food company."[76] In describing Jack's coaching process, the authors state:

For example, Jack saw that he had no problem empathizing with people when things were calm, but once he began to feel stress, he'd tune out other people completely. *That lack of self-control* sabotaged his ability to listen to what people were telling him in the very moments he most needed to do so. Jack's learning plan, therefore, focused on handling emotions effectively.[77]

Calling Jack's emotional behavior a "lack of self-control" is a judgmental position that shames Jack.[78] Falling into the success/failure trap by dismissing Jack's response as a "lack of self control" fails to respect Jack's inherent creativity. In the Black Belt Way of leading people, every emotional response is seen as having value and purpose. Strong leaders know that blaming and/or shaming people are never functional leadership strategies.

Fortunately, there is another way to approach the dilemma—through the perspective of creative adjustments.

Creative Adjustments

A more profitable leadership strategy towards people's emotional responses draws on an understanding of *creative adjustments*—unique, personal, and creative emotional and behavioral responses made by people in order to succeed in their environment. The concept of creative adjustments is much more in keeping with the *both-and* view of Black Belt Leadership, enabling leaders to hold a position that recognizes the fundamental goodness of people. The direct result of holding such a position is a non-judgmental, non-shaming, and ultimately more effective leadership strategy.

Had the coach who worked with Jack helped him explore his behavior in light of an understanding of creative adjustments, the two of them would have discovered that Jack's emotional "tuning out" of other people was a creative adjustment made in response to situations in Jack's past. Validating the strengths in Jack's skill of "tuning out" would have gone a long way toward creating a much more effective coaching experience, especially for Jack.

Leading people relationally means making the commitment to understand that people are doing the best they can, and that problems arise when people's emotional responses—which served them so well in the past—are no longer effective in the present. In Jack's case, his "tuning out" may have been effective for him when he was in grade school or even when he was a pre-management employee. As a leader, however, his inability to listen was hampering his current success. Rather than labeling as wrong his emotional response of not being able to hear people when he was under stress, a Black Belt Leader, using the concept of creative adjustment, could assist Jack in developing alternative emotional responses more effective in his present role.

The goal of a leader using the concept of creative adjustments is to acknowledge and validate a variety of emotional responses as being authentic and valid, while assisting people in selecting the most effective response(s) for current situations. Less effective leadership approaches ignore the validity of emotional responses altogether, believing that emotions are weak and ineffective. When these types of leadership approaches are used, employees simply disengage emotionally from the organization, with disastrous consequences for the bottom line over time.

The concept of creative adjustments offers leaders a more positive approach than other leadership perspectives, enabling those leaders to focus on people's strengths and abilities rather than their weaknesses. In a case like Jack's, this approach recognizes that tuning people out can sometimes be a useful skill. For example, let's say that Jack is required to attend a company golf outing in which he is put in a foursome with a major client. Further, let us suppose that the major client is a complete boor—rude, given to angry outbursts at missed shots, and bragging about his golf game *ad nauseum*. Should Jack be stranded on the golf course with such a person, his skills at being able to tune out another person could serve his—and his organization—quite well. Rather than something to be eliminated, his skill at "tuning out" could become part of Jack's effective emotional response repertoire, as well as helping him strengthen his emotional intelligence.[79]

❋ ❋ ❋
A Key to Leading People:
Leading people with an understanding of creative adjustments keeps harmful judgments out of working relationships.
❋ ❋ ❋

Key #3: Use The Gestalt Cycle of Experience

"The privilege of a lifetime is to be yourself."
- Joseph Campbell

If emotions are always in process, then superior leaders need a process model in order to better understand and utilize the emotional experience. The Gestalt Cycle of Experience (GCOE) can be just such a tool as you strive to become an emotionally intelligent leader.[80] The content of leadership will change, but the process remains the same. Let's take a look at the Gestalt Cycle of Experience to understand how the tool can help leaders navigate the rocky waters of process.

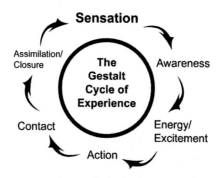

The GCOE begins with a **sensation**, which can be produced either externally or internally. **Awareness** then develops, followed by a **mobilization of energy** or **excitement**. Subsequently, an **action** is performed, and **contact** is made. Finally, **assimilation/closure** occurs, and the cycle is complete.

An Example of the Gestalt Cycle of Experience (GCOE)

To better understand the GCOE, let's take a look at a simple example. On a cool fall evening, my young children are asleep in their beds. My wife, after working hard all week teaching first graders, is dozing in her usual Friday evening spot on the sofa in the living room. I sit down to answer some e-mails and, hopefully, do some writing.

As I am sitting at my computer, I notice that I am thirsty. Presumably, the **sensation** of thirst has been present for some time, but I only become **aware** when the feeling gets strong enough to interrupt my concentration. I may have a short internal debate with myself as to when I am going to get up and get a drink. If I am in the middle of writing something where the words are flowing easily, then I am usually loath to interrupt my writing process. But, whether I attend to my thirst sooner or later, I eventually begin to shift my attention from the words that I am writing to the thought of, "What am I going to drink?" This begins the **excitement phase** where **energy** begins to mobilize. I get up from my computer and go to the refrigerator for a glass of ice tea (**action**). I drink until I feel satisfied (**contact**), and then I return to my computer (**assimilation/closure**). In the GCOE, closure is seen as a positive, important action, a stepping back to assimilate in order to move forward. The GCOE is a model that describes how people experience the world, and the assimilation/closure phase allows the experience to sink into our bones.

The above is a simple example of a single trip around the Gestalt Cycle of Experience.[81] The awareness of needing a drink drew my attention ("becomes figural for me," in Gestalt language) and I was able to satisfy that need. If, for any reason, I had not been able to get a drink, this would have been a problem for me. In the same way, problems arise for leaders when, for whatever reason, people or organizations are not able to fully complete the cycle, which results in what is often referred to as "unfinished business." Like excess baggage on an airplane, too much unfinished business in an organization can ground the entire enterprise.

As a model of individual and organizational behavior, the GCOE scales incredibly well and can be used to understand and intervene at the individual, team, or organizational level. The GCOE can be used to assist leaders in assessing, diagnosing and intervening on any missing process components that are keeping an individual, team or organization from reaching their fullest potential.

Though the Circle Be Unbroken

Completing an entire cycle through the GCOE is an emotionally satisfying process. An incomplete cycle is where emotional difficulties arise, and this is particularly true when group dynamics come into play. I once worked with a team of people who interacted with each other very, very quickly. Team members would frequently answer for each other, guessing what the other was going to say and completing sentences for each other. This was a highly intelligent, passionate group of people who had worked together for a considerable time. Thoughts came quickly to team members and opinions were held strongly. The intelligence and passion of the members made working on the team exciting.

However, there was a twofold downside, which could only be seen in the light of the GCOE. First, team members frequently bypassed (or even trampled) the **awareness** stage in a rush to get to the high level of energy/excitement created by the group. Then the team members would often leap into **action** without sufficient planning or a clear direction of where they were going. This would result in a significant amount of time lost when, in the middle of the action phase, they discovered that half the team was on one page and half was on another. The second downside could be seen in how the team moved through the **assimilation/closure** stage. In a rush to accomplish as much as possible during a meeting, some team members would often launch into a discussion of a new problem that needed attention while other members were still completing the first issue. Now the team had two cycles of experience competing for the same space. The leader of this group had forgotten that teams of people can only work on one issue at a time. An astute observer who was familiar with the GCOE would have noticed that not everyone was fully engaged in the new topic area because closure and assimilation had not been fully achieved with the first topic before the team moved onto the second topic.

※ ※ ※

A Key to Leading People:
Using the process approach of the Gestalt Cycle of Experience helps leaders navigate the ever-changing emotional landscape within their organizations.

※ ※ ※

Five Tips for Leading People with the Gestalt Cycle of Experience

While there is no 10-Easy-Steps list for to moving through the GCOE, I *am* able to offer several tips:

1. Watch the Charge.

Different situations carry different emotional "charges," or levels of intensity. The more intense the emotional charge is, the greater the likelihood that the process is going to be short-circuited in some way. A greater emotional charge requires greater emotional containment by the leader. To understand this concept, think of a fire hose. Professional fire-fighting hoses are more reinforced than ordinary garden hoses because the fire hoses need to handle greater pressure. If you hook up a garden hose to a fire hydrant, the garden hose will simply explode. Increasing your emotional intelligence as a leader requires developing your ability to contain and provide direction for emotions as you lead people. When strong emotional charges arise within a group of people, your responsibility as the leader is to structure the group in such a way that emotions can be dealt with effectively and safely. People are far more productive when they see that a leader can consistently provide appropriate levels of emotional containment.

2. Watch the Numbers.

The number of people involved in any given process will impact the way that the group moves through the GCOE. Generally, the larger the group, the more time is required to make sure everyone is moving most effectively through the GCOE.

3. Watch Your Pace.

Today's work environment often calls for leaders and subordinates to work at speeds that feel super-sonic. When you are leading people, keep in mind the skills, abilities and talents of your team in relationship to the task at hand, and then establish an appropriate pace from the top of the project (that's you) on down. You set the example. Paradoxically, when leading through process, going slower will often yield quicker results.

4. Watch Your Balance.

As you work through the GCOE, make certain that you shuttle back and forth between your personal experience and the experiences of those you lead. As a leader, you may not have the same experiences in common with the others. Pay attention (and give support) to both sides of the equation.

5. Watch your Expectations.

Establish realistic timeframes for completion of each GCOE phase. The goal here is to achieve the most effective and productive result possible for each business objective being mapped with the GCOE. Avoid putting stakes in the ground that represent arbitrary or unrealistic timeframes. These not only do a disservice to the business objective, but also to the hard-working people who will become emotionally flattened by long stretches of twelve-hour days required to meet unrealistic deadlines.

Embodied Exercise #4
Walking Through the Gestalt Cycle of Experience (GCOE)

Learning to think in terms of the GCOE will help you become better at thinking about the leadership process as a whole. Let's begin with the following exercise:

Take a recent situation at work and outline that situation according to the Gestalt Cycle of Experience. Note the specifics about where each phase of the cycle began for you and what emotions or other physical sensations you experienced at each of the five stages:

Sensation:
Awareness:
Energy/Excitement:
Action:
Contact:
Withdrawal/Closure:

Notice:

Did you complete the full cycle? If a team was involved, did the other members of your team complete the full cycle? If yes, what data lets you know that everyone completed the cycle? If not, what was missing? Were there steps in the cycle that were **easier** for you to identify? If so, which ones? Were there steps in the cycle that were **harder** for you to identify? If so, which ones? Are you satisfied with the outcome of the task involved? If not, how might you handle the situation differently next time?

Chapter Summary
Congratulations!

By unlocking the power of process, you have taken the next step toward becoming a Black Belt Leader!

Chapter Summary:
We began with a story about a martial artist who wisely followed the process and stayed detached from outcomes. We learned about the importance of unlocking the power of process for leadership, and we learned that the three keys unlocking the power of process are:

Key #1: Realize that Creativity Follows Technique.

Key #2: Creative Adjustments Need to be Understood.

Key #3: The Gestalt Cycle of Experience (GCOE) Needs to be Utilized.

Finally, we discussed the Five Tips of Leading Through the GCOE: Watch the Charge, the Numbers, Your Pace, Your Balance, and Your Expectations.

Suggested further reading:
Flawless Consulting by Peter Block

Beyond Individualism by Gordon Wheeler

Enlightened Leadership by Ed Oakley

Looking Ahead:
In the next chapter, we'll explore what every leader needs to know about change.

*"Black Belt Leaders wait for
problems and opportunities to manifest themselves,
and then they respond quickly and decisively."*

Story
Hand Closed, Hand Open

Once upon a time, a man and woman lived and worked in a small Japanese village, running their own restaurant. Their restaurant became quite prosperous, so the wife wanted to donate money to the more unfortunate people in the village. The husband always refused. "If we give our money away," he insisted, "there may not be enough left for us!"

Exasperated, the wife sought out the village martial arts teacher and explained her dilemma. "Sensei, could you please speak to my husband about his money?" she implored.

The sensei went to the couple's house. The husband invited their esteemed guest in for tea. After serving tea, the husband asked the nature of the sensei's visit. "Your wife told me that you do not wish to donate extra money to the village poor." "Oh yes, sensei," exclaimed the husband, "for if we do there will be little for us."

The sensei sat quietly for a moment. Then, he held out his hand clenched in a fist. "What would you call my hand in this position?" the sensei asked. "Why," said the husband, "I would call it tight-fisted and closed."

"And what," asked the teacher, relaxing his hand and revealing a tiny baby mouse sitting in his palm, "would you call my hand when I hold it like this?"

"Open," responded the husband.

"In order for the mouse to breathe," asked the sensei, "how must I hold my hand?"

"Again, open," answered the man.

"So it is with all living things," responded the sensei. "Think on this." With that, he bowed, got up, and left the house.

After that, the wife never had a problem getting her husband to share their wealth with those less fortunate.

Chapter 8
Leading Through Change

"Everything changes. Nothing remains without change."
-Buddha

Today's organizations are all about change. Any organization that insists on remaining the same today will find another organization eating its lunch tomorrow. Great leaders know this and therefore study and practice the art and science of leading people through change. In this chapter you will learn how to approach the process of organizational change from the perspective of Black Belt Leadership.

Four Rules of Change for Leaders:

1. Know that Change is Always Present.
2. Attend to Process.
3. Develop a "Leading Presence."
4. Understand that Change is Never Completely Predictable.

1. Know that Change is Always Present.

Change is an intrinsic, fundamental part of life, and therefore always present. Change happens whether leaders do anything or not. Some leaders mistakenly talk about "implementing change" or "creating change" in their organizations. But change is not something that can be turned on and off—and talking about "implementing change" in your organizations is as ludicrous as talking about "implementing breathing" in the people within your organization. Wise leaders have a different perspective because they know that a key to success lies in how effectively leaders move their organizations through change. Wise leaders are proactive rather than reactive. Rather than leading in a reactive mode—responding to the change—they seek to identify what's going on and then lead the change in the direction they want to go.

2. Attend to Process.

Great leaders view relationships as assets and the language of relationships is process, which you just learned about in Chapter 7. For example, consider the coach of a professional sports team. The coach uses play diagrams to let their team members know what to do—to understand the *process* of how the team will work together as a whole—in order to achieve victory. In a similar manner, great leaders of organizations monitor their own "play diagrams"—employee morale and emotional engagement, departmental structures and organizations, quota methodologies and attainment, customer satisfaction approaches and statistics, competitive analyses, and more—to determine how their company teams are working together. Effective leaders unlock the power of process using the three keys that you learned about in Chapter 7 to evaluate and make adjustments to their organizational "play diagrams."

3. Develop a "Leading Presence."

Communication in leadership is a two-way street, with messages being sent and received. More and more, research is showing that for every message communicated between people, the most valuable information is expressed non-verbally. Consequently, leaders who pay attention only to words are missing priceless information—information that may determine whether the change they want succeeds or fails in their organizations. In order to leverage the greatest value out of every interaction, leaders need to develop what I call a "Leading Presence," a leadership response to change that flows out of the embodied leadership we discussed in Chapter 4. Developing a Leading Presence is far more than merely having an intellectual understanding of "body language." The response is the difference between reading a book about golf versus actually playing a round of 18 holes yourself.

As we saw in the story at the beginning of this chapter, a critical factor in the development of a Leading Presence is the quality of openness. Many leaders make the mistake of working from inside a closed bubble, surrounding themselves with people who shield the leader from anything but carefully filtered information. Leaders who operate in this manner are dooming their organizations to failure. When leaders wall themselves off from the rest of the organization, bad news is frequently discovered at decision-making tiers only when the time for effective intervention has passed. Remarkable leaders stay open to all types of information, the good and the bad, from every sector within their organizations.

❋ ❋ ❋

"If there is one thing that the way of transition and the path of the life-journey teach, it is that when we neglect the process and try instead to copy the outcome, we fail completely to get what we were after."
William Bridges

❋ ❋ ❋

4. Understand that Change is Never Completely Predictable.

Individuals, teams and organizations are complex systems. Nobody can fully predict the outcome of change in any given complex system. In fact, attempting to do so can actually cause more problems than the prediction may solve, decreasing your ability to respond to changes that do occur and impairing your ability as a leader to be in an effective relationship with change.

For example, consider the act of sparring in martial arts. Two partners spar with one another in order to better hone both of their skills. If I try to predict how my partner is going to attack me, then I have already lost. Once I decide that I am going to defend against a punch to my face, my opponent can easily overcome me with a leg sweep. By constantly thinking about my partner's next move, I am less aware of the present moment, giving my partner a window through which a punch or kick can be slipped past my defenses.

The same principle holds true in organizations. If leaders are too focused on where they think change *will* come from, they will miss where change actually *does* come from. When compact disks (CD's) were developed in the mid-1980's, many record-making companies went out of business because they failed to see the writing on the wall. Conversely, the history of business is replete with examples of leaders who made synchronistic discoveries while involved in an activity unrelated to their work. For example, I once worked with a business leader who came up with an idea for a new multi-million dollar product while reading a bedtime story to his five-year-old daughter. Remaining open at all times to all possibilities made the difference.

Black Belt Leaders cultivate patience and the ability to wait for a problem or opportunity to become manifest. Then they respond effectively, quickly, and decisively. In the martial arts, there is a maxim that states: *strike second, arrive first.* The ability to respond quickly with such an immediate, almost intuitive, response does not come from our heads, but rather from being fully embodied with a Leading Presence. Only by drawing on the full resources of our entire being as leaders can we effectively respond to change.

❋ ❋ ❋

"There is no change that is unconditionally valid over a period of time. Life has always to be tackled anew."
C. G. Jung

❋ ❋ ❋

People's Responses to Change

Many leaders believe that people either fear or resist change. This is only partially true. The nature of the actual change is not what people typically resist. Instead, people often resist change because there is unresolved conflict in the organization that stems from the power and control tactics manifest in the company's leadership style. People do not like to be forced, so any mandated change, or change created without consensus, is bound to encounter resistance. What people resist is a change in which they had no voice.

Wisdom in Resistance—Sometimes

Great leaders remember that for many people, change is something that does not always produce the desired results. In the best of us, change produces some small degree of anxiety. For those of us who have been hurt in the past, change can be downright terrifying.

Whether leaders wish to acknowledge this or not, people carry their pasts with them into their business life—their memories and dreams, hopes and fears, and things long-forgotten. In addition to my consulting and coaching work, I also work as a clinical counselor with people who have lived through various types of trauma, the recollection of which is not just "in their heads." Research in neuropsychology shows that experiencing a traumatic event can actually "re-wire" a person's central nervous system.

In a very real way, people carry their history with them in every cell of their body.

So what does this have to do with leading change in an organization? Part of being an emotionally intelligent leaders means being aware that change can be very frightening for anyone who's been traumatized or hurt in some way,[82] and the number of people working in organizations who have been hurt can be staggering. For example, statistics on sexual abuse victimization indicate that approximately 1 out of every 4 women and 1 out of every 6 men have been sexually abused, a fact that cannot help but impact our organizational structures,[83] Wise leaders understand the importance of keeping these things in mind.

By citing these statistics, I'm attempting to dramatize the point that people cannot easily separate their work from the rest of their lives. But this is not to imply that everyone who resists change has been traumatized in some way. In fact, there may be quite legitimate organizational reasons for people to resist change, beginning with the simple reason that the change-at-hand might simply be a mistake for the company. Perhaps knowledgeable employees recognize that not enough technical research has been completed. Perhaps a product flaw has been discovered. But citations of these sorts of truths are few and far between in the leadership literature, due to what psychologists call *reporting bias*. Since most leadership books are written by the leaders themselves, the rare description exists in which those leaders made a decision to go in a direction actively resisted by people within their organizations, only to discover later on that those people were correct. *Reporting bias* exists because leaders-turned-authors want to be seen in the best light. This leaves little room, however, for writing about the common occurrence of a leader making a decision that was pointed out as a mistake by a subordinate employee. Rather than seeing this as a fault, such a leader should rejoice that a subordinate is emotionally engaged in the process enough to point out the leader's mistake.

Whether reacting out of personal trauma or an important line staff insight, people who resist change in organizations are important voices of stability. As Barry Johnson points out in his book *Polarity Management*, change and stability are important dimensions that exist at every moment in every organization. Rather than focusing exclusively on one or the other, wise leaders focus on both. The concept of polarities is so crucial to effective leadership that we will cover the subject in even greater detail in the next chapter.

❋ ❋ ❋
**"We are not merely perishable at the end of our lives.
Most parts of us perish during our lifetime only to be substituted
by other perishable parts. The cycles of death and birth repeat
themselves many times in a life span...most of the cells and tissues
that constitute our bodies today are not the same we owned when we
entered college."
Antonio Damasio M.D.**
❋ ❋ ❋

Where Change Begins

Some leaders make the mistake of believing that change has to begin outside the walls of their offices. One of the questions most frequently asked of consultants is "How can I get [fill in the blank: subordinates, front-line staff, etc.] to [fill in the blank: change, be more productive, finish by deadlines, etc]?"

If these questions sound familiar to you, you might be approaching the subject of change from the wrong angle, because in order for a change to be effective, that change has to begin with you.[84] A simple principle of the martial arts states that if you *control the head, the body will follow.* Regardless of your opponent's size, if you control his head, you control *him.* "Controlling the center" is a similar martial arts concept. On the Aikido mat, when I am responding to an attack from another person, if I do not control his or her center, the speed and strength with which I execute the technique will matter little. In fact, without controlling the center, the technique will fail in the end.

The same is true with business. As a leader, you are the center of the business. Any change that is made to the periphery of the business (i.e., a change that does not involve you) is change that will have very little effect on the company in the long run. If, as a leader, you want to develop a more emotionally engaged culture within your organization, then the impetus must begin with you, and you need to lead the way in both words and action.

There is a story told about Gandhi that serves to illustrate this point. A mother brought her son to Gandhi and said, "My son eats sugar all of the time. It is not good for him. Please tell him to stop eating sugar." Gandhi sat quietly for a moment, and then said, "Please bring your son back to me next week." A week passed, and the mother brought her son to again see Gandhi. "You should stop eating sugar, as it is not good for you," said Gandhi. Frustrated, the mother asked Gandhi, "Why did we have to wait a week just for you to tell him that? Couldn't you have just told him that last week, and saved us another trip?" Gandhi replied, "*I* had to stop eating sugar first before I could tell your son to stop."

Systemic Influences on Change

Do either of these experiences sound familiar?

1) *Bob is a mid-level manager at your organization who has been having difficulty with his job for some time. After following the appropriate steps, you decide to terminate him. His replacement, Steve, appears to work out well in the beginning. But several months later, Steve's job performance begins to look very much like Bob's.*

2) *Joanna is one of your best IT staff members. She is witty, kind, and courteous to everyone with whom she interacts. She understands your organization's IT system from front to back, and her annual performance reviews are impeccable. When a newly created IT management job becomes available, you gladly offer the position to Joanna. One year later, Joanna is a different person. She is struggling with her position, and many people have commented on her lack of humor. Worse yet, the IT performance numbers are down for the year.*

While, on the surface, these vignettes might look like individual performance problems, they actually describe the impact of dysfunctional systems on people's behavior. Systems theory recognizes people's mutual interdependence on one another's behavior, rather than viewing them as completely independent, stand-alone entities within an organization. A pole stuck firmly in the ground might represent the stand-alone view of human potential, whereas a child's toy mobile might represent the systems view. Touch the pole and only the pole moves. However, if you touch one part of the mobile, the entire object moves. Your organization is a system—closer in form to the child's mobile than a pole set in the ground. Changing a single aspect of that system will affect all of the other parts.

One of the fascinating characteristics of systems is that dysfunctions affecting the whole often show up in only one area, component, or person—and too often, repair strategies are wrongly targeted only at that single entity. Such an approach erroneously assumes that the entity stands alone in isolation. If you have a blood disorder that is causing damage to the liver or some other major organ, prudent treatment regimens will not just be aimed at the weakened liver. They will, instead, target the blood disorder, which is the overriding systemic dysfunction.

Organizations are analogous to the human body, in that they are led from the top and all parts must work together for optimal results. When a person is feeling physically out-of-sorts, rather than rushing to label one particular component as "the trouble," the best course of action is for the person to undergo a complete physical in order to identify the source of the problem. With regards to organizations, no less a figure than the legendary quality consultant W. Edwards Deming stated that, instead of scapegoating individuals, only by focusing on systemic issues within an organization could a company's problems be effectively solved.[85] To initiate any type of meaningful change, leaders must be willing to lead the charge toward analyzing and modifying systems within their own business structures. Otherwise, there is a very great chance that the problems will go on repeating themselves and nothing will change for the better. At best, the organization will remain stuck. At worst, a slow downward spiral is inevitable.

❋❋❋

"Win over yourself, the Taoist teachings advise. Win over yourself and you will conquer your enemy. The true victor is one who leaves the conflict without encountering bloodshed on either side."
Master Ueshiba

❋❋❋

The Paradox of Change

While leaders need to understand the importance of change, they also need to be aware that doing something differently may not be as effective in reality as the idea appeared on paper. This is because change contains a paradox. Effective leaders account for this paradox by following the Paradoxical Theory of Change, which states that the fastest way to change is to become more fully who we are in the present moment.[86] This, of course, flies in the face of leadership thinking that believes we have to do something different in order to change—so we keep trying "something different," despite the fact that time and time again, the new approach doesn't work. How many times have you reorganized or rearranged departments, for example, resulting in people being shifted around and cubicles being reconfigured? What was the original problem? Did the musical chairs ever bring resolution to that problem? Do you even remember what that original problem was?

The Paradoxical Theory of Change holds that change occurs more readily when leaders pay attention to increasing an awareness of "what is" before attempting to change any system. Fully appreciating the "what is" of any complex system allows leaders to intervene as change agents in a way that *leads* people rather than *pushing* or *pulling* them. An example of the point I am trying to make can be found in a recent coaching session I had with a woman we'll call Christine, a lawyer who was being offered a significant promotion at a prestigious law firm. At our first meeting, Christine was struggling with whether or not to "go for it." Keeping the Paradoxical Theory of Change in mind, I invited her to explore both sides of the dilemma. As we considered the promotion from an aerial perspective, some surprising information came to light. Although she initially thought that she would be "insane" to turn the offer down, we discovered that she had a number of very valid reasons for not accepting the promotion. Her "what is" that came to light for her was a conflict of priorities between her career and her personal life. If the struggle was already this intense with her current job, how much worse would things get with even greater responsibilities in the new position? After several sessions, Christine did decide to accept the promotion, but she did so with a greater awareness of her "what is" and was thus able to strike a balance less overwhelming for her and her loved ones.

❋ ❋ ❋

"We know that all is impermanent; we know that everything wears out. Although we can buy this truth intellectually, emotionally we have a deep-rooted aversion to it. We want permanence; we expect permanence."
Pema Chodron

❋ ❋ ❋

Reasons Why Change Fails

In their book *Primal Leadership*, leadership experts Goleman, Boyatzis, & McKee discuss the lack of sustained change that often follows training, and describe the brief period of change that occurs immediately after training as the "honeymoon period." Since more than $60 billion dollars are spent in North America on training alone, the reasons why change often fails are matters for serious consideration:[87]

1) Lack of Support. True organizational change can only occur within the context of support, which I would define as *the conditions required for a process to grow and evolve.* Support is both an individual, personal process, as well as one of a collective, communal nature. There are ways in which we support ourselves (or do not support ourselves) internally, and there are ways we receive support (or do not receive support) from the environment around us. An example of self-support is the way leaders have conversations with themselves. By and large, most of the leaders I've coached reported that they have very strong internal critics. How and when we give voice to our internal critics goes a long way toward supporting ourselves or cutting ourselves off from the self-support that every leader requires. Environmental support can be seen easily in the decisions that are made within an organization. Whether the decision being made addresses a change in the company's emotional culture or the computer server, a project will only succeed when there is enough support—financial and otherwise—within the organization. This is especially true with upper management, the people who have the most input over the allocation of resources.

2) Lack of Awareness about *Figure* & *Ground.* Many leaders find the Gestalt concepts of "figure" and "ground" to be quite helpful in leading people through change. *Ground* is everything we bring into a situation—our histories, our previous experiences, our fears, our desires, wants and needs. *Ground* is also the composite of everything that is happening at the present moment. *Figure* is what "stands out" in our subjective experience—the most important, or the thing that is paid the most attention, at any given moment. The concept of figure has to do with the interest and energy in each situation. What attracts me? What repels me?[88]

There is simply too much data happening around us for us to attend to everything all at once. We have incredibly sensitive filtering instruments (otherwise known as our bodies) that support us in *attending to only a few manageable things at a time.* This is *figure.* Usually we share the same figure with those in the same setting or situation. Sometimes, however, especially in the event of unclear communications that often accompany conflict, we may be focusing on different figures. For example, we may be in a meeting with someone and think that we are discussing the same thing, but then we find out (either in the meeting, or worse, later on) that we were actually discussing two entirely different matters. As you and I have different ground, what might be figural for me in that particular setting might *not* be figural for you. These differences in figures, as we shall see later, can create conflict.[89]

Recall the example that we discussed when you learned about the Gestalt Cycle of Experience (GCOA), where I was sitting at my computer and experiencing thirst. *Ground* was everything that was happening at the present moment (which also included the emotions I was experiencing as I typed). *Figure* was the thirst I began to experience.

Our figures come out of our ground. In order for something to become figural, there has to be energy. Used in a broad sense, this energy is the interest, power and strength needed to create action that comes from our ground. If there is not enough energy in the figure, then the figure that emerges will not be very strong, and most likely will not exist for a long period of time.

All of this is simply to show why structured training often fails. After any seminar, retreat, or time of reflection, we may have all the best intentions in the world to create a change in our lives. But when we get back into our day-to-day lives, we often find that the changes we have vowed to make are slipping away. Why? Using the GCOE, we can see that the change(s) we had hoped for are failing because the figure we are trying to attend to does not have enough support, or energy, to maintain.

3) Absence of Both-And Thinking. One of the things I see consistently in the leaders I coach is that most of them carry an extremely critical judge inside. High achievers generally do an exemplary job of putting themselves down, which can also translate into *focusing heavily upon themselves at the expense of others.*

Humans are group creatures by nature. We are hard-wired biologically to gather together, influenced by others and by our environment, each of us susceptible to influences from the larger systems within which we work and move. However, understanding this does not relieve us, as individuals, of the responsibility for our own behavior. *Both-and* thinking is important here once again. We are *both* individuals *and* members of larger systems (our organizations and environments). In order for change to succeed, we need to become more of who we are. In order to become more of who we are, we also need support from our environment. The fine balance between personal responsibility and environmental/organizational support is such an important one that the subject needs to be explored in a deeper way.

4) Absence of Personal Responsibility for Mistakes. Human nature makes us want to avoid personal responsibility. Even when we are trying to accept responsibility, avoiding personal responsibility is an easy trap to fall into. I had the good fortune of working for the same supervisor for the nine years I worked at a community mental health center. My supervisor, Debbie, also become a mentor to me. There were many times in those nine years (many of which I can recall to this day as points of transformation for me) when Debbie supportively confronted me about some behavior of mine that was not fitting the environment. There were times when I would react with anger or even indignation. But when I allowed the smoke to clear (which sometimes took days), I was usually able to see the value in the information that Debbie was giving me, and I was able to accept personal responsibility for my actions. Now, when I look back, I see that Debbie was absolutely correct in confronting me, and I have become a more effective intervener as a result of her supportive confrontations. Learning to understand and be aware of my "what is" was very helpful at that time in my professional development.

Ineffective leaders often avoid taking responsibility for organizational changes that don't work by simply blaming others for not being motivated or working hard enough to meet the objectives. Salaried employees, who labor 50 or 60 hours a week without overtime pay, understandably take exception to this approach. Even an employee who's normally shot out of a canon every morning will find his or her drive and motivation whittled away in an environment where leaders don't accept responsibility for their own mistakes.

❋ ❋ ❋
A Key to Leading People
Use the momentum of naturally occuring change in your organization to lead people into change that is best for your organization.
❋ ❋ ❋

Remember: Focus on Balance Rather than Blame

Striking a balance between individual and environmental responsibility can be very tricky. Individuals can easily rely upon "lack of support" as an excuse for not doing anything. In some ways, there is never enough support, because a simple fact of life is that resources are limited. I wrote much of this book in the wee hours of the morning, averaging about 4-6 hours of sleep per night. As I began to meet other writers, I learned that this is a common pattern. If all writers waited until there was "enough time" to write, then no books would ever be written. Conditions are never perfect. As leaders, we still need to make decisions, even in the face of limited time and resources, for we as leaders are the ones ultimately responsible for the outcome.

If you envision leading your organization in a way that creates emotionally engaged relationships with both your customers and your employees, doing so will require serious, extensive dialogue about the barriers within your organization that are interfering with emotional engagement. Those dialogues need to encompass all the points we've discussed in this chapter, from the Four Rules of Change that we addressed in the beginning, to the Reasons Why Change Fails, and the importance of Balance versus Blame. Leaders also need to remember that change has to take place over time. Leaders at various levels of an organization collectively need time to identify the ways that they are inadvertently failing to support their people. People (including the leaders) individually need time to understand how they might be inadvertently shooting themselves in the foot—and all parties need to be singing off the same page of the organization's Mission & Goal Hymnal.

Initiating this creative and supportive process falls within your purview as a leader; and this process can produce engaged employees who will ultimately help you increase your company's bottom line.

The process awaits you. The choice to begin is yours.[90]

Embodied Learning Experiment #5

Changing Your Views about Change

Black Belt Leaders understand the importance of changing our beliefs about change. Hopefully, you, too, have begun to acquire this understanding.

Let's take a moment to examine your views:

1. Write down at least one thing that is different about your perspective on change after reading through the book thus far.

What I used to believe about change was:

But now I believe:

2. When change fails, one way I tend to affix blame in my organization is:

3. One way I avoid taking responsibility for change in my own life is:

4. One change that would increase people's emotional engagement in my organization is:

5. When I think about change, I notice these physical reactions in myself:

6. Identify at least one area of your personal life and one area of your professional life where you would like to lead change. Identify one way these changes will become manifest.

7. In the past, when people saw me go through change, they would have seen me:

8. Now they will see me:

9. One change that I would like to see within in my organization during the next year is:

10. One way that I will take more personal responsibility for leading this change is:

Chapter Summary
Congratulations!

By recognizing the importance of change to emotionally engaged leadership, you have taken the next step toward becoming a Black Belt Leader!

Chapter Summary:
We began with a wife using resources effectively to lead her husband through change. You learned the Four Rules of Change for leaders and examined how people respond to change. We discussed how thinking systemically can impact leaders' perspectives on change, and finally, we covered four reasons why change fails.

Suggested further reading:
Facilitating Organization Change: Lessons from Complexity Science by Edwin Olson & Glenda Eoyang
Integral Psychology by Ken Wilber
Leadership Without Easy Answers Ronald A. Heifetz

Looking Ahead:
In the next chapter, you will learn about two key leadership qualities and how to use them to make yourself an even better leader.

BROWN BELT
Section 3:
Take Action!

"We need to encourage habits of flexibility, of continuous learning, and of acceptance of change as normal and as opportunity—for institutions as well as for individuals."
- Peter Drucker

"Black Belt Leaders understand the importance of both hard and soft skills in leading people."

Story
Heaven & Hell

Once upon a time a samurai warrior went to a famous Zen master. "Sensei," asked the samurai, "could you please instruct me about heaven and hell?"

"How could I teach anything to a samurai as stupid as you? You couldn't learn anything!" shouted the Zen master.

Enraged at the blatant insult, the samurai drew his sword, intending to hack the Zen master to pieces.

Unruffled, the Zen master said, "Here lie the gates of Hell!"

Catching himself (and the point of the lesson), the samurai took a deep breath and returned his sword to his sheath.

"And here," said the Zen master calmly, "open the gates of Heaven."

Chapter 9
Two Key Qualities Required to Lead People

"The test of a first-rate intelligence is the ability to hold two opposed ideas in the mind at once and still retain the ability to function."
- F. Scott Fitzgerald

Two Key Qualities: Balance and Flexibility

As you learned in Chapter Four, we are all embodied beings, and superior leaders always keep that fact in mind. Leaders who practice embodied leadership are successful because they are sustained by two important qualities: **balance** and **flexibility**. Just as we need to maintain balance in order to walk, ride a bike, or perform any other physical activity, so too do we need to remain balanced as a leader in order to stay at the top of our game. Without flexibility, we are unable to lean over to tie our shoes or to reach up to retrieve an item from the top closet shelf. In the same way, without flexibility, leaders create rigid organizations that are unable to meet today's requirements of adapting to constant change.

Leadership balance and flexibility are required in the emotional realm as well. The connection between balance, flexibility, and emotions is significant, and that significance is reflected in our language. When people perceive leaders as being very emotionally consistent, we talk about them as being *stable* and *rock-solid*. Leaders who are flexible are *in high demand*. One of the best ways to attend to balance and flexibility as a leader is by attending to *polarities*.

A Problem to Solve or a Polarity to Explore?

In the physical realm, as in leadership, balance is not only related to gravity, but also to training all parts of ourselves. A martial artist would never consider practicing punching with only one hand and not the other. If he trained only one side of his body, he would end up with less flexibility and less ability to defend himself. In the martial arts, as in business, one needs to be wholly prepared to meet the challenges that will come from all sides.

In this era of global organizations, very few decisions have clear, cut-and-dried answers. A great deal of grey area generally lies between two choices. People and operational factors often fall within this grey area, as well. The "right" answer to a problem can be difficult to determine at times, and must be based upon an intelligent analysis of this grey area.

Some leaders do not believe in grey areas and see leadership only in terms of black-and-white terms, with one "right" answer. This approach to leading people is a holdover from Scientific Management, a management practice established by Frederick Taylor in the early 1900's.[91] Scientific Management was developed at the dawn of the 20th century when leadership was needed for an uneducated workforce engaging primarily in manual labor at the end of the Industrial Revolution. But applying the out-dated principles of Scientific Management in today's highly educated, information-driven workforce is like driving a Model T Ford on our superhighways. Contemporary leadership strategies need to be exponentially more complex than those required in Mr. Taylor's day.

Finding the right way to lead people in your organization means uncovering the leadership processes that fit best within your organization. As I've stated before, this takes time, and also involves a certain degree of trial and error. Black Belt Leaders develop a large tolerance for mistakes. Not having to be right all of the time means that you will be wrong some of the time. Guaranteed. You will be anxious and sometimes even lose sleep over difficult decisions that you need to make—and no matter how much you struggle and analyze, you will occasionally make a wrong choice. This simply comes with the territory of being a leader.[92] The best way to minimize these occurrences is to weigh all of the factors and seek answers that create the "best fit" for the situation, the people, and the other variables that need to be considered.

So how do effective leaders approach the task of finding the best fit? The answer lies in understanding polarities.[93] Polarities are tools that can help leaders effectively use *both-and* thinking in a way that provides a process and structure for making decisions. Exploring a polarity recognizes that there are always two sides in every situation. Consider the idea of light and dark, for example. Just as most of the light in our world falls somewhere between blinding light and complete darkness, most of our leadership decisions fall somewhere in the middle between "absolutely right" and "absolutely wrong."

✳ ✳ ✳

A Key to Leading People:
Use polarities in a balanced and flexible manner
to build relationships with people you lead.

✳ ✳ ✳

Let's say that you have been given the chance for a promotion, one which would involve moving to a different city and taking a position higher up in the organization. You feel torn between wanting to stay at your current level and wanting to accept the new position. You enjoy your job and your co-workers. You have a beautiful home in an area where the cost-of-living is very manageable, and your family is happy and settled. On the other hand, you are excited about the prospect of taking on a new position with greater challenges, more money, and best of all—the relocation city is one where you and your partner have always talked about living. In this case, as with most problems leaders face, there is no clear-cut answer.

You have a dilemma on your hands. In the language of polarities, your dilemma would look something like this:

Wanting to stay at present job   Wanting to accept new position

$$\longleftarrow \longrightarrow$$

The examination of polarities is a process tool to be used as a guide through decision-making and change implementation. When we view a problem as a polarity, the issue shifts from an *either-or* problem to a *both-and* dilemma.

✳ ✳ ✳

"Both the journey and the destination are important.
Don't choose between them."
Peter Block

✳ ✳ ✳

In our example about your promotional opportunity, there are important and valid reasons for staying at your present job *and* for taking the new position. In order to make a "best-fit" decision, you need to explore both ends of the polarity, with your head *and* your heart—and because "best-fit" may vary among the members of your family, you need to initiate and lead the discussion with all parties involved.

Use the polarity continuum presented above, moving across from left to right during your discussions while employing the old "Benjamin Franklin scale" of pros and cons beneath each extreme to help guide the process. In addition to obvious criteria such as cost-of-living, schools, housing styles and availability, a job for your spouse, geography, weather, etc., incorporate the four considerations we covered when discussing why change fails: 1) Lack of Support, 2) Lack of Awareness About Figure & Ground, 3) Absence of *Both-And* Thinking, and 4) Absence of Personal Responsibility for Mistakes.

When all parties have weighed in on all areas, there will probably not be one clear, right or wrong point on the horizontal polarity line. But there should be an obvious best-fit point that is further toward one end than the other. Furthermore, because you wisely involved everyone in the decision making process, and because the components of successful change were part of your dialogue, your whole family will have ownership of the decision, whether you take the promotion or stay where you are.

Yin and Yang

Asian martial arts are well-versed in the language of polarities. In Asian thought, there is the symbol of the *T'ai Chi T'u* (frequently referred to in the West as the "yin/yang"), which looks something like this:

This symbol represents the polarities of the world: hot/cold, male/female, up/down, hard/soft, and so forth. As you can see, each side of a polarity incorporates a drop of the other side. Both sides are needed to complete the whole. In the same way, a leader must attend to the tensions between two ends of a particular polarity. However, the point on any given polarity that is best for you and your organization is a question that only you and the people you lead can answer together. There is no one single "right" answer that fits for every organization.

❊ ❊ ❊

"Whatever it is that you intend to achieve
by whatever it is that you doisn't likely to be
the thing you actually accomplish by doing it."
William Bridges
❊ ❊ ❊

Don't Lead Like Daedalus!

Some leaders frequently make the mistake of over-identifying with one side of a polarity or decision point. Doing this too early in the decision-making process is a path that can lead to chaos and damage. Consider the ancient Greek legend of Icarus & Daedalus:

Icarus was the son of Daedalus, the man who designed the labyrinth where King Minos imprisoned the monster known as the Minotaur. A talented inventor, Daedalus built the labyrinth in such a way that no one who was placed inside the labyrinth could find his way out again without assistance. After building the labyrinth, Daedalus fell out of favor with King Minos, and he and his son Icarus were imprisoned in a tower. In order to escape, Daedalus designed wings fashioned out of wax and feathers. Before leaving on their flight, Daedalus cautioned Icarus not to fly too low or the water would soak his feathers. Nor should he fly too high, or the sun would melt the wax in his wings. Father and son began to fly, and Icarus ignored his father's words. In his excitement at being able to fly like the gods, he flew too high. The sun melted his wings and he fell into the sea and drowned.

The Greek legend of Icarus & Daedalus holds several important lessons for leaders. The first lesson is not identifying too strongly with one end of a polarity over the other. In ancient Greece, only the gods could fly. For Icarus and Daedalus to attempt to fly was an attempt to over-identify with the gods. Identifying with the gods created a condition of narcissism, which is an easy trap for leaders to fall into. In identifying himself with the gods, Icarus literally played with fire (the sun) and got burned (the wax on his wings melted), and he died as a direct result of his arrogance.

Another lesson about leading people comes from a closer look at Daedalus' error. His name meant "cunning worker," and he was "...the embodiment of skill in the mechanical art," which is another way of saying that Daedalus was a technical genius.[94] However, Daedalus lacked the emotional intelligence to realize that he worked for an unjust tyrant. Daedalus continued to work for King Minos despite the fact that Daedalus knew the king was exacting a yearly "tribute" from the country of Athens. This "tribute" required that seven young men and seven young women be sent every year to the Minotaur, a monster with a bull's body and a human head, who would eat the fourteen "offerings."[95] After building Minos his labyrinth, Daedalus and his son suffered the wrath of this unjust tyrant and were imprisoned themselves. In a very real way, Daedalus' lack of emotional intelligence contributed to the death of his son.

The legend of Daedalus & Icarus teaches leaders that focusing only on technical mastery is a mistake. By striving exclusively for technical mastery absent any commitment to their emotional growth, leaders risk becoming imprisoned by their own tyrants, regardless of whether those tyrants might be coming from within or without. They also risk the well-being of those who depend upon them. This dependence can be either literal, in the case of children or the elderly, or symbolic, in the sense of people within an organization over whom the leader holds power.[96]

Some leaders believe they know everything and have all the answers. Wise leaders understand how little they actually know. Great leaders understand that an over-identification with one end of any polarity creates an *Unbalanced* Polarity. In the next section, we will further examine the phenomenon of Unbalanced Polarities and explore several typical polarities with which leaders struggle.

✻ ✻ ✻

A Key to Leading People:
Without a strong commitment to their own growth, leaders run the
risk of becoming imprisoned by a tyrant. And whether that tyrant is
internal or external, the imprisonment occurs all the same.

✻ ✻ ✻

Unbalanced Polarities: A Common Leadership Problem

While there is literally an infinite number of polarities to examine, let's take a look at some examples using these four:

1. "Hard" and "Soft" Skills
2. Content and Process
3. Conformity and Individuality
4. Challenge and Support

Please note that I specifically did not use the word "versus," which instantly forces the conversation back into *either/or* thinking. Instead, I used the word "and" when speaking of polarities, in order to stay in a *both-and* frame of mind.

As I mentioned previously, one side of a polarity is often over-valued at the expense of the other side in many organizational discussions. For example, in the four polarities described above, most leaders tend to overvalue hard skills over soft skills, content over process, conformity over individuality, and challenge over support. In the section that follows, you will learn the problems that can develop from such one-sided overvaluation. You will also identify the benefits that can accrue from increasing your awareness of the undervalued side.

Polarity

Overvalued Side	Undervalued Side
Hard Skills	Soft Skills
Content	Process
Conformity	Individuality
Challenge	Support

Now, let's take a look at these four polarities and discover how their unbalanced nature impacts organizations.

1) Hard Skills   Soft Skills

Hard skills involve the cognitive, technical aspects required in fields such as accounting, engineering, and information technology, to name just a few. Hard skills are more easily quantified or measured. *Soft* skills, on the other hand, are more subjective and are found in fields such as sales, marketing, and even teaching. Soft skills involve "people skills," which are vital for leaders. The degree to which leaders possess these skills directly correlates with their success. Effective leaders understand the importance of strengthening both their hard and soft skill sets in order to maintain balance. This affords them the flexibility of drawing upon whichever skill set might be required, or more appropriate, at any given time.[97]

❋ ❋ ❋

"Learning can be more like an exploration of a new territory than a heavy-handed accumulation of knowledge and its associated illusion of power."
Wendy Palmer

❋ ❋ ❋

Recall our discussion of the *Tai Chi T'u* ("yin/yang symbol") and how Asian martial arts recognize that there is always a small portion of one extreme inside the opposite extreme. The world of business is no different. Labor negotiators in the automobile industry, for example, need to have at least a rudimentary understanding of the assembly line workers' job responsibilities in order to negotiate their contracts. But that same labor negotiator also needs a solid grasp of any number of other *soft* techniques such as *give-and take, win-win,* and *active listening*—skills which can't be tracked and calculated like the parts along an assembly line. More soft skills are required as a negotiator than hard, but a balance of both is always necessary. Conversely, just because someone graduated at the top of his or her Finance class, holds an Ivy League MBA, and can crunch numbers like a computer, these skills do not insure that superior leadership will automatically follow in a major accounting firm. If leadership success is going to be achieved, this hard-skilled genius will need a balance of soft skills as well.

2) Content   Process

⟵ ─────────────────────────────────── ⟶

Recall from our discussion in Chapter Three that Cornerstone #3 of Black Belt Leadership is the Power of Process. In any interaction involving emotions—which is to say *every* interaction—leaders need to find a balance between content and process. In Chapter Three, you learned that content is the *what* of any conversation, or the basic information being discussed. Process, on the other hand, is the *how*—the series of actions, changes, and functions that take place in order to bring about a result.

For example, a team may meet to decide the best way to launch a particular product into the marketplace. The content of the discussion is the *what*—the product, the features, and the bells-and-whistles that will be attractive to potential buyers. The process is the *methodology* used to introduce the product—the steps of the marketing campaign, the budget, timeframe, and how the team is conducting the meeting.

Content is fairly cut-and-dried—the product specifications are as stated. But *process* is fluid, highly affected by the dynamics of team members, and laden with emotional elements. The configurations of process are every bit as important as the features of the product. Every task within an organization—regardless of industry or department—contains elements of both content *and* process. Effective leaders help their teams find the appropriate balance in each situation.

3) Conformity   Individuality

During this past holiday season, I had to contact a large company to resolve a problem with an order I had placed with them. Over the course of an hour, I spoke to five different employees. Each and every one answered the phone with, "Happy Holidays from ABC Corporation. How many I help you?" in a tone that sounded like death warmed-over. The employees sounded neither happy nor interested in helping me, and they were clearly emotionally disengaged from their jobs. They had obviously been pushed to comply with a script that had little meaning to them. The problem I was trying to resolve, while simple, did not fit neatly within the rules and procedures that each employee was accustomed to following, so the answer each time was to transfer me to a different department. After an hour of repeating my problem to person after person, I gave up in frustration. As a direct result of the way I was handled on the phone, I became a disengaged customer, and I vowed never to do business with ABC Corporation again.

Leaders must approach the polarity of conformity and individuality carefully. Companies that fall too far on the conformity side of this polarity often create working conditions that suck the emotional life out of every employee. These organization then turn into "The Business of the Living Dead," staffed by emotionally disengaged employees. These employees infect every customer with whom they come into contact. Emotionally disengaged employees create disengaged customers, and disengaged customers are not *paying* customers. The ultimate effect on the bottom line goes without saying.

Obviously, enabling employees to have absolute individuality isn't the answer either. After the dot-com crash, the media was overflowing with stories about dot-com start-ups that had been heavy on toys, extravagant launch parties, and annual junkets to the Bahamas, but light on the business models. Balance, balance, balance! Did I mention balance? Great leaders only need to hear the point made once.

Even in establishments like McDonald's or Denny's, where conformity is the selling point, individuality still needs to be factored in for success. Regardless of where the restaurant is located—San Francisco, Dallas or New York—I know the menus will be the same. My kids drag me to McDonalds because they are looking for sameness and familiarity. But the franchise owners in the different cities always incorporate a nuance or promotion unique to that city—and intra-franchise establishments within the same city customize their operations even further to remain competitive. (Did you ever notice that some have playgrounds and some do not?) McDonald's franchise owners can't assume success just because the golden arches are out in front. They know that the *customers* know there's another McDonald's not too far away. Balance means keeping both the adults and kids happy while they're all munching away at those award-winning French fries.

4) Challenge   Support

$$\longleftrightarrow$$

If those who are led are not challenged enough, they become bored and disengaged. But disengagement can also occur if there is too much challenge and too little support. The trick is to find the proper balance for each situation.

Many leaders, particularly men, have the most difficulty with the support end of this polarity, because men are not culturally conditioned to easily give or receive emotional support. In Western culture, men are expected to know all the answers, solve all the problems, and kill all the bugs. Consequently, "needing help"—especially for men— implies a certain level of inferiority, weakness, or lack of knowledge. Many leaders mistakenly believe that effective leaders must be strong enough to work through decisions and situations independently, without the need for assistance and support. But wise leaders understand that cutting oneself off from all support is like going scuba diving and cutting your air supply when you are fifty feet below the surface. Knowing how to balance the needs for support and independence is a hallmark of effective leadership.

❀ ❀ ❀

"One does not learn leadership in a vacuum as an intellectual exercise for its own sake. Leadership is a social phenomenon that has meaning inside of an already existing set of commitments and anticipated future concerns."
Richard Strozzi-Heckler

❀ ❀ ❀

Ten Tips for Incorporating Polarities into Your Leadership Style

1. Give yourself permission to make mistakes.

As you begin to use *both-and* thinking and look at the world in terms of polarities, you are learning new and valuable skills—and as with any new skill, mistakes are common. Don't beat yourself up when they happen. There will be times when you are exploring an underdeveloped side of polarity that you may not lean far enough toward that end of the scale. At other times, you may lean *too* far. As you grow into a Black Belt Leader, you will begin to develop a deep knowledge of how far is *far enough*. Making mistakes teaches smart leaders to increase their perception and awareness of their immediate situation.

2. Use feedback from others to gain information.

Gather—and use—information and feedback from other people. Those around you have a different perspective (remember our discussion about the concept of multiple perspectives?) that you can use to strengthen the underdeveloped side of any polarity. Harnessing the collective intelligence that exists around you is crucial to effectively implementing polarities.

3. Understand that each polarity is unique.

What works for you in one polarity is not necessarily going to work for you in another, or even for someone else in the *same* polarity. As an aspiring Black Belt Leader, you have to test out each polarity as you go. Furthermore, what works for you within each polarity may change from day to day, week to week, and month to month, as conditions change. Leading people calls for flexibility, strength, determination and resolve.

4. Take one polarity at a time.

If you try to change six different polarities in your organization at the same time, you will not succeed in changing any of them. Be patient. Think large, but work small. Learn from the wisdom of the martial arts. Experienced martial arts practitioners know the large advancements that can come from working on small changes, one at a time.

5. Practice thinking in polarities.

At first, you may have difficulty seeing the polarities that are operating in and around your organization. Therefore, you need to practice thinking and speaking about them. The more you practice thinking in terms of polarities, the easier they will be to see.

6. Practice using *both-and* language.

Pay attention to how you talk to others. Become aware of how many times throughout the day you give in to fear and say "but…" When you find yourself tempted to say "*but…*," stop and substitute the words "*both*" and/or "*and.*" Understand that making even this small change will have a large impact on how others receive your words.

7. Understand that multiple polarities are occurring at any given moment.

Every situation has multiple polarities. Consequently, do not put too much pressure on yourself to figure out which is the "right" polarity to focus upon. Organizations are holistic entities. Consequently, the polarity you start with doesn't matter that much. They will all get you to the same place.

8. Name both sides of a polarity.

Ancient cultures were well aware of the power of naming. Naming something brings clarity and reduces tension. You can solidify a polarity you're working with by giving each side a name. But don't turn the naming process into a project in and of itself. A simple name that fits will do.

9. Be patient.

Never force things. Forcing things against the natural order is a certain recipe for disaster. If you are struggling with a problem in your organization and the polarity does not immediately become clear, take a break and trust that the polarity will appear eventually.

10. Remember Icarus.

Remember that polarities are a process tool. In order to stay balanced as a leader, keep your eye on the *process* of the polarity. Remember that flexibility and balance go hand-in-hand. Do not expect to come up with every solution to every problem by yourself. Use the strengths of the effective people you have gathered around you in order to resolve the issue(s) du jour.

Embodied Learning Experiment #6
Practicing Polarities

Since most leaders have not been taught to think in polarities, they need some practice. Here is a learning experiment you can do to become more familiar with the process:

Chose a difficult situation with which you've been struggling. The situation can either be from your work or personal life (remembering that, in the emotional realm, there is no difference between the two).

Decide on a name for the difficulty—something short and sweet. Write that in the centered space below. On the left side of the polarity, label one choice you might make about this particular issue. On the right side, label a choice 180 degrees opposite from your choice on the left. The only criteria for the labels on either side should be that they are appropriate to the polarity.

———————————

(Polarity Name)

———————————   ———————————

(One side)   (Other side)

Now, take some time to think about each option and notice what happens to you physically. (As you do this, you might want to be in a quiet room with fewer external distractions). You may experience changes in muscle tension (tight or loose) or body temperature (hot or cold). You may notice these changes throughout your body, or more in one specific area than another.

Try not to make judgments about what you notice about yourself physically—just observe.

The point of this exercise is not to *do* anything with the dilemma. The point is to develop your own awareness about both sides of the polarity. Action without awareness is guaranteed to simply create more leadership headaches. Once a polarity is fleshed out, the solution often becomes clearer.

Chapter Summary
Congratulations!

By understanding the two key leadership qualities of balance and flexibility, and by learning how to think in polarities, you have taken the next step toward becoming a Black Belt Leader!

Chapter Summary:

We began with a story about a samurai who learned that his actions determined the presence of Heaven or Hell. We discussed the two key qualities of leadership—balance and flexibility. We then explored the important tools of polarities, and how they can be useful to leaders. We examined the leadership lessons contained in the ancient Greek myth of Icarus & Daedalus, and then we discussed approaches that leaders can take when polarities become unbalanced. Finally, we covered Ten Tips to help you incorporate polarities into you leadership style.

Suggested further reading:

Polarity Management by Barry Johnson
Presence: Human Purpose and the Field of the Future by Peter Senge, Otto Scharmer, Joseph Jaworski, and Betty Sue Flowers
Leadership on the Line by Ronald Heifetz & Marty Linsky

Looking Ahead:

In the next chapter, you'll explore how to better lead with harmony and discover what you can learn from Ebenezer Scrooge.

"The Black Belt Way of Leading People recognizes that there is no single answer that will best fit every leadership situation."

Story
Teacups & Martial Arts

Once upon a time, a young man joined a martial arts dojo (school). One of the tasks given to any beginning martial artist is to help clean the dojo. After several days of strenuous practice, the young student was given the task of cleaning the sleeping quarters for the sensei, the master of the school. In his eagerness to clean the teacher's quarters, the novice began to dust earnestly, and in doing so he knocked over the sensei's antique tea cup, an item of uncalculated beauty and cost. Turning around, the novice heard the sensei coming back to his quarters. Thinking quickly, the novice scooped up the pieces of the broken cup and hid them behind his back.
As the sensei entered the room, the novice walked toward him.

"Sensei," said the novice, "I have a question: Please instruct me about birth and death and their relationship to the martial arts."

The sensei responded, "Everything has a time to be born and a time to die. Everything changes. That is the nature of all things."

"Then sensei," responding the novice, holding the pieces of the broken teacup out in front of him "It was time for your tea cup to die."

Chapter 10
Leading with Harmony

"More than anyone else, it is the team leader who has the power to establish norms, maximizing harmony and collaboration to ensure that the team benefits from the best talents of each member."
- Daniel Goleman, Richard Boyatzis, & Annie McKee

What's More Important?

Leadership is about leading people—and people, as we have seen, are emotional beings, with feelings, dreams and desires that must be taken into account by leaders.

People become emotionally engaged when they know that someone cares about and appreciates the work that they do. Showing people genuine care and appreciation requires being in tune with those same people, and when leaders are in tune with those they lead, they are leading with harmony.

❋ ❋ ❋
"Leadership is a matter of intelligence, trustworthiness, humaneness, courage, and sternness."
Sun Tzu
❋ ❋ ❋

If you were forced to make a choice between your people or your technology, which would you pick? You have five seconds—one-one thousand, two-one thousand, three-one thousand... Quick! Decide!

If you chose technology, you would not be alone. In the past decade alone, technology has done much to make our work lives easier. While much of this technological progress has improved the economic and personal worlds within which we live, wise leaders understand that this trend can only go so far. Smart leaders understand that the most valued assets in their organizations are still their people. Period.

But many leaders quite frankly feel more comfortable with technology than with people, because they have a greater understanding of technology. As with all of our previous *both-and* discussions, effective leaders realize that success means developing an understanding of people as well.

You would never consider taking off on a cross-country motor vacation without checking the basics of your vehicle—gas, oil, tires, etc., both at the start of the trip and throughout your journey. Moreover, you wouldn't have to learn about those automobile basics in advance of your departure because you already know what they are and understand their importance. Similarly, if you view each objective and task that you're responsible for at work as a cross-country trip of sorts, you'll see that your people are the vehicles you need in order to arrive at your destination in one piece and on time. *Their* basics must also be identified and monitored to ensure that those people become, and remain, emotionally engaged.[98]

Here's a thought to chew on: Without a significant proportion of emotionally engaged people in your organization, your customers will eventually take their business elsewhere.

❃ ❃ ❃

"When a leader triggers resonance, you can read it in people's eyes: They're engaged and they light up."
Goleman, Boyatzis, & McKee

❃ ❃ ❃

Leadership Styles: Resonant & Dissonant

In their best-selling book *Primal Leadership*, Goleman, Boyatzis, & McKee identify two states of leadership: *resonant* and *dissonant*. In describing a particular manager as a resonant leader, the authors describe him as being "…attuned to people's feelings and [who] moved them in a positive emotional direction. Speaking authentically from his own values and resonating with the emotions of those around him, he hit just the right cords with his message, leaving people feeling uplifted and inspired, even in a difficult moment.[99] The authors then go on to define dissonance as the "lack of harmony," noting that, "Dissonant leadership produces groups that feel emotionally discordant, in which people have a sense of being continually off-key."[100]

Words like resonance, dissonance, and harmony are terms that have to do with sound, music, and movement. There is also a long tradition of using sound, music, and movement in a variety of spiritual traditions, all of which have some concept of harmony. Recall that the martial of Aikido is often translated into English as "the Way of the Spirit of Harmony."

One of the leadership pitfalls in considering dissonance, resonance and harmony is falling back into *either-or* thinking. Just as no baseball player hits a home run every time at bat, no leader is either consistently dissonant *or* resonant. Rather than considering resonance and dissonance as fixed positions to be achieved and then forgotten, think of them as opposing poles of a polarity:

Polarity of Harmony

Resonance   **Dissonance**

$\longleftrightarrow$

A leader needs to focus on finding the "best-fit" point on the continuum for each objective, task or situation—and that point for effective leaders will always be closer to resonance than dissonance. Those leaders also know that this process requires an understanding of what's driving each of their people, so that "best-fit" will apply as well to the act of matching each individual's talents with elements of the task at hand. An employee who knows that his or her skill set and individuality is valued for a particular task will be charged, energized, and emotionally engaged in that role. If a leader approaches each objective with an eye on how each employee can best be utilized, success will become exponentially greater.

Harmony & Resonance

Because effective leaders realize that harmony creates engagement, let's explore a little more fully exactly what *harmony* means. Many leaders have the misconception that harmony is a state of bliss, where no conflicts, problems or worries exist. But listen to what Aikido master Mitsugi Saotome's has to say about harmony:

> We talk of nature's harmony, our eyes soften, and we see in our
> imagination a blue sky with fleecy white clouds reflected in a quiet

pond. The song of the birds echoes from leafy branches. A soft, warm breeze lightly brushes our face as it waves in the tall grasses, and we smile as the lion lies down with the lamb. This image contains the too-sweet smell of decay. The lion will die of starvation. The sheep will overpopulate the area and destroy the tall grasses that anchor the soil. The rich topsoil will be washed away, the pond will dry up, and the sheep will die unnourished. The trees will die, and the only sound, the sound of the wind, will echo in a parched and lifeless desert.[101]

Rather than some idyllic dreamscape, harmony more accurately captures the notion of "fit" between the person and the environment. The emotionally intelligent approach chosen by a leader can be seen as harmonious—or *not* harmonious—only in relationship to the other people and the environment in which the leader works. The quality of "fit"— the harmony—between the leader and those being led (as well as the organization as a whole) is the true measurement. A style of leadership that would be viewed as quite harmonious in Organization or Department A might not fit at all in Organization or Department B, and the emotionally intelligent leader will know the difference.

Dissonance Personified—Four Coaches for Ebenezer

The psychology of the Swiss psychiatrist C. G. Jung has had a profound impact on American culture. Jung identified the idea of the archetype, which is an enduring pattern of behavior. Archetypes include the sage, warrior, lover, and magician,[102] and can be found in stories, movies, dreams, and fantasy, as well as in our everyday lives. The archetypal dissonant leader is Ebenezer Scrooge, the main character from Charles Dickens' *A Christmas Carol*.[103] Scrooge's transformation (or "reclamation," in Dickens' language) from dissonant miser to harmoniously resonant leader (and human being) holds many keys for those who seek to become better leaders.[104] In order to develop our own capacities for emotionally intelligent leadership, each of us, like Scrooge, needs to journey through our own emotional transformation. No one can experience the transformation for us—and the intensely personal work of transformation requires the skills of a martial artist: disciple, dedication, and willingness to travel the path of mastery without immediate rewards.

Most of us are familiar with the character of Scrooge. In *A Christmas Carol*, Dickens describes Scrooge this way:

> "...Oh! But he was a tight-fisted hand at the grindstone, Scrooge! A squeezing, wrenching, grasping, scraping, clutching, covetous old sinner! Hard and sharp as flint, from which no steel had ever struck out generous fire, secret, and self-contained, and solitary as an oyster..."

As the CEO of Scrooge & Marley, Scrooge is dissonant leadership in all its glory—written large with a capital "D." He is the embodiment of cold rationality, refusing to heat the office to a reasonable degree, either for himself or his clerk, Bob Cratchit. He refuses his nephew Fred's invitation to Christmas dinner, and although extraordinarily wealthy, he refuses to donate to the poor. He chases away a caroler and begrudgingly gives Bob Cratchit the next day (Christmas day) off, complaining that the holiday is "not fair" and "a poor excuse for picking a man's pocket every twenty-fifth of December."

As the story progresses, Scrooge is visited by four ghosts. (Yes, there were *four* ghosts. The ghost of Jacob Marley counts, too). In the course of their visits, these ghosts proceeded to lead Scrooge's transformation from a dissonant leader to a harmonious leader, and to a much more connected and pleasant person as well.

Dickens uses the words "ghost" and "spirit" interchangeably, which is fitting since the connection between emotional life and spirits is deeply embedded in our language. When referring to someone's emotional state, we often speak of the spirit. If someone is joyous, we might say he is in *high spirits*. If depressed and sad, we might say his *spirits are low*. With friends, we might try to do something to *lift their spirits*.

Let's re-examine Scrooge's visits from the spirits in light of what you have been learning about leading people:

Coach #1—The Spirit of Jacob Marley

The first ghost to coach Scrooge was the ghost of Jacob Marley, Scrooge's old business partner—with a ghastly surprise in store for old Ebenezer! Initially, Scrooge refused to believe what he was seeing:

> "...[Scrooge's] colour changed, though, when, without a pause, it came on through the heavy door, and passed into the room before his eyes. Upon its coming, the dying flame leaped up, as though it cried, 'I know him, Marley's Ghost!' and fell again..."

> "Why do you doubt your senses?" Marley asked him.

> "Because," said Scrooge, "a little thing affects them. A slight
> disorder of the stomach makes them cheat…"

Scrooge became somewhat flippant as he struggled to reign in his fear—
something many of us do when we're confronted with new information or
changes that threaten to undermine our worlds as we've come to know
them. In Dickens' words:

> "…Scrooge was not much in the habit of cracking jokes, nor
> did he feel, in his heart, by any means waggish then. The truth is,
> that he tried to be smart, as a means of distracting his own attention,
> and keeping down his terror; for the spectre's voice disturbed the very
> marrow in his bones…"

Marley showed Scrooge the chains suffered in the afterlife as a
consequence of the greedy decisions he made during his time on earth.
He then informed Scrooge that his own chains were destined to be even
longer and heavier now than Marley's, but that he (Marley) has intervened
on Scrooge's behalf with the powers that control the afterlife. To Scrooge's
dismay, Marley's intervention involves separate visits from three additional
ghosts. Scrooge is about to receive the coaching of his life.

Here are the Black Belt Leadership lessons that the ghost of Jacob
Marley teaches:

1) Leaders Need Honest Friends.

Jacob Marley was Scrooge's friend in life, and friends can be vital in letting
us know when we are getting out of balance. One of the things I often hear
from the executives I coach is, "I have acquaintances, but no real friends."
Executive power isolates, and isolation is an enormous threat to our emotional
intelligence. You cannot be isolated by executive powers for long periods of
time and remain either emotionally intelligent or effective as a leader.

"Friendship" might be too strong of a word to use to describe Scrooge
and Marley's relationship. "Companions in greed" may be more in keeping
with the flavor of their pairing. Still, Marley was the closest thing that
Scrooge ever had to a friend, and so Marley was the one sent to confront
Scrooge, by the powers of Heaven (or whoever manages the afterlife). The
powers of Heaven, like us, are required to work with what they have.

2) Denial: Leaders Often Fear the Messenger That Calls Them to Growth.

In her excellent book, *On Death and Dying*, psychologist Elizabeth Kubler-Ross identified the stages that people go through when they experience impending death.[105] Kubler-Ross identified the first stage that people move into when they experience a death as *denial*—the thought that "this is not happening." Kubler-Ross' groundbreaking insights have had significant impact on the fields of psychology, counseling, and social work. Building on Kubler-Ross' work, behavioral health professionals have identified that people go through similar impending-death stages when they encounter a change or other significant event. Perhaps this is because any event that calls us to change—a job loss, a child leaving for college, or the sale of a family home—is, in actuality, a "mini-death" for us. Our old environment or way of doing things is dying, and a new one is being born.

As with Scrooge and Marley, when leaders encounter their own harbinger of change, they often become frightened and go into denial. When first confronted with the ghost of his dead partner, Scrooge retreated behind "science" and claimed that Marley was probably a hallucination caused by indigestion. ("There's more of gravy than of grave about you, whatever you are!") How often do we retreat into the security of denial, hiding behind "Science" and "Research" as an excuse to keep us from moving forward?[106]

3) Leaders Must Appreciate and Acknowledge Their Direct Experience.

The last words the Buddha is said to have uttered are, "Don't believe something just because I said it. Compare it to your own experience and see if it makes sense." But comparing something to our own experience requires a realistic grasp of where we are in our lives—and more importantly, where we've been—and this process of assessment can be difficult. Going back to Scrooge for a moment, his confrontation by Marley's ghost forced a serious challenge to his understanding of reality.

> "...[Marley's ghost] held up its chain at arm's length, as if that were the cause of all its unavailing grief, and flung it heavily upon the ground again.

"At this time of the rolling year," the spectre said, "I suffer most. Why did I walk through crowds of fellow-beings with my eyes turned down, and never raise them to that blessed Star which led the Wise Men to a poor abode! Were there no poor homes to which its light would have conducted me!"

Scrooge was very much dismayed to hear the spectre going on at this rate, and began to quake exceedingly.

"Hear me!" cried the Ghost. "My time is nearly gone."

"I will," said Scrooge. "But don't be hard upon me! Don't be flowery, Jacob! Pray!"

"How it is that I appear before you in a shape that you can see, I may not tell. I have sat invisible beside you many and many a day."

It was not an agreeable idea. Scrooge shivered, and wiped the perspiration from his brow.

"That is no light part of my penance," pursued the Ghost. "I am here to-night to warn you, that you have yet a chance and hope of escaping my fate. A chance and hope of my procuring, Ebenezer."

"You were always a good friend to me," said Scrooge. "Thank `ee!"

"You will be haunted," resumed the Ghost, "by Three Spirits."

Scrooge's countenance fell almost as low as the Ghost's had done.

"Is that the chance and hope you mentioned, Jacob?" he demanded, in a faltering voice.

"It is."

"I -- I think I'd rather not," said Scrooge.

"Without their visits," said the Ghost, "you cannot hope to shun the path I tread. Expect the first tomorrow, when the bell tolls one."

"Couldn't I take `em all at once, and have it over, Jacob?" hinted Scrooge.

"Expect the second on the next night at the same hour. The third upon the next night when the last stroke of twelve has ceased to vibrate. Look to see me no more; and look that, for your own sake, you remember what has passed between us!"[107]

As Marley began to tell his former partner about the horrors of being infinitely and unmercifully chained in the hereafter, two things began happening to Scrooge. First, he slowly recognized the impossible, irrational vision of an apparition in front of him, not to mention three more to come, as being disturbingly real. This new information began to change Scrooge immediately. Next, this new information permeated his awareness and altered the composition of the man he'd been up to that point. A new bar had now been set for taking a situation and "comparing it to your own experience to see if it makes sense," as Buddha said.

By the time Marley had finished his foretelling of the three Spirits to come, Scrooge was already beginning his personal transformation and his awareness was expanding.

> "…The apparition walked backward from him; and at every step it took, the window raised itself a little, so that when the spectre reached it, it was wide open. It beckoned Scrooge to approach, which he did. When they were within two paces of each other, Marley's Ghost held up its hand, warning him to come no nearer. Scrooge stopped.
>
> Not so much in obedience, as in surprise and fear: for on the raising of the hand, he became sensible of confused noises in the air; incoherent sounds of lamentation and regret; wailings inexpressibly sorrowful and self-accusatory. The spectre, after listening for a moment, joined in the mournful dirge; and floated out upon the bleak, dark night.
>
> Scrooge followed to the window: desperate in his curiosity. He looked out.
>
> The air was filled with phantoms, wandering hither and thither in restless haste, and moaning as they went. Every one of them wore chains like Marley's Ghost; some few (they might be guilty governments) were linked together; none were free. Many had been personally known to Scrooge in their lives. He had been quite familiar with one old ghost, in a white waistcoat, with a monstrous iron safe attached to its ankle, who cried piteously at being unable to assist a wretched woman with an infant, whom it saw below, upon a door-step. The misery with them all was, clearly, that they sought to interfere, for good, in human matters, and had lost the power forever…
>
> Scrooge closed the window, and examined the door by which the Ghost had entered. It was double-locked, as he had locked it with his own hands, and the bolts were undisturbed. He tried to say "humbug!" but stopped at the first syllable. And being, from the emotion he had

undergone, or the fatigues of the day, or his glimpse of the Invisible World, or the dull conversation of the Ghost, or the lateness of the hour, much in need of repose; went straight to bed, without undressing, and fell asleep upon the instant…"[108]

❋ ❋ ❋
A Key to Leading People:
Your capacity to lead successfully depends, in large measure, on your ability to be aware of, and assimilate, your immediate experiences— but more importantly, your ability to understand and value the ways those experiences have changed you.
❋ ❋ ❋

Coach #2—The Spirit of Christmas Past

The first Spirit who appeared to Scrooge after Marley's departure was the Ghost of Christmas Past, a specter of contradictions.

"…It was a strange figure -- like a child: yet not so like a child as like an old man, viewed through some supernatural medium, which gave him the appearance of having receded from the view, and being diminished to a child's proportions. Its hair, which hung about its neck and down its back, was white as if with age; and yet the face had not a wrinkle in it, and the tenderest bloom was on the skin…"[109]

This ghost took Scrooge on a trip to view his personal past, beginning with his isolated childhood and traveling forward to very recent yesterdays.

They walked along the road, Scrooge recognising every gate, and post, and tree; until a little market-town appeared in the distance, with its bridge, its church, and winding river. Some shaggy ponies now were seen trotting towards them with boys upon their backs, who called to other boys in country gigs and carts, driven by farmers. All these boys were in great spirits, and shouted to each other, until the broad fields were so full of merry music, that the crisp air laughed to hear it.

"These are but shadows of the things that have been," said the Ghost. "They have no consciousness of us.

The jocund travellers came on; and as they came, Scrooge knew and named them every one. Why was he rejoiced beyond all bounds to see them! Why did his cold eye glisten, and his heart leap up as they went past? Why was he filled with gladness when he heard them give each other Merry Christmas, as they parted at cross-roads and-bye ways, for their several homes? What was merry Christmas to Scrooge? Out upon merry Christmas! What good had it ever done to him?

"The school is not quite deserted," said the Ghost. "A solitary child, neglected by his friends, is left there still."

"Scrooge said he knew it. And he sobbed.

"...They went, the Ghost and Scrooge, across the hall, to a door at the back of the house. It opened before them, and disclosed a long, bare, melancholy room, made barer still by lines of plain deal forms and desks. At one of these a lonely boy was reading near a feeble fire; and Scrooge sat down upon a form, and wept to see his poor forgotten self as he used to be..."[110]

Finally, after re-visiting a variety of scenes from Scrooge's youth, Scrooge and the Ghost of Christmas Past came upon the sight of Scrooge as a young man sitting with a young woman to whom he'd once been engaged.

"In a changed nature; in an altered spirit; in another atmosphere of life; another Hope as its great end. In everything that made my love of any worth or value in your sight. If this had never been between us," said the girl, looking mildly, but with steadiness, upon him; "tell me, would you seek me out and try to win me now? Ah, no!"

He seemed to yield to the justice of this supposition, in spite of himself. But he said with a struggle," You think not?"

"I would gladly think otherwise if I could," she answered, "Heaven knows. When *I* have learned a Truth like this, I know how strong and irresistible it must be. But if you were free to-day, to-morrow, yesterday, can even I believe that you would choose a dowerless girl -- you who, in your very confidence with her, weigh everything by Gain: or, choosing her, if for a moment you were false enough to your one guiding principle to do so, do I not know that your repentance and regret would surely follow? I do; and I release you. With a full heart, for the love of him you once were."

He was about to speak; but with her head turned from him, she resumed.

"You may -- the memory of what is past half makes me hope you will -- have pain in this. A very, very brief time, and you will dismiss the recollection of it, gladly, as an unprofitable dream, from which it happened well that you awoke. May you be happy in the life you have chosen."

She left him, and they parted.

"Spirit!" said Scrooge, "show me no more! Conduct me home. Why do you delight to torture me?"

"One shadow more!" exclaimed the Ghost.

"No more!" cried Scrooge! "No more, I don't wish to see it! Show me no more!"[111]

Here are the lessons of leading people that the Ghost of Christmas Past teaches:

1) Leaders Must Risk the Choice To Go Forward.

Scrooge had to make the choice to step out into the journey of self-discovery when his past was replayed for him. Becoming a successful leader means stepping out into a similar journey, sometimes in a positive way through a sought-after promotion or transfer, and other times in a negative way through a layoff or downsizing. At each juncture, we may not have complete control over the circumstances, but we always have full control over what we do *about*—and how we react *to*—the circumstances. Swallowing our fear of the unknown gives us the courage we need to choose a direction. If we cave into that fear, we become immobilized; and not only do we fail to move forward, but we often regress. In order for his emotional transformation to occur, Scrooge had to begin by making the choice—*taking the risk*—to accompany the ghost, even though he did not know, and remained fearful of, where the ghost was leading him.

Developing ourselves as leaders always involves risk. Many of us put off taking a risk by over-analyzing a situation to death. Scrooge didn't do that. He did not waste time by asking how long the trip would take, or if any other executives in his position had undergone a similar process, and, if so, what their outcomes had been. He did not ask how his transformation would be statistically measured or with which instruments. He did not ask if there might be more popular ghosts who could coach him through the process. He simply accepted a risk and stepped out onto the path of mastery appearing before him. The process of leading people is messy and complex, and each step forward involves a risk with no guarantees. Who would have guessed that such a lesson would come from someone like Ebenezer Scrooge?

❋ ❋ ❋

A Key to Leading People
Wise leaders understand that moving
toward success always involves some degree of risk.

❋ ❋ ❋

2) Leaders Often Must Go Backward in Order To Move Forward.

Scrooge needed to go backwards to revisit his past in order to move forward into a new level of leadership. Moving backwards to go forward is a very wise approach. In order for healing and wholeness to occur—a requirement for leading people—leaders often have to revisit those parts of their lives where hurt and pain reside. Some believe that unresolved hurts from the past are best "put behind" or thought of as merely "water under the bridge." But believing that an emotional sore spot "is water under the bridge" is an excellent formula for remaining stuck.

The concept of moving backwards to go forward is a strategy used effectively in the martial arts as well. Aikido—the art of yielding—is about giving, in order to get your way. Since I am a physically small man, if a very large man attacks me and I attempt to slug things out toe-to-toe with him, I will always lose. However, if I can yield to his on-coming energy, which initially looks as if I am retreating (or going backwards), there is greater potential for me to redirect the attacker's energy so he ends up defeating himself. This principle of yielding is one you can use in your own leadership interactions, and the principle is so important that we will devote much of the next chapter to the subject.[112]

3) Leaders Must Deeply and Fully Experience Their Emotions.

When the ghost took Scrooge to see his childhood school, Scrooge began to cry. At first, Scrooge denied his tears, claiming, "...it was a pimple." Later on, Dickens tells us that Scrooge completely broke down. Those who aspire to become stronger leaders strive to fully and deeply experience their emotions, both past and present. When we are moved to tears (of sorrow or of joy) by recalling some incident from the past, those tears appear because we carry our full history with us at the cellular level— and like wiper fluid on a dirty windshield, those tears make things easier to see. If we don't clear away the soil that we carry from the past, our vision remains clouded and we will have a difficult time focusing upon what is really happening in the present moment.

4) Leaders Must Be Able To Embrace Paradox.

The Spirit of Christmas Past is a paradox—a child and an old man at the same time. The ability to contain both sides of a paradox is paramount if we desire to increase our capacity for becoming a more effective leader.[113] The Chinese sage Lao Tzu said, "the words of truth are always paradoxical."

Human interactions are messy, complicated, and alive, and because they are so organic, creating the definitive list of "ten-things-to-do-to-handle-every-interpersonal-interaction" is impossible. Emotionally engaged leadership is a process in which there are no set answers. Human interactions—as emotional and messy as they are—call for us to be creative, passionate, and fully present as best we can in our interactions with one another. Great leaders embrace paradox.

Coach #3—The Spirit of Christmas Present

The second Spirit who appeared to Scrooge in Marley's wake was the Ghost of Christmas Present, a "jolly Giant, glorious to see," bare-chested, covered with a wreath of holly branches and icicles, and surrounded by a Christmas feast consisting of all manner of great food. Accompanied by this colossal Spirit, Scrooge ventured out into the world to experience the full glory of Christmas Day.

> "...For, the people who were shovelling away on the housetops were jovial and full of glee; calling out to one another from the parapets, and now and then exchanging a facetious snowball--better-natured missile far than many a wordy jest--laughing heartily if it went right and not less heartily if it went wrong. The poulterers' shops were still half open, and the fruiterers' were radiant in their glory. There were great, round, pot-bellied baskets of chestnuts, shaped like the waistcoats of jolly old gentlemen, lolling at the doors, and tumbling out into the street in their apoplectic opulence. There were ruddy, brown-faced, broad-girthed Spanish Onions, shining in the fatness of their growth like Spanish Friars, and winking from their shelves in wanton slyness at the girls as they went by, and glanced demurely at the hung-up mistletoe. There were pears and apples, clustered high in blooming pyramids; there were bunches of grapes, made, in the shopkeepers' benevolence to dangle from conspicuous hooks, that people's mouths might water gratis as

they passed; there were piles of filberts, mossy and brown, recalling, in their fragrance, ancient walks among the woods, and pleasant shufflings ankle deep through withered leaves; there were Norfolk Biffins, squat and swarthy, setting off the yellow of the oranges and lemons, and, in the great compactness of their juicy persons, urgently entreating and beseeching to be carried home in paper bags and eaten after dinner. The very gold and silver fish, set forth among these choice fruits in a bowl, though members of a dull and stagnant-blooded race, appeared to now that there was something going on; and, to a fish, went gasping round and round their little world in slow and passionless excitement.

...But soon the steeples called good people all, to church and chapel, and away they came, flocking through the streets in their best clothes, and with their gayest faces. And at the same time there emerged from scores of bye-streets, lanes, and nameless turnings, innumerable people, carrying their dinners to the bakers' shops. The sight of these poor revellers appeared to interest the Spirit very much, for he stood with Scrooge beside him in a baker's doorway, and taking off the covers as their bearers passed, sprinkled incense on their dinners from his torch. And it was a very uncommon kind of torch, for once or twice when there were angry words between some dinner-carriers who had jostled each other, he shed a few drops of water on them from it, and their good humour was restored directly. For they said, it was a shame to quarrel upon Christmas Day. And so it was. God love it, so it was.[114]

The Ghost of Christmas Present and Scrooge then journeyed to the home of Bob Cratchit, Scrooge's employee, where they saw Bob sitting with his lame son, Tiny Tim. Returning to Dickens' telling:

"A Merry Christmas to us all, my dears. God bless us."

Which all the family re-echoed.

"God bless us every one!" said Tiny Tim, the last of all.

He sat very close to his father's side upon his little stool. Bob held his withered little hand in his, as if he loved the child, and wished to keep him by his side, and dreaded that he might be taken from him.

"Spirit," said Scrooge, with an interest he had never felt before, "tell me if Tiny Tim will live."

"I see a vacant seat," replied the Ghost, "in the poor chimney-corner, and a crutch without an owner, carefully preserved. If these shadows remain unaltered by the Future, the child will die."

"No, no," said Scrooge. "Oh, no, kind Spirit. Say he will be spared."

"If these shadows remain unaltered by the Future, none other of my race," returned the Ghost, "will find him here. What then? If he be like to die, he had better do it, and decrease the surplus population."

Scrooge hung his head to hear his own words quoted by the Spirit, and was overcome with penitence and grief…"[115]

Here are the lessons of leading people that the Ghost of Christmas Present teaches:

1) Leaders Must Attend to the Here-and-Now.

Every spiritual tradition speaks of the power of the present moment. Nothing can be done about the past or the future. Leaders can only act in the present, and that moment is a giant space of time, teeming with unlimited possibility and potential. Yet most leaders (this author included) hold a partial fear of the present, for the present provides enormous freedom. We have many strategies for keeping ourselves from taking full advantage of the benefits of the present moment. We entomb ourselves with our frantic schedules, our PDAs and cell phones, and our hectic routines. To live deeply in the knowledge that each and every present moment is full of unlimited potential and possibility is very frightening for most leaders, and most of us prefer to stay cocooned within the false safety of our fears and our anxieties.[116]

2) The Present Is the Only Place Where Leaders Experience Emotions.

In the description of the Ghost of Christmas Present, Dickens' gift as a writer truly comes to life. His passages quoted earlier demonstrate the varied riches in each "present moment," but also how quickly one moment can give way to the next. Once gone, that moment—along with the rich palate of opportunity therein—becomes part of the past. The old saying, "Luck is where preparation meets opportunity," speaks to the importance of cherishing each moment and anticipating the value so you can be ready when the moment arrives.

Emotionally engaged leadership—which is where I'm attempting to take you with this book—is a centered, sensual (in the fullest sense of the word) participation in the joys and sorrows of life. In one of his interviews with PBS journalist Bill Moyers, mythologist Joseph Campbell said, "Life is just like a play. Except that it hurts."

To paraphrase Campbell for leaders, *leadership cannot be separated from life, and both hurt.* Both can be joyful, too, when leaders learn to fully appreciate the gifts of the present moment.

3) Leaders Must Be Flexible.

The Ghost of Christmas Present had the "remarkable quality...that notwithstanding his gigantic size, he could accommodate himself to any place with ease." In the same way, the present moment calls for leaders to remain flexible and open to whatever events impact their lives, and to the people who enter, stay and leave their lives. Many leadership strategies require people and surroundings to change to accommodate the leader, but these strategies have things backwards. Effective leaders understand that their own flexibility to meet people where they are is what truly empowers them.

While he accompanied Scrooge, the Ghost of Christmas Present did not insist that the places they visited accommodate his giant size. Instead, he used his power to change himself to fit the present moment, making his form smaller or larger as required. Rather than being the same enormous size all the time (a.k.a. aggrandized), leaders who instinctively know when they should be small or large are those who become assets to their people and their organizations. Or, as Aikido master Mary Heiny sensei says, "You have to give up the strength to get to the power."

4) Leaders Must Be Connected with Others.

The Ghost of Christmas Present took Scrooge on a journey throughout Christmas Day, where they watched unseen as people interacted with one another. They stopped at the home of Bob Cratchit, Scrooge's clerk. They visited the streets of London where, in Dickens' words, "if you had to judge from the numbers of people on their way to friendly gatherings, you might have thought that no one was at home to give them welcome when they got there." They went to see a family of miners, a group of lighthouse keepers, the crew of a sailing ship, and finally, the house of Scrooge's nephew.

All of the people they encountered were actively involved in relationships with at least one other person. Scrooge, the archetypal dissonant, was the only one who stood alone—who was involved in relationships with *no one*—in the drama of Christmas Present. Author John Donne's famous meditation, "No man is an island..." should be emblazoned across the office walls of every leader.

Coach #4—The Spirit of Christmas Yet-to-Come

For many readers, Dickens' final ghost of Christmas is the scariest of all four. The mere presence of this ghost causes Scrooge to genuflect.

> "..for in the very air through which this Spirit moved it seemed to scatter gloom and mystery…[Scrooge] felt that [the Spirit] was tall and stately when it came beside him, and that its mysterious presence filled him with a solemn dread. He knew no more, for the Spirit neither spoke nor moved."[117]

By this point in the story, Scrooge's eyes were wide open regarding his own *what-is* and *what-was*. He was facing reality—both intrinsic and emotional—for the first time in his life, and he was filled with foreboding about the mess he could very possibly have made of his future. His mean-hearted mockery of life's emotional elements had come perilously close to chaining him to a destiny like Marley's.

> "…A churchyard. Here, then, the wretched man whose name he had now to learn, lay underneath the ground. It was a worthy place. Walled in by houses; overrun by grass and weeds, the growth of vegetation's death, not life; choked up with too much burying; fat with repleted appetite. A worthy place!
>
> The Spirit stood among the graves, and pointed down to One. He advanced towards it trembling. The Phantom was exactly as it had been, but he dreaded that he saw new meaning in its solemn shape.
>
> "Before I draw nearer to that stone to which you point," said Scrooge, "answer me one question. Are these the shadows of the things that Will be, or are they shadows of things that May be, only?"
>
> Still the Ghost pointed downward to the grave by which it stood.
>
> "Men's courses will foreshadow certain ends, to which, if persevered in, they must lead," said Scrooge. "But if the courses be departed from, the ends will change. Say it is thus with what you show me."
>
> The Spirit was immovable as ever.
>
> Scrooge crept towards it, trembling as he went; and following the finger, read upon the stone of the neglected grave his own name, EBENEZER SCROOGE.
>
> "Am I that man who lay upon the bed?" he cried, upon his knees.

The finger pointed from the grave to him, and back again.

"No, Spirit! Oh no, no!"

The finger still was there.

"Spirit!" he cried, tight clutching at its robe, "hear me. I am not the man I was. I will not be the man I must have been but for this intercourse. Why show me this, if I am past all hope?"

For the first time the hand appeared to shake.

"Good Spirit," he pursued, as down upon the ground he fell before it: "Your nature intercedes for me, and pities me. Assure me that I yet may change these shadows you have shown me, by an altered life."

The kind hand trembled.

"I will honour Christmas in my heart, and try to keep it all the year. I will live in the Past, the Present, and the Future. The Spirits of all Three shall strive within me. I will not shut out the lessons that they teach. Oh, tell me I may sponge away the writing on this stone!"

In his agony, he caught the spectral hand. It sought to free itself, but he was strong in his entreaty, and detained it. The Spirit, stronger yet, repulsed him.

Holding up his hands in a last prayer to have his fate aye reversed, he saw an alteration in the Phantom's hood and dress. It shrunk, collapsed, and dwindled down into a bedpost..."[118]

Here are the leadership lessons taught by the Ghost of Christmas Yet-to-Come:

1) The Future Does Not Provide Leaders With Much Information.

A friend of mine who is somewhat tall and shy told me that when she was in elementary school, she was selected to play The Ghost of Christmas Yet-to-Come. The role, she explained rather tongue-in-cheek, was easy since the ghost had no lines. Like the Ghost of Christmas Yet-to-Come, the truth is that our future is silent. As the Ghost of Christmas Yet-to-Come literally points out to Scrooge, the only thing that we know for sure about the future is that, at some point out there, we will all die.

There is one other thing we know, however, at this point in our Black Belt leadership discovery: Tomorrow holds our future's present moments. By planting the seeds of effective leadership now, you will reap the benefits of success in the years ahead.

2) Leaders Must Recall Their Mortality.

As the famous economist John Maynard Keynes wryly noted, "In the long run, we are all dead." While at first glance this might seem to be an overwhelmingly depressing thought, there is some light within the melancholy. Staying rooted in the knowledge of our collective mortality helps leaders be more supportive and gentle with others, as well as with themselves. Being aware of our limited lifespan also enable us to put mistakes into context—both our own and those of others. Remembering our collective mortality keeps us cognizant of the fact that we're each operating on a time continuum of unknown duration and that the responsibility lies within each of us to become the best possible leaders we can be during the time that is given us.

3) Leaders' Actions Impact Future Generations.

The decisions we make and the actions we take today impact our future generations, just as the decisions that Scrooge made impacted whether Tiny Tim lived or died. History tells us that when Native American councils used to gather to make a decision, they would attempt to take into account the impact their decision would have on the next *seven generations*. If only we could be so wise!

❊ ❊ ❊

"The starting point, as with all change,
is to get clear within ourselves."
Peter Block

❊ ❊ ❊

Christmas Day—Transformation

Scrooge awakened on Christmas day as a new, emotionally transformed leader. Overjoyed, he jumped around his bedroom and laughed for the first time in many years. He shouted, "I will live in the Past, the Present and the Future…The Spirits of all Three will strive within me!" A changed man, Scrooge increased his emotional intelligence to the point where he had the capacity to grasp the paradox that past, present, and future are all contained in the present moment. This is reality viewed through a three-dimensional, holistic lens. With the support of his ghostly coaches, Scrooge underwent an emotional transformation, which became embodied in every aspect of his being. As Dickens relates:

> "...He went to church, and walked about the streets, and watched the people hurrying to and fro, and patted children on the head, and questioned beggars, and looked down into the kitchens of houses, and up to the windows, and found that everything could yield him pleasure. He had never dreamed that any walk—that anything—could give him so much happiness...
>
> Scrooge was better than his word. He did it all, and infinitely more; and to Tiny Tim, who did not die, he was a second father. He became as good a friend, as good a master, and as good a man, as the good old city knew, or any other good old city, town, or borough, in the good old world. Some people laughed to see the alteration in him, but he let them laugh, and little heeded them; for he was wise enough to know that nothing ever happened on this globe, for good, at which some people did not have their fill of laughter in the outset; and knowing that such as these would be blind anyway, he thought it quite as well that they should wrinkle up their eyes in grins, as have the malady in less attractive forms. His own heart laughed: and that was quite enough for him...
>
> He had no further intercourse with Spirits, but lived upon the Total Abstinence Principle, ever afterwards; and it was always said of him, that he knew how to keep Christmas well, if any man alive possessed the knowledge..."[119]

Two points summarize Scrooge's emotional transformation:

1) Leaders Are Who They Are Who They Are.

In order to lead with harmony, you must first and foremost become a harmonious person. Scrooge wasn't a fellow who was mean and stingy with Bob Cratchit and then went home to be a loving spouse and father who had a close-knit group of devoted friends. No, he was humbugging with *everyone*. When someone is a dissonant leader, he or she tends to create dissonant relationships in most areas of their lives. Conversely, a leader who practices harmony will have generally harmonious lives outside of the workplace as well. The odds are slim that you will be a harmonious leader in the office and then go home and kick the dog, scream at your children, and ignore your spouse. You are who you are who you are.

2) Emotional Experience—Not Logic or Rationality—Is What Transforms Leaders.

Why did Dickens choose ghosts to be the catalysts for Scrooge's emotional transformation? Simply put, ghosts are emotional beings, and only emotional experiences have the power to change us. Ghosts—those shadowy entities that haunt the edges of our awareness—stand firm against an over-emphasis on rationality. Leaders who rigidly over-value cold, logical rationality at the expense of any emotional awareness or exploration could use a visit from a few ghosts.

Cool logic simply does not have the heat that is required to transform us, and this limitation of logic to bring about change is exactly why the process of becoming a leader takes longer than most people expect. Change and growth are much more powerful and long-lasting when they occur in ways that emotionally engage us, and this emotional engagement takes time.

❋ ❋ ❋
"All that is gold does not glitter,
Not all those who wander are lost;
The old that is strong does not wither,
Deep roots are not reached by the frost."
Bilbo Baggins
❋ ❋ ❋

Scrooge and the Gestalt Cycle of Experience

We can discover some additional important insights when we consider our friend Scrooge's emotional transformation in light of the Gestalt Cycle of Experience (GCOE) that we discussed in Chapter Seven. Through the multiple dissonant choices Scrooge made in his life, he deadened his sensations. Consequently, there were many things outside of his awareness—the pain of his isolated childhood, Tiny Tim's illness, and the tragedy of poverty in his environment, to name a few. In the same way, dissonance in leadership tends to deaden sensations and awareness. Like suddenly going tone deaf, we can no longer hear when the emotional music of our organization is out of tune.

For a number of reasons, Scrooge had intentionally moved much of his emotional life outside of his awareness and sensation.[120] The task of the ghostly coaches of Christmas was to support Scrooge as he developed the ability to sense again, and to once again become aware of his pleasure and pain—past, present, and future. The Spirits of Christmas helped Scrooge create energy in order to take action—the actions of remembering his past, participating in Christmas Present, and experiencing glimpses of Christmas Yet-to-Come. Scrooge was transformed by moving through the GCOE and making complete, whole contact (which includes his emotional life) with the past, present, and future. When their work was complete, the Spirits of Christmas withdrew, allowing Scrooge to awaken to the wonders of Christmas Day and to assimilate the experiences he learned through his coaching.

Final Words on Scrooge

Any type of transformational changes that leaders go through will involve risk. One of the most painful risks for many leaders is that of feeling of embarrassment or even shame, which can occur when others thoughtlessly make light of something important. The following line from *A Christmas Carol* bears repeating:

> Some people laughed to see the alteration in
> [Scrooge], but he let them laugh, and little heeded
> them, for he was wise enough to know that nothing
> ever happened on this globe, for good, at which
> some people did not have their fill of laughter in
> the outset....

To be able to "little heed" those who laugh at and scorn our ideas around emotional engagement requires leaders to cultivate the discipline of a martial artist. Scrooge does not judge those who laugh at him, nor does he seek them injury. He is content with the make-up of his own heart, and that is enough. Dickens' wisdom echoes that of Lao Tzu, who many centuries before wrote:

> The wise student hears of the Tao and practices it diligently.
> The average student hears of the Tao and gives it thought now and again.
> The foolish student hears of the Tao and laughs aloud.
> If there were no laughter, the Tao would not be what it is.

Finally, we need to remember that while each of us can learn from Scrooge's emotional growth, every leader needs to undergo his or her own transformation. Nobody else can make the changes for us. And so we bid farewell to our friend Scrooge as we consider lessons learned from this point:

Seven Leadership Lessons for Leading with Harmony

1. Trust Yourself. As we learned in Chapter Four, when properly trained, your body/mind is capable of detecting exquisitely subtle changes in emotional states. Trust your ability as a leader. If something feels off, something probably *is* off. In that same vein, if something feels emotionally right, that feeling can probably be trusted. Scrooge did not wait around for an "expert opinion" on the reality of the ghosts. He trusted himself and went with his experience.

2. Trust the People in Your Organization. Keeping yourself open to multiple perspectives is critical in order to stay in tune with the people you are leading. In order to be in tune with someone, you must first trust him. Scrooge was ultimately able to trust Bob Cratchit, but not until he first trusted himself.

3. Cultivate Friendships. A basic rule of life says that, "Nobody makes it here alone, and nobody gets out alive." As the song goes, "you gotta have friends." Friends can act as stable rudders when the storms of life threaten to overwhelm us. Scrooge's reclamation never would have occurred without the friendship of Jacob Marley.

4. Embrace Paradox. *Both-and* thinking and Polarities are paradoxes. In order to become a more successful leader, you need to be able to accept, embrace, and manage paradoxes. Scrooge was having the most important conversation of his life with Marley, and Marley was <u>dead</u>. Leadership is full of paradoxes. Embrace them.

5. Lead in the "Here-and-Now." *Here* is where change occurs and *now* is when polarities present themselves. The present moment brings us the gift of never-ending possibilities and potential. By allowing himself to more fully experience the here-and-now, Scrooge was able to transform himself into an even more successful leader.

6. Recognize Interdependence. We are all interconnected. Our actions and decisions as leaders have a tremendous impact on the lives of those we lead, because those people we lead (and mentor) today will go on to lead and impact others tomorrow. Recognize that your actions and decisions as a leader are interdependent with countless people, and help set the stage for the quality of leadership in your organization down the road.

7. Laugh at Yourself. Be cautious about taking yourself too seriously as a leader. Part of the struggle behind someone who is far too serious all the time comes from being unable to find the humor in even the smallest mistakes they (and we) make. We are all human and therefore imperfect, and imperfections are inherently funny, as the David Lettermans and Jay Lenos of the world continuously point out to us every night. Find the humor in your work, and let others see you laughing.

❋ ❋ ❋
"Our basic argument, in a nutshell, is that
primal leadership operates at its best through
emotionally intelligent leaders who create resonance."
Goleman, Boyatzis, & McKee
❋ ❋ ❋

Conclusion

As we say farewell to our wise teacher Ebenezer Scrooge, remember the most vital lesson that he brings to the table: **As a leader, you must undergo your own emotional transformation. No one else can make the changes for you.**

Embodied Learning Experiment #7
Embodying Harmony

Harmonious leaders make people more productive because they instill positive emotions. For this experiment, think about two people for whom you have worked—supervisors, coaches, managers or mentors—who have been harmonious leaders. Now picture yourself being around one of those harmonious leaders. Take some time and imagine that you are with them now. What types of feelings do you experience when you think about them? Write at least two of those feelings below.

Next, identify the physical data within yourself on which you base those feeling you just listed. For example, you may feel "comfortable" when you imagine yourself being with a particular mentor. The physical data identified with being comfortable might include your stomach relaxing or softening. See if you can identify two pieces of physical data for each feeling you list.

Now, complete the same exercise using the name of two leaders you worked for who were dissonant—not harmonious.

Harmonious Leader:
>   Feeling:
>>   My physical data:
>>   My physical data:
>   Feeling:
>>   My physical data:
>>   My physical data:

Dissonant /Not Harmonious Leader:
>   Feeling:
>>   My physical data:
>>   My physical data:
>   Feeling:
>>   My physical data:
>>   My physical data:

Chapter Summary
Congratulations!

By recognizing the importance of harmony in leadership and by being willing to participate in your own transformation to expand your emotional capacity for leadership, you have taken the next step toward becoming a Black Belt Leader!

Chapter Summary:

We began with a story about what happens when teacups die. Then we discussed the importance of harmony in creating resonance in your organization. We explored being in tune with those we lead, and we talked about the *Polarity of Harmony,* which includes the polar extremes of *Dissonance* and *Resonance.* Next we watched how Ebenezer Scrooge moved from being a dissonant leader to one with more resonance, and we observed how he was coached along the way. We learned about Scrooge's journey through the Gestalt Cycle of Experience (GCOA), and finally, we learned several important steps to becoming a more harmonious leader.

Suggested further reading:

Creating Effective Teams: A Guide for Members and Leaders by Susan Wheelan
The Hero with a Thousand Faces by Joseph Campbell
The Way of Transition: Embracing Life's Most Difficult Moments by William Bridges

Looking Ahead:

In the next chapter, you will learn about the important principle of yielding, and how you can actually gain power by giving up power.

"When an ineffective leader hears something he does not like, he stops listening and starts talking. When a Black Belt Leader hears something he does not like, he stops talking and starts listening."

Story
Who Do We Hire?

Once upon a time there was a small village in Japan that was under constant threat from bandits. The bandits were extorting "safety money" from the villagers each month. As time went on, the villagers realized that something needed to be done about the situation before the bandits exhausted their community's financial resources.

So, the villagers held a secret meeting where they agreed that they would hire a martial artist who could protect the village from the bandits. In secrecy, the village dispatched runners to find suitable candidates. The runners returned, accompanied by three different martial artists, who were then quartered in various locations around the village apart from each other. The elders met and agreed upon a test to determine which martial artist they would hire. Choosing a hut in which they would meet, the elders hid two strong young men armed with sticks on either side of the door.

The elders then sent for the first martial artist. As he entered the hut, he was set upon by the men and was knocked unconscious. The elders knew that this was not the martial artist for them, and they had him taken away to be cared for.

The elders stationed the youths as before on either side of the door and then sent for the second martial artist, who was a woman. When she entered the hut, the two youths emerged once again and set upon her. But she effortlessly disarmed them and was about to kill them when the elders quickly explained to her the test they had devised. At that point, she relented.
The elders then sent her away to be fed and entertained.

Finally, they sent for the third martial artist, setting up the test as they had for the first two. As he approached the hut, he stopped short. Sensing that something was wrong, he called out, "Hey, you in there! Why do you wish to hurt me?" Somewhat startled, the youths sheepishly stepped out of their hiding spaces.

The village elders smiled at each other.
They had found the martial artist to hire.

Chapter 11
The Secret To Doubling Your Leadership Power

Yield and overcome;
Bend and be straight;
- Lao Tzu

Double Your Leadership Power

Black Belt Leaders have a broad understanding of power. Recall our discussion of polarities from Chapter Nine where we talked about the *T'ai Chi T'u* (commonly called "yin/yang"), represented once again in the graphic below:

This figure almost looks like two fish swimming nose to tail with each other. In traditional Chinese philosophy, the lighter "fish" was considered *yang* and the darker "fish" was considered *yin.* Many people mistakenly consider the *T'ai Chi T'u* and the qualities of yin and yang to be in *either-or* language. This is incorrect thinking, because yin and yang both come from the Tao—the Ultimate One. The T'ai Chi T'u represents the essence of holistic thinking, which is recognizing that all things are interconnected and interrelated. While yin and yang have particular qualities ascribed to them, these qualities are meant more as *both-and* rather than *either-or.* Some polar qualities ascribed to yin and yang include:[121]

Yin	Yang
Dark	Light
Hot	Cold
In	Out

Most leaders understand power only in the narrowest of forms. They do not appreciate that power can be both yin and yang, but instead see only the yang aspect. In other words, they only associate the use of power only with aggressive, in-your-face, leadership styles. Leading people the Black Belt Way invites you to double your power by incorporating yin power into your leadership strategies.

Yin Power—Strength in Yielding

Understanding both yin power *and* yang power is important because both are needed for effective leadership. Yin power is the side that draws upon the authority of yielding, flexibility and flow. Most leaders underestimate yin power, and some even go so far as to ignore the yin altogether, using only the yang form of power that shoots out, moves forward, and gets ahead. Our weapons, such as guns and missiles, are very yang in their nature. Many leaders erroneously believe that exercising yin power in any way will be viewed as powerless and weak.[122] When I work clinically with aggressive adolescents, one of the most frequent reasons the teens give for getting into a fight at school is, "I couldn't back down. People would think that I'm scared." When I coach executives (particularly male executives), one of the most frequent reasons they give me for their conflicts at work is, "I couldn't back down. People would think that I was scared or didn't have what it takes to do my job."[123] See any patterns here? Regarding the use of power, there doesn't seem to be any major difference between teenagers and executives. In most organizational cultures, whether in the hallways of a high school or the executive boardroom of a Fortune 500 company, yielding is seen as a sign of weakness.[124] This is a misunderstanding of the fundamental nature of power. Wise leaders know that yielding can be a sign of strength.

The non-violent teachings and work of both Martin Luther King, Jr. and Mahatma Gandhi are examples of yin power, which the martial art of Aikido masterfully utilizes as well. For example, Aikido uses an attacker's energy to defeat that attacker. The best way to keep yourself safe around Aikido practitioners is simple: *Do not attack them*. If there isn't any energy coming in the form of an attack, then there is nothing for the Aikido practitioner to do.

✹ ✹ ✹
"The practice of Aikido demands that we live in contradiction and paradox; answers and solutions are guided by what is presented in the moment, not by fixed predispositions."
Richard Strozzi-Heckler
✹ ✹ ✹

Understanding what yin power teaches leaders about power is vastly different from leaders' typical conception of power. To most leaders, power comes from being highly defended. With yin power, power comes from being open. Many leaders deal with problems in a straightforward, linear fashion. With yin power, problems are resolved in a circular fashion.

Yin power makes use of a potent tool known as *blending*, which is a different way to approach an on-coming force. Blending is a highly sophisticated, intelligent, and sensitive use of power that seeks to join with the flow of events as they are, neither slamming into an on-coming force head-on nor allowing oneself to be hopelessly overwhelmed. As I've mentioned before, human beings are biologically hard-wired to oppose force with force. Without specialized training, leaders will lead in this force-against-force way, negatively impacting people and processes throughout their organization.

Aikido practitioners, who make full use of the power of blending, understand that if we simply oppose force, then whichever force is stronger wins. If you've ever gone swimming in an ocean or a lake on a windy day when the waves were high, you probably had a lesson in blending. When the waves came crashing in and you tried to stand strong against them, you were knocked down. Waves are much stronger than any person. However, if you intelligently "go with the flow" inside the movement of the waves, you will discover that you may lose your footing temporarily, but you can regain your footing once the power of the wave has passed. That is *blending* with the waves.

How does blending work in organizations? A typical leadership problem I have observed involves resistance that arises in team meetings. A common scenario is that a leader will give his team a new requirement that must be developed, for example, as a result of a customer requesting a new product feature, or management mandating a new internal process (one usually involving a myriad of paperwork). The team members' first impulse will generally be to resist this new requirement, either in whole or in part, for a variety of reasons that seem both valid and important. A leader who uses a yang approach toward leadership would fight against the team's resistance, either laying down the law by edict or trying to intellectually convince the team about the correctness of the new approach. Either tactic is doomed to failure from the beginning, and soon thereafter, the team and the leader find themselves mired in conflict.

On the other hand, a leader who uses a yin style of leadership to blend would approach the team differently from the onset. Rather than trying to force the issue or intellectually debate the point, a leader who seeks to blend with the team will become positioned physically, mentally and emotionally to see the problem from the team's point of view. A leader who blends is one who honors the importance of resistance and openly explores the fears and concerns that the team might be holding. Much like a surfboard riding on top of the waves, blending allows leaders to ride out the natural emotional upheaval brought about by new processes and procedures, and also orchestrate resolution in a manner that keeps the team on track and moving forward.

Blending allows leaders to join with the energy of the problem, moving in the direction that the problem is moving, and then leading toward a successful resolution. Skillful leaders also manage to do all of this with only a minimal amount of energy expended.

In short, blending is smart leadership.

❊ ❊ ❊

Of yielding, Lao Tzu says,
Men are born soft and supple;
dead, they are stiff and hard.
Plants are born tender and pliant;
dead, they are brittle and dry.
Thus whoever is stiff and inflexible
is a disciple of death.
Whoever is soft and yielding
is a disciple of life.
The hard and stiff will be broken.
The soft and supple will prevail.
Tao Te Ching
❊ ❊ ❊

Yin Power & Negative Capacity

Some leaders believe that they are always expected to know all the answers. Superior leaders know they will never have all the answers. "Always" is a setup for failure because "always" is an inflexible, rigid position that turns into a trap.

Incorporating yin power into your leadership style develops your capacity for being able to say, "I don't know." You cannot be an effective leader if you are so invested in making sure the world knows you have everything under control that you cannot admit what you do not know. When you are unable to admit that you do not know, you leave no room for solutions to present themselves.

Every leader is faced with uncertainty and difficult decisions, and today's leaders must deal with problems that do not offer simple resolutions. Using yin power during times when direction is uncertain is a superior leadership strategy, because yin power offers leaders a way to lead through the unknown. The poet Keats referred to the ability to lead without always knowing as "negative capability." Keats considers negative capability as a way of being in relationship with mysteries, doubts and uncertainty in a manner that allows for new opportunities and new directions.

When uncertainty arises, smart leaders value emptiness and open space—space for appreciating "what is not" in order to develop a new "what is." When leaders can stay in relation with the "I don't know" that is Keats' negative capability, they find that they discover a resolution much more quickly than when they somehow try to force a solution through exclusively intellectual means.

❋ ❋ ❋

"Empowerment means that each member is responsible for creating the organization's culture, for delivering outcomes to its customers, and especially for the quality of their own experience."
Peter Block
❋ ❋ ❋

Four Tips to Help Leaders Increase Their Yin Power

1. **Empower People Effectively.**
2. **Increase Your Power by Sharing Knowledge.**

3. **Walk Your Talk.**
4. **Listen Openly.**

1. Empower People Effectively.

People perform better when they are empowered to do the job they were brought into your organization to do. Trust that you have selected competent people and let them get to work. In this information age, information is power. A key factor to being empowered is having the information necessary to make appropriate decisions. Leaders who hoard power by centralizing all information make an enormous tactical mistake. People at all levels of an organization need information in order to make quick, effective decisions. When leaders limit the scope of information available, the entire organization suffers because processes unnecessarily slow down to a snail's pace. This creates a formula for certain disaster in today's fast-paced world.

My brother Patrick once worked for a high-end hotel chain with a computerized reservation system that would automatically create a brand new file every time a customer registered. As a result, the only place that the hotel's repeat customers had a history was in the minds of the employees. As long as employment was strong and morale was high, customer service levels remained at acceptable levels, because the employees knew the customers. But when company fortunes, management issues, and employee morale took a downturn, a large number of employees left the organization, taking customer histories along with them. Suddenly, every customer was treated as a brand new customer, a fact that did not sit will with established clientele. Wise leadership would understand the importance of capturing all customer data and then making that data consistently available to the front-line employees. This would maximize high customer satisfaction because even new employees would have access to customers' historical information.

※ ※ ※
**"More than anything else, information is the
top necessity for every employee."
Coffman & Gonzalez-Molina**
※ ※ ※

2. Increase Your Power by Sharing Knowledge.

You can create yin power by giving up control over much of your information. Have you ever heard a person say, "This organization keeps me too well informed?" Probably not. The old way of doing business, where information was restricted to the upper levels of management, simply does not work these days. Try to imagine giving up your cell phone and searching instead for a public pay phone every time you need to make call. How much time would be lost? How frustrated would you become?

The old adage that "information is power" was true in the past because, in the old way of doing business, all power (i.e., information) was consolidated and retained at the organization's upper levels. This methodology used to work well because there wasn't nearly as *much* information. But since the proliferation of desktop technology and the Internet, the world has changed exponentially. Today, effective organizations are built upon the twin foundations of the Information Revolution and the Emotional Economy. While "information is power" is still true, the adage has a very different meaning in the 21st century. Hoarding information at upper management levels now *decreases* the associated power (as well as the emotional engagement of your employees), while sharing information effectively throughout the organization dramatically *increases* the power and engagement value of that same information.[125]

In today's current environment, the old adage has been tweaked to say, "the sharing of knowledge is power." Having appropriate access to increased information allows all members of your organization to function more effectively, thus making the organization stronger—and more profitable—as a whole. The key to empowering the people you are leading is giving them knowledge—keeping them well-informed at the appropriate levels.[126]

❈ ❈ ❈
**"Instead of idle talk and vapid ideas,
action and performance are greatly esteemed here."
Akira Tohei, Shihan, founder of Midwest Aikido Center**
❈ ❈ ❈

3. Walk Your Talk.

Excellent leaders mean what they say, and they do what they say they are going to do. Anyone who has been part of an organization for any length of time has seen leaders who say one thing but do another. In the same way, standing on the side of an Aikido training mat and talking about harmony, yielding, and so forth, is easy. Eventually, however, you have to stop talking and step onto the mat. This is a crucial point of embarkation, because your *off-the-mat theory* and *on-the-mat practice* had better match each other, or else you will lose credibility as a leader.

Off-the-Mat Theory: What leaders say they do.
On-the-Mat Practice: What leaders really do.

Off-the-mat theory is talked about in business meetings and on brochures. An example of off-the-mat theory is, "We believe all of our employees should be fully empowered." But if on-the-mat practice actually allows employees to make very few independent decisions, then your employees will quickly become disengaged.[127] A proliferation of disparities between on-the-mat practices and off-the-mat theories can wreak havoc in any organization—even yours.

Leaders take an important step toward empowering people when they become willing to share the power. You, as a leader, decide the degree of empowerment your staff will have, and this is something you need to think about very seriously. Whatever you decide to do regarding empowerment of people, lead from a place of congruency in your thoughts, actions, and intentions. Different leaders in different organizations will arrive at different conclusions. You may be in an organization where your employees should not be fully empowered. For example, a fire chief can more effectively put out a fire by using a "command and control" style of leadership. Most of us are not fire chiefs, though, and leaders today would do well to follow the example of the Ritz Carlton, a high-end hotel chain that empowers all of their employees—from the housekeeping staff on up—to be able to make decisions on their own that affect the comfort of their guests. At the Ritz Carlton, any (repeat: *any*) staff member is able to offer a guest a free night's stay if something is not satisfactory.

If you say, "I empower my staff," and then turn around and support organizational practices and procedures that severely limit the empowerment of your staff, you are not exercising effective leadership. That approach is like trying to move a car by having two people pushing against the front while two more people push against the back at the same time. You will simply not get anywhere.

But you also need to recognize that any form of empowerment has limits. Empowering employees does not give them the "right" to address stockholders or to sell the company. Just as in family life, empowerment looks very different for a four-year old than for a 16-year-old. In the corporate world, empowerment also has variances. As a leader, whatever limits you set, make sure that you clearly communicate those limits to all members of your organization. Effective leadership requires a delicate balancing act between sharing too little power, which denies necessary support to your people, and sharing too much power, which can result in a free-for-all.

Many leaders wonder how they can tell when people in their organizations are feeling empowered. There is a simple assessment tool you can use that does not require bringing in outside consultants or distributing expensive questionnaires. The assessment tool is simply this: Try *asking* your people if they feel empowered. Then listen to what they have to say. Discovering the range of empowerment that exists in your organization, done in dialogue with the people themselves, brings about an even greater sense of empowerment—temporarily, at least—even if no immediate changes are made to the way operations are carried out. If people feel like a name instead of a number, and if they believe that what they do matters, then what they do *will* matter. This brings us to our next point: the importance of listening.

❋ ❋ ❋

**"In the end, this is what compassion really is;
just that deep, deep, open listening.
Without outflows, without grasping."**
**Norman Fischer, former Abbot of the San Francisco Zen Center
and founder of The Everyday Zen Foundation.**
❋ ❋ ❋

4. Listen Openly.
Superior leaders ask, and then they listen—carefully.

Listening is one of the most fundamental skills of a leader and also the one skill that is most often ignored by ineffective leaders. Individuals who believe they already know the answers are those who listen half-heartedly at best, or at worst, not at all—that is, of course, if they even bother to pose a question in the first place. Furthermore, when ineffective leaders do ask a question, they become defensive when they receive a response they don't like. If you are leading people and you believe you already know the answer, and/or if you don't care what anyone else thinks, then why ask the question? People appreciate being asked to participate with their ideas and opinions, but they tend to shut down and disengage if the asking turns out to be lip service.

Unlike the ineffective leader, when a skilled leader hears something he doesn't like, he stops talking and start listening—even more so than he was previously. You can't learn anything about what's going on in your organization if you're always talking, and trying to argue someone out of a perspective is rarely effective. Being a leader is not the same as being the captain of the debate team. If you ask a person whether or not he or she feels empowered and the answer is "no," then quietly ask "why" and listen to what is said. You will inevitably learn something you did not know. If, on the other hand, you become defensive and begin arguing about how empowered the person should be feeling, then you were not ready to ask the question in the first place.

In his book *The E-Myth Revisited,* author Michael Gerber tells a pleasurable story about checking into a hotel in Northern California. What he described was a traveler's dream. He writes about coming into a comfortable hotel, being assigned a room within three minutes despite having no reservation, and having dinner reservations made for him at the on-site restaurant. He described the seamless customer service between the hotel and the restaurant, in that the restaurant staff asked his coffee preference and then the same brand of coffee appeared in his hotel room coffee machine the next morning. He described returning to his room after his meal, only to find firewood set up in his fireplace, with a long match ready for striking laying across the logs, the bedcovers turned down, and a mint on his pillow. The next morning, he awoke to find his choice of newspaper outside of his door. Mr. Gerber said he happily recommended that hotel to everyone he knew.

What, one might ask, was the cost to the hotel for these glowing recommendations? A match, a mint, a newspaper, and a cup of coffee! In Gerber's words, "But it wasn't the match, the mint, the cup of coffee or the newspaper that did it. *It was that somebody had heard me.*"[128]

The critical point here is that people—whether they are your employees or customers—are much more likely to become emotionally engaged with your organization when they believe they're being heard. Empowerment is in the eyes of the empowered.

Embodied Learning Experiment #8
Embodying Yin Power

Next time you are out in a large crowd of people, try this experiment in yielding. You'll find this easier if you select a time when you are relaxed and don't have a particular goal that you must accomplish or a place you need to be. Remember, this is a learning experiment, and being relatively relaxed is more conducive to learning. Awareness is the key learning point here, and awareness takes time to develop, so be patient with yourself.

Stand a little apart from the crowd. Take a moment and watch how the people move. You may see a pattern to the crowd's movement. Then enter yourself into the movement of the crowd. Yielding is learning to go with the direction of existing powerful patterns rather than against those patterns.

As you move through the crowd, notice your feeling when you move with the crowd. Then go against the movement of the crowd and notice how your feeling changes. Try the following and see what you discover:

- Yield.
- See if you can pay attention to the rhythm and flow of the crowd.
- Move in when there is an opening, and go around when there is no opening.
- Smile at people.
- If people are nasty or surly towards you, simply regain your balance as best you can.
- Don't stifle your reaction, as the goal is not to eliminate emotions, but to experience the emotions and then let them go.

As you move through the crowd, consider "leaning in" to a side that is not familiar to you. For example, if you tend to talk with people easily, considering going through this experiment without saying a word to anyone. If you tend to keep to yourself, consider striking up a conversation with someone. Pay attention to what you notice.

Remember: Feel free to adjust the experiment to fit your needs. The purpose of doing this is to learn more about yourself, not to overwhelm you. If, as you are doing this experiment, you find that yielding is difficult and find yourself snapping at other shoppers or pushing your way through crowds, stop. On the other hand, if you find that you can keep your center and balance for a long period of time, keep going.

When you have completed this experiment, consider the following questions:

1. What did you learn most about yielding in this experiment?
2. What surprised you the most?
3. What is one new thing you have learned about yourself as a result of trying this experiment?

Chapter Summary
Congratulations!

By recognizing the secret of gaining more power of through yielding, you have taken the next step toward becoming a Black Belt Leader!

Chapter Summary:

We began with martial artists being tested by village elders, with the most skilled martial artist being selected to lead the village to safety. We then learned how to double leadership power by increasing yin power. We examined the importance of being able to *blend* in order to create more effective leadership strategies, and we explored four strategies for increasing yin power.

Suggested further reading:

Kinds of Power by James Hillman

The Right Use of Power: How Stewardship Replaces Leadership by Peter Block

The Zen of Creativity: Cultivating Your Artistic Life by John Daido Loori

Looking Ahead:

In the next chapter, you will learn important rules that leaders need to understand for managing conflict.

"Change requires movement.
Movement creates friction.
Friction means conflict.
Therefore, people cannot be led
through change without conflict."

Story
Crossing the River

Long ago in Japan, two monks, one older and one younger, were walking down the road when they came to the edge of a river. A recent storm had washed away the bridge, and a young woman was standing by the side of the river. The current was rather strong, and she was unable to cross.

The older of the two monks stopped and offered to carry the woman across. The woman gladly accepted, and the monk did so.

The younger monk watched in silence, aghast. He knew that it was against the rules of their order to have any physical contact with women. As the monks continued on with their journey, the younger monk stewed in the memory of his elder breaking one of the rules of the order. Finally, he could stand it no longer. "How could you?!?" the younger monk cried out.

Startled, the older monk replied, "How could I? How could I what?" "How could you carry that woman across the river when the rules of our order tell us otherwise?" said the young monk.

"Ah," said the older monk gently, "I left that woman back on the other side of the river. I see you are still carrying her."

Chapter 12
Leading Conflict

"Honest differences are often a healthy sign of progress."
-Mahatma Gandhi

Conflict. How amazing that one simple word creates so many problems and opportunities in organizations? Leadership is about moving people forward, which means change. Conflict, as Gandhi's quote teaches, goes hand-in-hand with change.

Many organizational leaders have pointed out that in today's business, change is a constant. What many leaders have not pointed out is the relationship between change and conflict. Change and conflict are two sides of the same coin. You do not get one without getting the other, and both change and conflict are tremendously misunderstood in leadership circles today. Like so many other things, they come in different shapes and sizes, and leaders need to be prepared for them all.

The Four Conflict Management Tools of Black Belt Leaders

One of the great gifts that Morihei Ueshiba gave the world through Aikido is the creation of a safe arena for learning about how we engage in conflict. For me, practicing Aikido is like having a laboratory where I can go and attempt to physically embody the things I teach in my consulting and coaching practice. This book is a small version of that laboratory for you.

Four Conflict Management Tools of Black Belt Leaders:
1. Understand the True Nature of Conflict.
2. Develop <u>Even More</u> Self Awareness.
3. Develop Creative Leadership Skills.
4. Develop <u>Even Better</u> Skills to Manage Conflict.

Let us look at each tool in turn.

Conflict Management Tool #1: Understand the True Nature of Conflict.

As we have already observed, conflict is greatly misunderstood in leadership circles. Ineffective leaders believe that conflict is a sign that something is wrong, and that conflict is something to be feared and avoided at all costs. Superior leaders know differently.

Just as change is a normal and natural part of life, so too is conflict. Conflict was required to create the Grand Canyon. The water of the Colorado River was in conflict for millions of years with the surrounding rocks before such a scenic place was created. Conflict between your car's tires and the road is required in order for the car to move forward. In the same way, conflict is required to move your organization to the next level. The main point is to recognize that many business leaders sing the praises of change while ignoring the vital and crucial role that conflict plays in creating change.

Why do we so easily discuss change but ignore conflict? There are three reasons: 1) Conflict can be painful; 2) Conflict can be difficult; and 3) Conflict is often interpreted as a threat.

While change can be fun and exciting to talk about, conflict resolution requires effort but pays dividends in the long run. You have probably attended seminars where the presenters bragged and boasted about how much they enjoy conflict. You will not hear that from me. Just between the two of us, I do not like conflict one bit, and I'm not going to write about how I love a good skirmish and cannot wait for the next experience to occur. I always feel nervous around people who say those sorts of things, since I believe they are either not being truthful, or they've never been in a genuinely intense conflict with someone else. There is something deep within human nature that seeks to avoid conflict. [129]

While I personally do not enjoy discord, I have participated in some highly confrontational meetings and conversations that—because the parties were committed to the outcome—resolved themselves with spectacular results. Thus, despite my own aversion to such encounters, I have learned an important lesson from those meetings: *The heat of conflict is required to produce golden results.*

I have also learned that conflict creates added difficulties, which leaders should value. In his excellent book, *A Path with Heart,* author Jack Kornfield observes that difficulties are considered of such great value that a Tibetan prayer recited before each step of practice actually <u>asks</u> for them. The prayer goes like this:

> *Grant that I may be given appropriate difficulties*
> *and sufferings on this journey so that my heart may*
> *be truly awakened and my practice of liberation and*
> *universal compassion may be truly fulfilled.*[130]

Conflict Management Tool #2: Develop <u>Even More</u> Self Awareness.

Long before combat enters their lives, martial artists begin practicing for the eventuality. Olympic athletes begin training years, and sometimes decades, before the day of their Olympic competition. Famous musicians begin practicing in their childhood. The secret for martial artists and Olympic athletes and famous musicians lies in preparation. If you want to become a World-class leader, then you need to prepare in the same manner. The time for learning how to lead people through conflict is *not* when the conflict has already erupted.

Ineffective leaders believe that, as some magical function of their elevated position, the necessary skills to handle conflict will somehow materialize. This makes about as much sense as believing that you can skydive just because someone took you up in a plane and called you a skydiver. When the inevitable stress of conflict arises (and I mean inevitable), unprepared leaders will regress to either a *Pushing* or *Pulling* style. Guaranteed.

How does a leader prepare for managing conflict? Some use coaches and mentors. Others use books such as this one, and some draw upon multiple sources of support. But all effective leaders know one thing for certain: You cannot manage or lead people through conflict if you haven't spent time analyzing and understanding how you deal with—and respond to— conflict yourself. Begin with these important questions and observations:

- What do I like about conflict?
- What do I hate about conflict?
- The easiest part of conflict for me is…
- The hardest part of conflict for me is…
- One thing I tell myself when conflict arises in my organization is…
- One physical change that happens to me during conflict is…
- The physical part of myself that I'm <u>least</u> aware of during conflict is…
- One way my breathing changes during conflict is…

Make a habit of running through this checklist—and making notes as much as possible—each time you find yourself in a conflicted situation. The more time you invest in doing this, the more automatic the process of awareness will become for you. Your leadership responses need to be automatic because, in the heat of a situation, you can quickly discover that you have lost your way. Increasing your awareness about how you respond to conflict—in mind, body and spirit—can provide you with critical information that can help you lead people through conflict to a successful resolution.

Conflict Management Tool #3: Develop Creative Leadership Skills.

Achieving creative leadership requires overcoming the hard-wiring of physiology. This requires reprogramming yourself in order to remain open in the face of conflict. Let's take a closer look at how this reprogramming works for leaders.

Biologically, people experience conflict as a stressful situation, and our bodies are wired to manage stress in particular ways. In general, in the face of conflict, people tend to pull inward, narrowing and constricting themselves in mind, body, and spirit. Breathing becomes shallow, vision narrows, muscles tighten, heart rates increase, and minds race. These are primal "fight-or-flight" responses, which were essential during the early stages of human development. But in the modern world, they are exactly the opposite of what needs to happen in order to creatively lead anyone through—and out of—conflict.

A number of "tools" are now available to help override our natural biological instincts and train our bodies to "open up" while slowing down in the midst of confrontation. One tool in particular, from the martial arts, is the practice of *mindfulness*. Drawn from ancient meditation practices, mindfulness is a method for training, focusing, and clarifying the mind. Unless you have been practicing meditation full time for a decade in a monastery, this practice takes into account the knowledge that you won't be able to stop your mind from thinking and jumping from subject to subject. Zen teachers of old referred to this as "monkey mind." A leader with a racing heart and monkey mind cannot possibly be prepared to address and resolve conflict. Although we rarely have control over the pace of external events bombarding us, we are able to control the tempo of internal events, especially the pace of our thoughts.

Requiring only a few minutes each day, here is a simple mindfulness exercise you can use to put this theory into practice:

> Sit comfortably in a chair so that your feet are flat on the floor and your back/spine is in a gentle but straight vertical alignment, as if a string were running from the top of your head to the ceiling above you.
>
> For five minutes, simply sit there, without moving your body, as you try not to think about anything. When thoughts rush in (which they will do one after the other), do your best to shut them down and try again to have an empty mind. Just be. Focus on your breathing, counting from one to ten. When you reach ten, return to one and count to ten again, repeating the process over and over.
>
> Let your whole being function as a 360-degree open sphere of listening. When you find yourself drifting off in thought again, return to your counting from one to ten.
>
> If you find your back bending or slouching, straighten up again and return to your count, starting from one.
>
> Any time you find yourself thinking, daydreaming or even dozing, return to one and begin again.
>
> For a short and simple five minutes, please just let yourself be.

Once you've comfortably built these five minutes into your daily routine, you can increase the time to ten minutes, or even longer, if you wish. If you pursue your mindfulness practice for only 10 minutes a day, though, over a six–month period, you will experience a profound improvement in your leadership effectiveness—especially during conflicts and crises—all without going anywhere or spending a cent.[131]

❅ ❅ ❅

**"When problems arise,
we do not rise to the level of our expectations –
we fall to the level of our training."
Bruce Lee**

❅ ❅ ❅

Conflict Management Tool #4: Develop <u>Even Better</u> Skills to Manage Conflict.

Effective leadership is a never-ending work-in-progress, and there is always another new skill or tool just around the bend. No matter how successful you become, there is always room for improvement—and if you think you know all there is to know about the craft of conflict resolution, you're probably going backwards.

Five Skills for Even Better Conflict Management

1. **Breathe.**
2. **Separate the Person from the Problem.**
3. **Listen!**
4. **Clarify Positions from Interests.**
5. **Take Time.**

1. Breathe.

In the middle of an intensely inflamed situation, breathing can be easier said than done. You may be surprised to hear this, but my professional observations of conflict have documented that people involved in highly confrontational situations frequently hold their breath for long periods of time. Holding your breath, as you might imagine, is not an optimal state if you're a leader to whom people are turning for resolution.

In order to learn how to stop holding your breath during conflict, you not only need to recognize that you *are* holding your breath, but you also need to anticipate ahead of time that this will be your body's natural reaction.

A key element of early training for professional dancers, athletes, martial artists and the like is learning how to become acutely aware of their breathing processes and mechanisms, as well as learning how to regulate and control their breathing during exertion and stressful (i.e., performance) situations. The scope of your leadership responsibilities requires that you have this same sort of training as well. There are many ways for you to begin, but here is an exercise to help you get started:

> Sit in a chair as before in the mindfulness exercise—
> this time with your feet a comfortable distance apart, your
> arms relaxed, hands in your lap, your body pushed fully

into the seat, with your shoulders resting against the chair back. Now, bring your attention to your breathing. Don't try and change the way you are breathing—just notice what "normal" breathing is for you. What is the quality of your breathing? Analyze with words like shallow, deep, irregular, even. Make mental notes for a minute or two. Pay attention to how you feel throughout your entire body. Don't try to change anything—just notice.

Now, allow your abdomen to relax and take in several full, deep breaths, exhaling at the same slow rate as you inhale. Do this ten times, for ten breaths, taking as long as necessary. When you have finished, focus on your breathing again, and make note of any changes. Are you using different words? Has *shallow* become *deep*? Is *irregular* now *regular*? In general, do you feel more *relaxed, aware, alive*?

You may also want to try this experiment again, this time concentrating on a deeper, more relaxed breathing, and compare your observations of the two separate exercises. This small investment of time and energy (which requires zero investment of money, gasoline, mileage, etc.) will not only contribute to a healthier you, but will also add to your effectiveness as a leader and your ability to steadily lead people (and yourself) through, and out of, conflict.

2. Separate the Person From the Problem.

From "shooting the messenger" to surrounding themselves with people who always say "yes," ineffective leaders make the critical mistake of confusing the person with the problem. What do I mean by this? Remember that the person bringing the problem to you is a competent and capable person in his or her own right. Honor the relationship you have with the person above the problem at hand. Remember that this person is not raising the issue with you to waste time or cause even more problems. Under most circumstances, the problem is what needs to be managed, not the person.[132]

Once you have developed awareness around your breathing, and you have separated the person from the problem, you are now ready to move onto the most difficult challenge.

3. Listen!

Great leaders are great listeners. Period. We talked about this at length in Chapter 11 when we discussed how to double the strength of your leadership position with yin power. But the subject of listening carries substantial import and bears briefly revisiting within the context of our present discussion of conflict.

Ineffective leaders operate under the misguided impression that listening quietly to someone is the same as agreeing with that person when, in fact, *listening to* and *agreeing with* are two completely separate activities. Sometimes you can agree with someone right up front, without expending any energy in dialogue. But generally, agreement is reached after some level of repartee where, after varying positions are presented, you find yourself in agreement with one another. In order for you to know where you stand, however, you have to have been listening.

In a conflict polarity, successful resolution will reside closer to the center of the continuum than to one end or the other. But prior to any resolution, while each end is "laying out the facts," a lot of talking is taking place. This discussion can become quite heated, but if nobody is listening, everyone is wasting time. The one who listens the most gains the most information—and information is power, no matter how the fish is fried.

There's an old saying taken from sales and marketing role-playing sessions that states, "The first person who speaks loses." Try implementing this theory the next time you're negotiating for an automobile. You'll walk out with a better deal—faster—if you just sit there silently looking at the numbers, with a concerned face, while the salesman is stewing over what you might be thinking. *The first person who speaks loses...* "Well, let me go back to my manager and see if we can do any better on this price." Congratulations on your new car!

While leadership is about much more than negotiating, or having someone lose, leaders can still learn something from the sales and marketing folks. As a leader, you have ample opportunities each day to practice your listening skills. The next time you're in a meeting, for example—unless you're the presenter, of course—do your best not to say a word. Listen, take notes, and as briefly as possible answer any direct questions. But otherwise, don't say anything. Not speaking is not about winning, as in the scenario above, but instead about gathering important leadership information. Just make listening to everyone else your primary objective for this one meeting.

Afterwards, back in your office, take note of how much you learned by listening and by observing others while *they* were doing the talking. You will be astonished at how this simple change in your behavior can lead to enormous gains in your effectiveness as a leader.

❀ ❀ ❀

**"In effect, you can change the game
simply by starting to play a new one."
Fisher & Ury**

❀ ❀ ❀

4. Clarify *Positions* From *Interests.*

In their classic book *Getting to Yes*, Roger Fisher and William Ury identify the crucial difference between interests and positions: **Interests** are what I need; **Positions** are what I think will get me there. Let's look at an example from my coaching practice. David is an executive who had been working with me to learn embodied leadership. Let's drop in on a meeting that took place in his organization:

ABC, Inc. is a multi-national company that manufactures software for accounting systems. The top-level managers of ABC, Inc. are having their monthly conference call. Among those present at this teleconference are David, ABC's CEO; Robert, the director of ABC's United States marketing division; and Carol, the director of ABC's European marketing division. Robert is arguing for speeding up production of the company's newest software program, which Robert is convinced will be next year's killer application and a runaway best seller for the company. He wants the new program on the market one full month ahead of schedule. Carol, on the other hand, is arguing that several of the software packages that ABC is currently marketing are over-priced. She reports that they are being outsold by other software companies who have recently entered the market sector that ABC has dominated for the past several years. Furthermore, Carol strongly maintains that they shouldn't introduce a new product until their pricing structure is revisited. Robert and Carol have been in conflict over the issue for more than 15 minutes.

What's going on here? Both Robert and Carol are locked into their respective positions, and the meeting could probably go on for several hours without much being accomplished. But because David has been practicing embodied leadership, he understands the difference between interests and positions. He begins to help Robert and Carol identify the interests behind the positions they are taking. The economy has recently taken a downturn, and both Robert and Carol are concerned about ABC's bottom line. Robert believes that bringing the new software to market one month earlier will increase profits, while Carol believes that cutting the software's price will produce the same results. Having arrived at some common ground, David is able to help Robert and Carol identify ways whereby each can meet their own individual interests. A decision is soon reached to release the software program two weeks ahead of schedule while offering customers a 15% discount during the first two months that the software is on the market.

Recall our discussion from Chapter Three about the importance of process. In the meeting just described, David demonstrated a masterful awareness of process. The final decision that the team reached was not as important as the process that David used. The content of the final decision is not critical because there were several equally valid solutions. Using his skills as an embodied leader, David was able to discover that both Robert and Carol held the same interest behind their opposing positions. He could just have easily learned that the two parties had different interests behind their positions. The critical learning point here for leaders is to remember that discovering people's interests is next-to-impossible when people are locked into their positions, unless someone is asking questions and listening to the answers. Then the art and science of being a true leader comes into play as you help conflicting parties effectively resolve their differences in ways that move your organization forward.

5. Take Your Time.

Keep these two simple leadership points in mind:

1. Leaders who slow down when they attempt to resolve conflict usually get quicker results. When you try to rush, you run the risk of missing the true source of the conflict, and any resolution will only be temporary. Proceed slowly and secure an effective solution that will contribute to your organization's success, and to yours and that of your people, as well.

2. The greater the number of people involved in any conflict, the more time will be expended to effectively resolve the conflict. Remember that you have to listen to all parties before any options for resolution can emerge. If there are a lot of people with an equal number of positions, a great deal of time is going to be involved in order to arrive at a successful resolution. Budget appropriately.

Embodied Learning Experiment #9
Breathing & Conflict

Breathing with conscious awareness during conflict is one of the most important tools a leader can employ. Try this exercise to help you become even better:

> Think about a person or situation in your recent past that you have felt very angry about. Imagine yourself back in that situation or with that person. Do not just use your mind for these thoughts. Think instead with your whole being. Imagine yourself in an angry situation, and then notice what happens within your body. Pay particular attention to the quality of your breathing.

Close the book for a moment and give the exercise a try...

Welcome back. Take a few deep breaths to help settle yourself. Now, what did you notice about your body in that experiment? What did you notice about your breathing?

Can you identify what you need to do in order to begin breathing normally again? If so, give that action a try. As you practice, challenge yourself to see how many other ways you can find to accomplish the same thing.

Chapter Summary
Congratulations!

By recognizing the value of conflict in your organization you have taken the next step toward becoming a Black Belt Leader!

Chapter Summary:

We opened with the story of two monks carrying a woman across the river. One monk carried the woman much further than was necessary. As a leader, how often do you carry someone further than required? We then went on to explore the important role that conflict plays in the life of an organization. We learned that conflict is a natural part of life, and that conflict and change go hand-in-hand. We discussed **The Four Black Belt Leadership Conflict Tools**:

1. Understand the True Nature of Conflict.
2. Develop <u>Even More</u> Self Awareness.
3. Develop Creative Leadership Skills.
4. Develop <u>Even Better</u> Skills to Manage Conflict.

Suggested further reading:

The Magic of Conflict by Tom F. Crum
Getting to Yes by Roger Fisher & William Ury
Difficult Conversations by Douglas Stone, et al.
The Power of Now: A Guide to Spiritual Enlightenment by Eckhart Tolle

Looking Ahead:

You're on the home stretch. Only one more chapter to go!

BLACK BELT
Section IV:
Assess Your Strategy

"A good head and a good heart are always a formidable combination."

- Nelson Mandela

"Black Belt Leaders understand that there is never only one right way to lead people."

Story
Many Ways to Right

A long time ago in Japan, a disagreement had erupted between two neighbors in a village. Neither side could reach an agreement, and the argument was disrupting life in the village.

The headmaster of the village decided to take the disputants and ask guidance from a famous martial arts sensei living nearby. Both parties to the disagreement decided to abide by whatever the teacher decided.

The first neighbor presented his case to the sensei.

"I think you are right," the sensei said.

Then the second neighbor presented his case, to which the sensei said,

"I think you are right."

The headmaster of the village exclaimed, "But, sensei, they cannot both be right."

To which the sensei responded, "I think you are right."

Chapter 13
Climbing the Mountain

"Leadership is daring to step into the Unknown."
- Stephen Hawking, physicist

Many Ways to Right

Of all the martial arts stories that I've ever read, the one leading into this chapter is one of the most evocative for me. "Decide!" I want to shout at the sensei. When I can be more honest with myself, I realize that asking someone to decide is really asking them to decide *for* me, which is really a very subtle way of giving up my power to another.

True leadership is about the effective use of power. Leaders need to understand the important human dynamic that, despite the importance we place on freedom and individuality, there is a huge pull in Western society to give our power to someone else. At some level, we all want mommy or daddy to come to the rescue. At various times in our lives, we all want the lone hero or heroine to come riding into the village and save the day.[133] But that is not going to happen. Effective leaders take just the right amount of responsibility when they lead people—no more, no less. Often, the worst mistake a leader can make is deciding *for* the group—and smart leaders know that the most important decision they make time and again, throughout each business day, is determining whether an issue is *theirs* to decide, or the *group's*.

Leaders Need To Be Right, Right?

Not exactly. Leaders need to succeed, and there is a big difference between succeeding and being right. By *right*, I mean an abstract, archetypal, Godhanded-down-to-Charleton-Heston-playing-Moses kind of right. Leaders need to understand that the concepts of "right," "better," and "more effective" are always grounded in a particular context.

Another example can be drawn from martial arts to illustrate this point. During my years of practicing Aikido, people interested in the martial arts have often asked me the question, "Which is the right martial art for me?" Before I can answer effectively, a counter-question needs to be asked: "What are you looking for in a martial art?" A 23-year-old Army Ranger has training needs that are entirely different from those of a 65-year-old retired schoolteacher.

While this dynamic may seem blatantly obvious in martial arts, the same dynamic occurs (and is often unrecognized) in organizations. Ineffective leaders value action over all else. Needing to be seen as right, these leaders will often leap into acting without fully understanding their problem, creating greater problems in the process. Wise leaders pay attention to action, but their focus on action is not blind. They consistently ask the question, "Right (or more effective) for whom, and in what context?" A solid, effective action for a conservative legal firm in New York City would not necessarily be advisable for a dot-com start-up in Tokyo. Leaders need stay open to the multiple solutions that can present themselves simply by keeping in mind the context of every organizational problem they face.

❋ ❋ ❋
**By now, however, it should have become clear that
there is no such thing as the one right organization.
There are only organizations, each of which has distinct strengths,
distinct limitations and specific applications."
Peter Drucker**
❋ ❋ ❋

No Simple Solutions to Climbing the Mountain

Simple solutions do not engender debate and discussion. For example, there are no debates raging about how many wheels a car should have or whether computers should have keyboards. For better or for worse, leadership has few solutions that are simple. If there were simple solutions to the challenges of leading people, someone would have discovered them years ago, and that would have been that.

Many ancient traditions use the metaphor of climbing a mountain to describe the journey of development, whether that development is spiritual, physical, emotional or mental. Even the term "mountain climbing" invokes formidable, complex images of human beings who look no bigger than ants picking their way slowly up the side of a precipitous peak. Some may feel that this metaphor is a little extreme in the context of leadership, while others feel the image isn't quite graphic enough to suit their own realities. But *all* attest to the complexities of leadership. Fortunately, the same ancient traditions that gave us the mountains also recognize that there are many ways scale those heights.

Into the Dark Forest

In Bill Moyers' interviews with Joseph Campbell, the two men discussed the legend of King Arthur. Campbell described how, when the knights of the round table went off into the Dark Forest in search of the Holy Grail, they "each entered the forest at a separate point of his choice."[134] Here Campbell was expounding on a theme he initially wrote about in *Creative Mythology*, where, citing Gottfried Weber, he offers the description of the knights' quest as follows:

> [The knights] had decided to ride forth, each in his own direction, because to start out in a group would have been shameful. And in the morning, at first light, the fellowship rose. When all had assumed their arms, they attended Mass and, when that was done, mounting, commended their good king to God, thanked him for the honors he had done them, and, issuing from his castle, "entered into the forest, at one point and another, where they saw it to be thickest, *all in those places where they found no way or path*...[135]

Campbell then goes on to eloquently express a vital truth discovered by the Western world—the importance of people contributing their uniqueness to the world. Paraphrasing Campbell in the context of leading people, we discover an important truth:

> **The great leadership truth is that each of us is a completely unique leader. If we are ever to give any gift to the world, that gift will have to come out of our own leadership experience and the fulfillment of our own leadership potentialities, not someone else's.** [136]

Each and every leadership situation is a wonderfully complex inter-weaving of people (including temperaments and personalities) and situations (including resources, supports and limitations), the likes of which have never been seen by the world to date and will never be seen again. The emotionally intelligent leader injects his own uniqueness into each situation and, together with the combined, empowered talents of his people, finds the *best-fit* path up the mountain du jour.

❋ ❋ ❋

A Key to Leading People:
Give yourself permission to develop leadership strategies
that are both powerful *and* connected with others.

❋ ❋ ❋

Skills for Continuing Your Journey

Remember that the process of leading people is both never-ending and cyclical. As you develop into a more emotionally intelligent, embodied leader, you may wish to re-visit sections of this book from time to time. As I've said, practice and repetition are key components to skilled leadership, just as in any other discipline you are trying to nourish.

In Aikido—as in leadership—there are actually relatively few techniques, and the basics do not take that long to learn. However, there are an endless number of variations on the basic themes. Mastering those variations requires—and is worthy of—a lifetime of study.

At the beginning of this book, you were introduced to the Seven Solutions of Black Belt Leadership, which were:

1. Know the Five Core Problems of Leadership.
2. Understand Leadership as a Relational Process.
3. Seek Harmony in Leadership.
4. Lead People Rather than Pushing or Pulling Them.
5. Cultivate Emotional Engagement.
6. Practice Embodied Leadership.
7. Follow *The Black Belt Cycle of Leading People.*

You then learned about the Five Core Problems facing leaders today, which are:

1. Organizations pay an enormous price when leaders ignore emotions.
2. Organizations suffer when leaders mistakenly believe there is only one right way to lead people.
3. Organizations fail when leaders refuse to believe there are wrong ways to lead people.
4. Organizations flounder when leaders think that there are easy answers to leading people.
5. Organizations lose viability when they follow the old structures that serve people at the top first.

Now that you have reached the end of this book, you should have a reasonable grasp of how you use the Seven Solutions to conquer the Five Core Problems. Of the Seven Solutions, the seventh—*The Black Belt Cycle of Leading People*—is especially important, since the solution provides you with a process by which you can approach the other six. On every page of this book, we have traveled in one form or another through the steps of *The Black Belt Cycle of Leading People*, which are:

1. Set Your Strategy.
2. Take Your Stance.
3. Take Action.
4. Assess Your Strategy.

Throughout our exploration of the Seven Solutions, you learned about the important role that emotions play in leadership, as well as the importance of cultivating your own emotional growth in order to increase your power and effectiveness. By using the Seven Solutions to achieve higher levels of emotionally intelligent, embodied leadership, you can expect to strengthen the emotional engagement of the people you are leading, which will result in increased levels of success for your organization.

Ultimately, leading people is a path of excellence that is both an art and a science. Once you've begun filling your toolkit with strategies, tips and techniques, the main ingredients you need to add are confidence and serenity. These come largely from your own belief in yourself. If you don't believe in yourself, no one else will either. Insecurity has a way of hitching a ride on your shoulder, and even if you can't see the interloper, others can.

❋ ❋ ❋
"Our deepest fear is not that we are inadequate.
Our deepest fear is that we are powerful beyond measure…
We ask ourselves, who am I to be brilliant, gorgeous,
talented, fabulous? Actually, who are you not to be?
You are a child of God.
Your playing small doesn't serve the world."
Marianne Williamson[137]
❋ ❋ ❋

Taking Your Space: Playing Big

Stop at this moment and write a one-sentence description of where you want to be as a leader in one year. Now write another sentence that describes where you want to be in five years; and then write a final sentence describing where you want to be in 10 years. Be specific. Saying "I want to be a better leader" does not make the grade. As you write, draw from all five of your physical senses. Putting your aspirations into a single sentence may be difficult, but clarifying your dream(s) into a succinct objective is the first step in plotting the path toward your achievement of that goal. Dream big!

Bringing dreams to life is rarely easy and requires that we own our full space in the world. When we were discussing how to manage conflict, one of the things we discovered was that, in the midst of conflict, people tend to shrink and take up less space. The truth is that most of us have never been given permission to take up our full space. On the Aikido mat, I constantly see this shrinking in others (and in myself as well). I also see this in boardrooms, meetings, and coaching sessions.

There are countless leadership and management perspectives that will tell you to think big. Few tell you to dream big. Even fewer prepare you to handle the pressures that follow when big dreams finally happen. But the truth is that success is both satisfying and difficult. Peter Jackson, director of the phenomenally successful *Lord of the Rings* film trilogy, was under enormous amounts of pressure throughout most of the filming. Neither he nor the film studio knew how successful the movies would be until after the first one was released. They lived under the three-year-long pressure of leading a production that cost over $300 million. Now that's pressure! If Peter Jackson had not been able to stand the pressure, he never would have succeeded in making the award-winning trilogy.

This leads us to The Black Belt Leadership Law of Success: *When you dream big and begin to bring your dreams into reality, expect enormous pressure to follow.* The phrase "Be careful what you wish for," comes to mind. Fate may put you through a great deal of pressure before awarding you your dream. As you move forward, research the realities of others who've already realized dreams similar to yours, and then plot those realities into your own plan for success. Always keep yourself open to the possibility that *not all dreams have a reality you can live with.* Then, when you are ready, dream big, commit yourself to that dream, and never let go until the dream is in your hands. Every ounce of progress in every industry came from dreamers (large and small) who wouldn't let go. There's no reason why you can't be the next one to reach a mountaintop!

❋ ❋ ❋
"Step by step walk the thousand-mile road."
Miyamoto Musashi, famous Japanese sword master
❋ ❋ ❋

Don't Just Sit There—Do Something!

You cannot become a martial artist by reading a how-to on martial arts, and you cannot become a better leader simply by reading this book or others on the subject of leadership. As the old joke goes about how you get to Carnegie Hall, you have to practice. Be bold!

Act! Make mistakes. Try something different. Risk running in circles, and become even more successful as a leader. But do something!

I had been practicing Aikido for several years when I had the opportunity to attend an Aikido seminar being taught by a well-known and well-respected Aikido sensei. This particular sensei was very open and welcomed questions. During one of the breaks, I found myself standing next to him at the water cooler, and I grabbed the opportunity to ask him a question about a particular technique I'd been struggling with. He looked at me quizzically for a moment and said—very gently—"Come back in three years and ask me that same question." We briefly talked about several other things and then went our separate ways. As I walked away from the sensei, I initially felt a little put off by the answer he gave me. He seemed to be answering *other* people's questions in great detail. "He didn't have to be so Zen about it, for crying out loud!" I found myself thinking. However, his answer had been given in such an affirming way that I thought I would chew on his words for a while. Back at my home dojo, I began practicing the troubling technique whenever I got the chance. Slowly, I began to discover that the answer to my questions was held in the very technique I was questioning.

By the time three years had passed, the sensei had—sadly—passed on, but I always thank him profusely for his teaching whenever I practice this particular technique. As you move forward beyond the end of this book, I challenge you to find the courage to live the techniques and philosophies we've discovered, and allow them to teach you. Without practice, these ideas remain idle chatter on paper. When you practice these leadership skills and attempt to embody them, the process of becoming a great leader will affect not only your leadership abilities, but the quality of the rest of your life as well.

❀ ❀ ❀

**"Progress comes to those who train and train;
reliance on secret techniques will get you nowhere."
Master Ueshiba**

❀ ❀ ❀

That's All Well and Good, But I Don't Have Three Years!

In the story above, I was fortunate enough to have the time to allow the technique to gradually be revealed to me while I worked on my own. Of course, not everyone has that kind of time. A more efficient approach is to consult an expert.

If you want to learn martial arts, you study under a sensei. If you want to learn to ride a horse, you find a good equestrian teacher. If you want to get into shape, you hire a personal trainer. No one—not a single person— ever made his or her way to the Olympics without a coach. Learning how to lead people is no different. As you read through this book, if there are particular issues you find yourself stuck on, consider working with an executive coach, therapist, a group of colleagues, or anyone else who can support your growth and provide you with honest feedback. Those are the people who can help you through the tough spots. Every great leader has a support network, as well a group of trusted people who can be consulted and relied upon for guidance.

Be Prepared.

As you practice becoming more of an emotionally intelligent, embodied leader, watch out for the *White Toyota Effect*. When we were first married, my wife and I needed a new car. After some research, we decided on a new model from Toyota that had just come off the production line. Talking over our intended purchase the evening before we were going to sign the contract, one of the concerns we had was that there might not be very many of these new models out on the road.

The next morning, I had to run a few other errands. In the course of about two hours, I counted 10 cars on the road that were the same make and model of the car we intended to purchase. I went home and told my wife about my experience. The next day, we bought the car, and on the way home, the same thing happened to her. Now, whenever we encounter this phenomenon after making a new purchase or trying out a new experience, we refer to the episode as the *White Toyota Effect*.

Recalling our discussion of the Gestalt Cycle of Experience (GCOE), this example points to the importance of awareness. Before I began car shopping, I had little interest in the new car models, so I had no awareness of what types of cars were on the road. Car makes and models were simply not *figural* for me. Once I became a consumer of that product, however, my awareness changed drastically.

So, you may ask, what does the *White Toyota Effect* have to do with leadership? Simply this: The more awareness you develop about the qualities of appropriate and engaging emotional interaction, the more you will become aware of the overall deplorable state of engaging emotional interaction in organizations today. From the receptionist in the front office to the highest boardroom office, there is an alarming absence of appropriate emotional interaction, and this deficit is hurting your organization.

❊ ❊ ❊

**"If you merely read this book you will not reach the way of strategy.
Absorb the things written in this book.
Do not just read, memorize or imitate, but so that you can realize the principle from within your own heart
study hard to absorb these things into your body."
Miyamoto Musashi**

❊ ❊ ❊

If You Meet a Leadership Program, Kill It!

In Zen, which influences many of the Asian martial arts, there is a saying: "If you meet the Buddha along the road, then kill him." This saying is a warning against not getting trapped in any particular system. In the Introduction, you read about how Black Belt Leadership is *not* a leadership system. The world does not need one more leadership system. What the world does need is great leadership that draws on the wisdom of the body and recognizes the treasury of emotions waiting to be tapped within every organization . Learning about emotionally intelligent, embodied leadership requires some form of structure, and I have given you one in this book. In day-to-day life, however, you must not allow a learning structure to become petrified into a system that places rules above people. An inflexible leadership structure that is set in stone will quickly suck the emotions—and the value—out of any organization.

Superior martial arts teachers train their students to surpass them on the mat. The purpose of an executive coach is to get you to the point where you no longer need the coach. In both cases, the students become the teachers and then offer their own wisdom to the next generation. With this understanding, I offer you the structure of Black Belt Leadership in order for you move beyond structure and into the realm of leadership mastery.

I invite you to use the principles contained in this book as a method of learning about and expanding your capacity for emotionally intelligent, embodied leadership for as long as—and *only* as long as—these principles are of help to you. Use the processes we've discussed to become the most effective and powerful leader you were meant to be—one who practices leading people in mind, body and spirit. Paths and structures, programs and rules can only point the way. You must find a leadership style that works best for you and your organization. Then, after you discover your own unique expression of emotionally intelligent embodied leadership, *throw this book away.*

In a way, what we've covered in these thirteen chapters is really very simple: basic respect, being sincere about who you are, and both allowing and encouraging other people to become more fully who *they* are. In their book *Lessons from the Top*, authors Thomas Neff and James Citrin recall Herb Kelleher, the CEO of Southwest Airlines as saying, "[People] want a program, and we've always felt that making it 'a program' murders it."[138] Always value your people over your programs.

Finally...Pay Attention to "We."

For the first time in the history of humanity, the collective "we" of civilization has the ability to determine the world's fate. After millions of years of habitation, we have, in the last half-century, acquired the technology to annihilate the planet. The course of our global future will be determined by our leaders, whether those leaders head a nation, a military power, a medium sized business or a small non-profit organization. Every leader counts. What an awesome responsibility! Success in leadership calls for leaders to move out of the "I" stage of individual agendas and into the viability of the larger "we."

In closing, I'll leave the final thought about the importance of "we" to Ken Wilber:

> In other words, if you and I are going to live together, we have to inhabit, not just the same empirical and physical space, but also the same intersubjective space of mutual recognition. We are going to have to fit, not just our bodies together in the same objective space, but our subjects together in the same cultural, moral and ethical space. We are going to have to find ways to recognize and respect the rights of each other and the community, and these rights cannot be found in objective matter, nor are they simply a case of my own individual sincerity, nor are they a matter of functionally fitting together empirical events: they are rather a matter of fitting our minds together in an intersubjective space that allows each of us to recognize and respect the other. Not necessarily *agree* with each other, but *recognize* each other – the opposite of which, simply put, is war.[139]

Good Luck!

Thank you for investing your valuable time in exploring the concepts between these covers. I hope that you have found one or two of my thoughts to be beneficial to you as a leader. Although this marks the book's ending, your growth as a Black Belt Leader has only just begun. An endless adventure awaits you as you discover avenues for leading people that are ever more successful. Best of luck to you. Enjoy—and *live*—the journey!

"Everything is in relationship to everything else. The ending of one thing is also the beginning of the next."

Story
Growing Books

Once upon a time, many years ago in China, a famous martial artist finished a book that he had been working on for the past ten years. Hearing that the book had been completed, one of his students came to him and said, "Master, you must be very relieved to have finished your book."

"Yes. And no," replied the master. "Finishing this book simply makes room for the next book to begin growing."

Afterword
Staying Open

"Superior performers intentionally seek out feedback; they want to hear how others perceive them, realizing that this is valuable information."
- Daniel Goleman

In an effort to practice what I've preached throughout this book, I invite you to dialogue with me (through email, snail-mail, or phone contact). Please feel free to offer any feedback, letting me know whether or not what I have written fits your experience(s) in the world of leadership.

Specifically, I would be interested in hearing:

- What was the most important helpful thing about this book?
- What was the least helpful part of the book for you?
- Is there anything vital that I left out that you discovered on your own path toward becoming a more emotionally intelligent, embodied leader?
- What other resources (books, websites, speakers, etc.) have you found helpful on your own path toward becoming an even better leader?

In addition to the above questions, I am also open to any other comments you might want to make. I can be reached directly via email at: *Tim@blackbeltconsultants.com*. I'll look forward to hearing from you.

Appendix I
Author's Notes

"Imagination is more important than knowledge."
- Albert Einstein

Leaders need imagination, and therefore, they need stories. Stories have a great deal to teach us about the emotional realm of leadership in business and organizations. In his book *How to Argue and Win Every Time,* nationally known trial lawyer Gerry Spence offers his wisdom based upon years of winning legal cases that many people thought were impossible to win. His secret? Stories. Observing that humans are "creatures of story," Mr. Spence shares, "[t]he strongest structure for any argument is the *story.*"[140]

Stories such as J. R. R. Tolkien's *Lord of the Rings* trilogy and J. K. Rowling's *Harry Potter* series are enormously successful. For example, J. K. Rowling's fifth title, *Harry Potter and the Order of the Phoenix,* broke publishing records with a first printing of 6.8 million copies and a second printing of an additional 1.7 million copies—figures previously unheard of in the publishing industry. These books are successful because the stories they tell strike a chord deep within us. They stir our imagination in ways that simple facts cannot. Each and every one of us longs to venture out on what Joseph Campbell referred to as the Hero's Journey (which applied to both males and females), with close friends and comrades to support us. Each of us wants to make something of ourselves in this world, to belong to something bigger than our own individual selves. In short, stories reach out to us and challenge us to offer our own unique dreams and visions to the world. Having the opportunity to lead others offers every leader the enormous gift of being able to work and play their dream into existence. There are few greater privileges in life.

Notes About the Asian References in This Book

Stories move us emotionally—both to joy and to tears. We cheer when we hear stories about winners. We weep at stories of successful romances. As a lover of both stories and all things martial arts, I have created the stories contained in this book having been influenced from a variety of sources. The martial arts world is ripe with stories, from ancient times to the present, stories that grow richer with each passing generation. Although the stories were not consciously drawn from any one source, I would like to convey appreciation for Paul Reps collection of Zen stories entitled *Zen Flesh, Zen Bones.*[141]

The Book of Balance and Harmony is a classic thirteenth-century anthology of Taoist writings from the School of Complete Reality, and was translated by Thomas Cleary. Unless otherwise noted, any quotes of Sun Tzu were drawn from Mr. Cleary's *The Illustrated Art of War.* I would like to expresses my gratitude and appreciation to Mr. Cleary for all of his translated texts and other works. Knowledge of Taoism and China in the English-speaking world has been infinitely enhanced by Mr. Cleary's work and dedication.

The quotes by Miyamoto Musashi were taken from *A Book of Five Rings.*

Unless otherwise noted, the quotes by Master Ueshiba were taken from John Steven's *The Art of Peace,* and the quotes of Lao Tzu come from *Tao Te Ching* version translated by Gia-fu Feng and Jane English.

On Martial Arts, Leadership & Spirituality

More than one person has asked me about living the combination of martial arts, leadership, and spirituality. Some people have even told me they consider the martial arts to be evil and hurtful practices (although I've noticed that none of these people seem to have ever actually *practiced* a martial arts). In an effort to dispel these stereotypes, I wanted to take a moment and address these concerns. The bottom line, for me, is I have never experienced an unhealthy tension between my martial arts practice and the practice of my spirituality.

My experience mirrors many of the superior martial artists with whom I have had the privilege to speak to about these matters. By all accounts, Master Ueshiba was a deeply, deeply spiritual man. His writings, recorded comments and embodied art of Aikido closely echo the perspectives of

Mahatma Gandhi, Martin Luther King, Jr., and Jesus Christ. For example, in John 10:10, Jesus said, "I have come that you might have life more abundantly." I believe that Jesus would agree that having "life more abundantly" includes our living fully and deeply through the miraculous physical structures of our bodies that God has given us.

One resource that I found quite helpful during the writing of this book was Fr. James Heft's chapter, *"Truths and Half-truths About Leadership: Ancient and Contemporary Sources,"* which remained at my desk, dog-eared and highlighted, through much of my writing of the second half of this book. At a recent celebration at the University of Dayton, Fr. Heft, S.M., who is the University Professor of Faith and Culture, Chancellor of the University, and also connected with the University's Center for Christian Leadership stated, "We should be clear at the outset that we Christians don't celebrate doctrines; rather we celebrate God's gifts where they are to be found: in people."[142]

If leaders walk away with nothing else from this present work, hopefully they will clearly experience my commitment to the importance of people over doctrines, theories and practices. If leaders will not value people because of higher-level ethical, spiritual and moral imperatives, then perhaps they will do so in light of recent and overwhelming evidence (only a fraction of which has been presented in this book) that valuing and supporting people simply makes good business and economic sense. Other spiritually-based books that I found helpful during this course of writing included: Gerald May's *The Dark Night of the Soul;* C.S. Lewis' *The Great Divorce;* and the writings of Ken Wilber.

About the Author

Tim Warneka wrote this book in response to the many clients and seminar participants who repeatedly told him, "Get this material in print!" A consultant, executive coach, speaker and author, Tim is the founder of *The Black Belt Consulting Group*, where he employs the principles he describes in this book to create success with individuals, groups, teams and organizations. Regarded as an expert in human performance, Tim holds a black belt in Aikido, a master's degree in counseling, certification as a massage professional, postgraduate training from the Gestalt Institute of Cleveland, and is an adjunct instructor at Bryant & Stratton College and Lakeland Community College.

Tim is available for coaching and consulting for individuals, families, groups, teams and organizations. You can reach him personally via email or phone: *Tim@blackbeltconsultants.com* 440-944-4746.

Bibliography/Webography

Aguayo, R. (1991). *Dr. Deming: The American Who Taught the Japanese About Quality.* Fireside Publishing. New York, N.Y.

Beisser, A. (1970). *The Paradoxical Theory of Change.* In *Gestalt Therapy Now,* (J. Fagan, Ed.). Science and Behavior Books, New York, N.Y.

Beck, D.E. & Cowan, C.C. (1996*). Spiral Dynamics: Mastering Values, Leadership, and Change.* Blackwell Publishing, Malden, MA.

Block, P. (2002). *The Answer to How is Yes: Acting on What Matters.* Berrett-Koehler Publishers, Inc. San Francisco, CA.

-----. (2002a). *The Right Use of Power: How Stewardship Replaces Leadership.* Audio Tape. Sounds True, Inc. Louisville, CO.

-----. (2001). *The Flawless Consulting Fieldbook & Companion: A Guide to Understanding your Expertise.* Jossey-Bass/Pheiffer, San Francisco, CA.

-----. (2000). *Hard Measures for Human Values.* Available online at: *http://www.designedlearning.com/insights/apr2000.asp.*

------. (1996). *Stewardship: Choosing Service over Self-Interest.* Berrett-Koehler Publishers, Inc. San Francisco, CA.

Brindle, M. C. & Stearns, P. (2001). *Facing Up to Management Faddism: A New Look at an Old Force.* Quorum Books. Westport, CT.

Bridges, W. (2001). *The Way of Transition: Embracing Life's Most Difficult Moments.* Perseus Publishing. New York, N.Y.

Brooke, R. (Ed.). (2000). *Pathways into the Jungian World: Phenomenology and Analytical Psychology.* Routledge. New York, N.Y.

-----. (1991). *Jung and Phenomenology.* Routledge. New York, N.Y.

Brunton, P. (1939). *Discover Yourself.* E. P. Dutton & Co. New York, N.Y.

Bulfinch, T. (1979). *Bulfinch's Mythology.* Random House Publishing. New York, N.Y.

Callanan, M. & Kelley, P. (1992). *Final Gifts: Understanding the Special Awareness, Needs, and Communications of the Dying.* Bantam Books. New York, N.Y.

Campbell, J. (1968). *The Masks of God: Creative Mythology.* The Viking Press. New York, N. Y.

-----. (1964). *The Masks of God: Occidental Mythology.* The Viking Press. New York, N.Y.

-----. (1949). *The Hero with a Thousand Faces.* Bollingen Foundation. New York, N.Y.

Capra, F. (2000). *The Tao of Physics.* Shambhala Publications. Boston, MA.

Carter, J. P. (1993). *Racketeering in Medicine: The Suppression of Alternatives.* Hampton Road Publishing Company. Norfolk, VA.

Cerf, C. & Navasky, V. (1998). *The Experts Speak: The Definitive Compendium of Authoritative Misinformation.* Villard Books. New York, N.Y.

Chodron, P. (2001) *The Places That Scare You: A Guide to Fearlessness in Difficult Times.* Shambhala Publications. Boston, MA.

Cleary, T. (trans.) (1989). *The Book of Balance and Harmony.* North Point Press. New York, N.Y.

-----. (trans.) (1998). *The Illustrated Art of War.* Sun Tzu. Shambhala Press. Boston, MA.

Coffman, C. & Gonzalez-Molina, G. (2002). *Follow this Path: How the World's Greatest Organizations Drive Growth by Unleashing Human Potential.* Warner Business Books. New York, N.Y.

Collins, J. (2001). *Good to Great: Why Some Companies Makes The Leap...And Others Don't.* HarperCollins Books. New York, N.Y.

Collins, J.C. & Porras, J. I. (1994). *Built to Last: Successful Habits of Visionary Companies.* HarperCollins Books. New York, N.Y.

Covey, S. (1990). *The Seven Habits of Highly Effective People.* Fireside Publishing. New York, N.Y.

Crocker, S. (1999). *A Well-Lived Life: Essays in Gestalt Therapy.* GICPress. Cleveland, OH.

Daido Loori, J. (2004). *The Zen of Creativity: Cultivating Your Artistic Life.* Ballantine Books. New York, N.Y.

Damasio, A. (2000). *The Feeling of What Happens: Body and Emotion in the Making of Consciousness.* Harvest Books. Harcourt Publications. New York, N.Y.

-----. (1995). *Descartes' Error: Emotion, Reason, and the Human Brain.* Quill Publishing. New York, N.Y.

Deming, W.E. (2000). *Out of Crisis.* The MIT Press. Cambridge, MA.

Dickens, Charles. (1984). *A Christmas Carol and other Christmas Stories.* NAL Penguin, Inc. New York, N.Y.

Drucker, P. (1999). *Management Challenges for the 21ˢᵗ Century.* HarperBusiness. New York, N.Y.

-----. (1985). *Innovation and Entrepreneurship.* Harper & Row Publishers. New York, N.Y.

Ehrenreich, B. (2002). *Nickel and Dimed: On (Not) Getting By in America.* Owl Books. New York, N.Y.

Eisler, R. (1987). *The Chalice & The Blade - Our History, Our Future.* HarperSanFrancisco. San Francisco, CA.

Feng, G. & English, J. (1972). *Lao Tzu: Tao Te Ching.* Random House Publishing. New York, N.Y.

Fisher, R. & Ury, W. (1981). *Getting to Yes: Negotiating Agreement without Giving In.* Penguin Books. New York, N.Y.

Flowers, B. S. (Ed.). (1988). *Joseph Campbell: The Power of Myth with Bill Moyers.* Doubleday Books. New York, N.Y.

Gerber, M. (1995). *The E-myth Revisited: Why Most Small Businesses Don't Work and What To Do About It.* HarperBusiness Publishing. New York, N.Y.

Gerstner, L.V. (2002). *Who Says Elephants Can't Dance?* Harper Business. New York, N.Y.

Goleman, D., Boyatzis, R., & McKee, A. (2002). *Primal Leadership: Realizing the Power of Emotional Intelligence.* Harvard Business School Press. Boston, MA.

------. (1998). *Working with Emotional Intelligence.* Bantam Books. New York, N.Y.

-----. (1995). *Emotional Intelligence: Why it can matter more than IQ.* Bantam Books, New York, N.Y.

Goleman, D., Kaufman, P., & Ray, M. (1992). *The Creative Spirit.* Penguin Books. New York, N.Y.

Goode, E. *The New York Times,* "The Heavy Cost of Chronic Stress", December 17, 2002. Available on-line at:

http://www.nytimes.com/2002/12/17/health/psychology/17STRE.html?pagewanted=print&position=top

Griffith, S. (1971). *The Art of War.* Oxford University Press. New York, N.Y.

Harris, V. (trans.). (1974). *A Book of Five Rings.* Miyamoto Musashi. The Overlook Press. Woodstock, N.Y.

Heckler, R. S. (2003). *Being Human At Work: Bringing Somatic Intelligence Into Your Professional Life.* North Atlantic Books. Berkeley, CA.

-----. (1990). *In Search of the Warrior Spirit.* North Atlantic Books. Berkeley, CA.

-----. (1985). *Aikido and the New Warrior.* North Atlantic Books. Berkeley, CA.

-----. (1984). *The Anatomy of Change: East/West Approaches to Body/Mind Therapy.* Boston: Shambhala Publications.

Heft, J. (1999). *"Truths and Half-truths About Leadership: Ancient and Contemporary Sources".* In *Catholic School Leadership: An Invitation to Lead,* Thomas J. Hunt, et al, (Eds). Garland, Inc. New York, N.Y.

-----. (1996). *Faith and the Intellectual Life: Marianist Award Lectures.* University of Notre Dame Press. South Bend, IN.

Heifetz, R. (1994). *Leadership Without Easy Answers.* Harvard University Press. Cambridge, MA.

Heifetz, R. & Linsky, M. (2002). *Leadership on the Line: Staying Alive through the Dangers of Leading.* Harvard Business School Press. Boston, MA.

Hellinger, B., Gunthard W., & Beaumont, H. (1998). *Love's Hidden Symmetry: What Makes Love Work in Relationships.* Zeig Tucker & Co. Phoenix, AZ.

Hillman, J. (1997). *Kinds of Power.* Currency Publishing. New York, N.Y.

Hudson, F. M. & McLean, P.D. (1995). *Lifelaunch: A Passionate Guide to the Rest of Your Life.* The Hudson Institute Press. Santa Barbara, CA.

Hyams, J. (1979). *Zen in the Martial Arts.* Bantam Books. New York: NY.

Kabat-Zinn, J. (2005). *Coming to Our Senses: Healing Ourselves and the World Through Mindfulness.* Hyperion Books. New York, N.Y.

Kash, P. M. & Monte, T. (2002). *Make Your Own Luck: Success Tactics You Won't Learn in Business School.* Prentice Hall Press. Paramus, NJ.

Kegan, R. & Lahey, L. (2001). *The Real Reason People Won't Change*. Harvard Business School Publishing Corporation, OnPoint Series, Product # 8121. Available at: *www.hbsp.harvard.edu/hbronpoint*.

Kepner, J. (1987). *Body Process: A Gestalt Approach to Working with The Body in Psychotherapy*. 1995 GIC Press. Cambridge, MA.

-----. (1995). *Healing Tasks: Psychotherapy with Adult Survivors of Childhood Abuse*. 1995 Jossey-Bass, Inc. San Francisco. CA.

Koestenbaum, P. & Block, P. (2001). *Freedom and Accountability at Work: Applying Philosophic Insight to the Real World*. Jossey-Bass/Pfeiffer. San Francisco, CA.

Kornfield, J. (1993). *A Path with a Heart: A Guide through the Perils and Promises of Spiritual Life*. Bantam Books. New York, NY.

Krawchuk, F. (2003). *"A Model for Decision Making for the Military Leader"*, in *Being Human at Work* edited by Richard Strozzi Heckler. North Atlantic Books, Berkeley, CA.

Kubler-Ross. (1969). *On Death and Dying*. Macmillan Publishing Company. New York, N.Y.

Lame Deer, J. & Erdoes, R. (1972). *Lame Deer: Seeker of Visions*. Simon & Schuster, Inc. New York, N. Y.

Lee, R. (Ed.) (2004). *The Values of Connection: A Relational Approach to Ethics*. Gestalt Press. Cambridge, MA.

Lee, R. & Gordon, W. (Eds.). (1996). *The Voice of Shame: Silence and Connection In Psychotherapy*. Jossey-Bass.

Leonard, G. (1991). *Mastery: The Keys to Success and Long-Term Fulfillment*. Penguin Books. New York: N.Y.

Leupnitz, D. A. (1988). *The Family Interpreted: Psychoanalysis, Feminism and Family Therapy*. Harper Collins, New York, N.Y.

Lewis, C. S. (1946). *The Great Divorce*. MacMillan Publishing Co. New York, N.Y.

McGonagill, G. (2002). *The Coach as Reflective Practitioner*. (pps. 59 – 85), chapter in Fitzgerald and Berger (Eds.), *Executive Coaching*, Davies-Black Publishing, Palo Alto, CA.

Linden, P. (2001). *Winning is Healing: Body Awareness & Empowerment for Abuse Survivors*. CCMS Publications. Columbus, OH. (Available as an e-book at *www.being-in-movement.com*).

May, G. (2004). *The Dark Night of the Soul : A Psychiatrist Explores the Connection Between Darkness and Spiritual Growth*. HarperSanFransisco, San Francisco, CA.

McCarthy, M.P., Stein, J. & McCarthy, M. (2002). *Agile Business for Fragile Times*. McGraw-Hill Trade, New York, N.Y.

Merton, T. (1955). *No Man is an Island*. Harcourt Brace Jovanovich Publishers. New York, N.Y.

Mitchell, S. (1992). *Tao Te Ching*. (Pocket Edition). HarperPerennial. New York, N.Y.

Moore, R. & Gillette, D. (1992). *The Warrior Within: Accessing the Knight in the Male Psyche*. William Morrow and Co., Inc. New York, N.Y.

Moore, T. (1996). *The Re-Enchantment of Everyday Life*. HarperCollins Publishers. New York, N.Y.

Morgan, F. E. (1992). *Living the Martial Way: a manual for the way a modern warrior should think.* Barricade Books. Fort Lee: N.J.

Musashi, M. (2000). (Victor Harris, trans.) *A Book of Five Rings.* The Overlook Press. Woodstock, N.Y.

Neff, T. & Citrin, J. (2001). *Lessons from the Top: The Search for America's Best Business Leaders.* Doubleday Publishing, New York, N.Y.

Nijsmans, M. (1995). *"A Dionysian Way to Organizational Effectiveness.",* chapter in Stein, M. & Hollwitz, J. (Eds.) *Psyche at Work: Workplace Applications of Jungian Analytical Psychology.* Chiron Publications, Wilmette, IL.

Nevis, E., Lancourt, J., & Vassallo, H. (1996). *Intentional Revolutions: A Seven-Point Strategy for Transforming Organizations.* Jossey-Bass Publishers. San Francisco, CA.

Olson, E. & Eoyang, G. (2001). *Facilitating Organization Change: Lessons from Complexity Science.* Jossey-Bass/Pfeiffer. San Francisco, CA.

Palmer, W. (1994). *The Intuitive body: Aikido as Clairsentient Practice.* North Atlantic Books. Berkeley, CA.

Parlett, M. *The Unified Field in Practice.* Gestalt Review, Volume 1, Number 1. 1997. Malcolm's article is available on line at: http://www.gestaltreview.com/1997/parlett.html.

Peat, F. D. (1987). *Synchronicitity: The Bridge Between Mind and Matter.* Bantam. New York, N.Y.

Peters, T. (2003). *Re-Imagine!* Dorling Kindersley Publishing. New York, N.Y.

Pfeffer, J. & Sutton, R. (2000). *The Knowing-Doing Gap: How Smart Companies Turn Knowledge into Action.* Harvard Business School Press. Boston, MA.

Pfeffer, J. (1998). *The Human Equation: Building Profits by Putting People First.* Harvard Business School Press. Harvard Business School Press. Boston, MA.

Pizzo, Stephen. *"Team Building Made Easy: Shut Up & Listen."* Article published in *Business 2.0.* July 2003, page 84.

Reicheld, F. F. (2001). *Loyalty Rules! How Today's Leader Build Lasting Relationships.* Harvard Business School Press. Boston, MA.

Reps, P. (1985). *Zen Flesh, Zen Bones.* Charles E. Tuttle Co. New York, N.Y.

Reynosa, L. & Billingiere, J. (1989). *A Beginner's Guide to Aikido.* R & B Publishing Co. Ventura, CA.

Ribis, A. (2000). *Name Your Potion,* an article published in *Fuse,* December, 2000.

Saotome, M. (1993). *Aikido and the Harmony of Nature.* Shambhala. Boston, MA.

Senge, P. M. (1990). *The Fifth Discipline: The Art & Practice of The Learning Organization.* Doubleday. New York, N.Y.

Sheldrake, R. (1995). *Seven Experiments that Could Change the World.* Riverhead Books. New York, N.Y.

Shipler, D. K. (2004). *The Working Poor: Invisible in America.* Knopf. New York, N.Y.

Silverstein, M. J. & Fiske, N. (2003). *Trading Up: The New American Luxury.* Portfolio. New York, N.Y.

Spence, G. (1995). *How to Argue and Win Every Time: At Home, At Work, In Court, Everywhere, Everday.* St. Martin's Press. New York, N.Y.

Stevens, J. (1987). *Abundant Peace: The biography of Morihei Ueshiba, founder of Aikido.* Shambhala Publications. Boston, MA.

Stevens, J. & Krenner, W. (1999). *Training with the Master: Lessons with Morihei Ueshiba, founder of Aikido.* Shambhala Press. Boston, MA.

Suzuki, S. (1988). *Zen Mind, Beginner's Mind.* John Weatherhill, Inc. New York: NY.

Turpin, J. & Kurtz, L. (1997). *The Web of Violence: From Interpersonal to Global.* University of Illinois Press. Chicago, IL.

Ueshiba, M. (Stevens, J., trans.). (1992). *The Art of Peace: Teachings of the Founder of Aikido.* Shambhala Publications. Boston, MA.

Voehl, F. (1995). *Deming: The Way We Knew Him.* St. Lucie Press. Boca Raton, FL.

Warneka, T. (2002). *Everyday Terrorism: The Long Shadow of Our Hidden Dragon - Shared Factors of Terrorism and Juvenile Violence.* In *The Psychology of Terrorism: Programs and Practices in Response and Prevention (Psychological Dimensions to War and Peace Series).* Chris Stout, Ed. Praeger Publications. Westport, Con.

-----. (2000). The body psychological and psyche embodied: Embodying peace in conflict resolution using the martial art of Aikido" *The Fourth R, 92,* 3-6. (Available on-line at: http://www.clevelandtherapists.com/warneka2embodyingpeace.html).

Warner, B. (2003*). Hardcore Zen: Punk Rock, Monster Movies & the Truth About Reality.* Wisdom Publication. Summerville, MA.

Watson, L. (1990). *The Nature of Things: The Secret Life of Inanimate Objects.* Destiny Books. Rochester, VT.

Wheeler, G. (2000). *Beyond Individualism.* Analytic Press. New York, N.Y.

Wheeler, G., & Jones, D. *Finding our Sons: a Male-Male Gestalt.* In Lee, R. & Gordon, W. (Eds.). (1996). *The Voice of Shame: Silence and Connection In Psychotherapy.* Jossey-Bass. New York: N.Y.

Wilber, K. (2000). *The Collected Works of Ken Wilber, Volume 6: Sex, Ecology & Spirituality.* Second, Revised Edition. Shambhala. Boston: MA.

-----. (2000). *Integral Psychology: Consciousness, Spirit, Psychology, Therapy.* Shambhala. Boston: MA.

-----. (1997). *The Eye of Spirit: An Integral Vision for a World Gone Slightly Mad.* Boston: Shambhala Publications.

-----. (1996). *Up From Eden: A Transpersonal View of Human Evolution.* Quest Books. Wheaton, IL.

Wilhelm, R. (trans.) (1962). *The Secret of the Golden Flower: A Chinese Book of Life.* Harvest/HBJ Books. New York, N.Y.

Woodman, M. (1985). *The Pregnant Virgin: A Process of Psychological Transformation.* Inner City Books. Toronto, Canada.

Whyte, D. (2001). *Crossing the Unknown Sea: Work as a Pilgrimage of Identity.* Riverhead Books. New York, N.Y.

-----. (1994). *The Heart Aroused: Poetry and the Preservation of Soul in Corporate America.* Doubleday. New York, N.Y.

Zinker, J. (1977). *Creative Process in Gestalt Therapy.* Vintage Books. New York, N.Y.

Websites

Tim Warneka increases human performance for individuals and organizations through coaching, consulting, training, keynote speaking and wellness services. Visit Tim on-line at: *www.blackbeltconsultants.com.*

Paul Linden's website is: *http://www.being-in-movement.com.*

Wendy Palmer's website is: *http://www.consciousembodiment.com/.*

Aiki Extensions website is: *http://www.aiki-extensions.org.*

The Gestalt Institute of Cleveland's website is: *www.gestaltcleveland.org.*

Endnotes

[1] In her groundbreaking book, *The Chalice and the Blade*, Dr. Riane Eisler makes the distinction between *dominator* models and *partnership* models. Leadership today primarily operates from the dominator model. Modern organizations continue to perpetuate what Dr. Eisler refers to as *dominator hierarchies* (hierarchies based on force or the expressed or implied threat of force), thus continuing to do violence toward individuals, groups, teams, and even organizations as a whole, which includes a negative impact on the organization's bottom line. Most of the research and data that I discovered in the course of researching this book supports the basic themes found in Dr. Eisler's book.

[2] I have drawn the analogy of food and cooking, as well as the basic outline of the story that begins this book from Bert Hellinger's book, *Love's Hidden Symmetry*.

[3] For purposes of simplicity, I will often refer to leaders and employees. If "employees" does not fit your leadership situation, please feel free to substitute a word that fits better, whether that might be *student, volunteer, associate, person with lower rank* or any other word(s) that suit your particular situation.

[4] This from John Stevens, author of *Abundant Peace: The biography of Morihei Ueshiba, founder of Aikido*:

> Morihei was undoubtedly the greatest martial artist who ever lived. Even if we accept every exploit of all the legendary warriors, East and West, as being literally true, none of these accomplishments can be compared to Morihei's documented ability to disarm any attacker, throw a dozen men simultaneously, and down and pin opponents without touching them, recorded scores of times in photographs, on film and by personal testimony." (p. 67)

[5] Aikido also embodies even the Win:Win:Win strategy. See *Spiral Dynamics* for more on Win:Win:Win strategies.

[6] Thanks to Mary Heiny sensei for these valuable insights.

[7] See Wilber's *Integral Psychology* for a full explanation/description of Wilber's four-quadrant model.

[8] *Integral Psychology*, pp. 70, italics in original.

[9] Ken Wilber's reference to "second tier" organizations is in reference to Spiral Dynamics, a model for the evolution of dynamic human systems. I refer interested readers to Ken

Wilber's *Integral Psychology* and to *Spiral Dynamics* by Don Beck and Christopher Cowan. Ken Wilber's statement about no second tier organizations being in existence can be found on *www.enlightenment.com* in the "Interviews" section of that site.

[10] I have chosen not to explicitly discuss Wilber's work in the main body of this book out of concern that adding Wilber's concepts overtly into the present work would overly complicate the issue (due entirely to the limitations of my own writing skills rather than anything intrinsic to Wilber's work). For those readers familiar with Wilber's work, this book focuses on the importance of the left-hand quadrants in order to bring both subjective and intersubjective experience into the leadership dialog. To use Wilber's concepts, this book presents the enormous amount of hard data that argues for an increased awareness by leaders of peoples' interior experience. In failing to recognize the interiority of individuals and collections of individuals (groups, teams, organizations, etc.), and focusing far too long on exteriors, today's organizational structures have hurt both individual members as well as the organizations themselves, financially and otherwise.

Although not often referenced in this book, Ken Wilber's works underlie, support, and weave through everything that I have written here. I owe Ken Wilber a great debt for clarifying and illuminating a framework that is powerful, effective, and humble (if you're reading this – "Thanks, Ken!"). I refer interested readers to any of Wilber's works, and especially *Up From Eden*, *Integral Psychology* and *Sex, Ecology & Spirituality*. For more explicit applications of Wilber's work to the human performance arena from this writer, stay tuned.

[11] I am deeply aware that I am standing on the shoulders of giants. Taking an example from business leadership literature alone, from Peter Drucker starting in the 1950's and '60's to D. Edwards Deming in the 70's to Peter Block in the '80's, to Peter Senge in the '90's, all of these men have made arguments that support the premise of this book. (As I write this, I am achingly aware that all of these are men. I will be grateful to the reader who points me in the direction of women Organizational Development writers.) Beside business leadership, I have drawn from experts in the field of human performance, psychology, religion, mythology, Eastern & Western thought, Aikido, Somatic Studies, and several other areas, all of whom I have attempted to give their proper due.

[12] Source: American Institute of Stress (www.stress.org).

[13] Source: American Institute of Stress (www.stress.org).

[14] *Follow this Path*, p. 76.

[15] Source: National Institute for Occupational Safety and Health (NIOSH). NIOSH's website is: *http://www.cdc.gov/niosh/homepage.html.* NIOSH's report on stress in the workplace can be found at: *http://www.cdc.gov/niosh/stresswk.html.*). If readers are not convinced by the data that has been provided, I suggest that they simply consider the enormous popularity of Scott Adam's *Dilbert* comic strip, which is a hilarious recording of the bitterness, anger and frustration that workers experience in daily corporate life. The popularity of *Dilbert* demonstrates that Mr. Adam has clearly struck a nerve in the psyche of corporate employees.

[16] Source for stress statistics is The American Institute of Stress (www.stress.org).

[17] For example, in *Primal Leadership*, on page 13, Goleman, Boyatzis, and McKee state, "…of all the interactions at an international hotel chain that pitched employees into bad

moods, the most frequent was talking to someone in management...These interactions were the cause of distress more often than customers, work pressure, company policies, or personal problems." I am enormously indebted to the work of the authors of *Primal Leadership*, a text which became my constant companion while I was writing this book.

[18] *Follow this Path*, p.136.

[19] *Primal Leadership*, p.17-18.

[20] *Follow this Path*, p. 138.

[21] According to the National Association of Manufacturers, "Underlying the looming workforce shortage is a demographic shift of historic proportions. The Baby Boom generation will retire in large numbers, beginning in just a few years and peaking in 2012. They are not being replaced by sufficient numbers of highly skilled workers. The result is a projected 10 million unfilled positions by 2020." For further information, see http://www.nam.org/secondary.asp?CategoryID=108.

[22] *Follow this Path*, p. 145.

[23] Pete's story is described in Luzmore's chapter *Leadership Development & Increased Productivity at Work*, which can be found in Richard Strozzi Heckler's *Being Human at Work*.

[24] Please let me know how your experiments go! My use of experiments comes out of the tradition of Gestalt interventions. Gestalt practitioners hold true to the original meaning of the word *experiment* by inviting people to become more curious about the outcome rather than becoming more judgmental.

[25] For examples, see *Primal Leadership*.

[26] I want to be crystal clear here that I am arguing against neither employee of the month parking spaces nor paper certificates given for any event, perfect attendance or otherwise. To believe that misses the point entirely. The problem is the co-creation of an unhealthy dynamic between leaders and those being led that occurs in some organizations. The leaders see the employees as passive beings with no internal motivation. (I have even heard corporate leaders take this concept so far as to refer to their employees as "children" or "kids"—behind the employees' backs, of course). The leaders then believe that almost every employee behavior needs to be reinforced positively with a reward. The employees, on the other hand, do their part to keep the unhealthy dynamic in motion by refusing more and more, over time, to actually *do* anything *without* an external reward. The problem lies more with a flatland perspective of human behavior on the part of leaders and employees rather than any one particular example of such behavior (such as a paper certificate). We need to fix the problem, not just treat the symptoms.

[27] *Good to Great*, page 26.

[28] ibid, page 26.

[29] In the same vein as endnote #26, I want to be clear that I am not arguing against having consequences within organization. There are always consequences in life, and organizations are no different. Successful organizations have healthy structures, which include clear, consistent, and appropriate consequences for behavior, both positive and negative. The important point here is recognizing that many leaders use their power inappropriately through almost constant threats of punishments, which is not a model for effective leadership.

[30] *Good to Great*, page 29.

[31] Or in Collins' experience, either. As he goes on to observe, Granted, the Scott Paper story is one of the more dramatic in our study, but it's not an isolated case. In over two thirds of the comparison cases, we noted the presence of a gargantuan personal ego that contributed to the demise or continued mediocrity of the company. (*Good to Great*, p. 29)

[32] This chapter (and entire book, to some degree) is an attempt to broaden the all-too-limited discussion on workplace violence. When "workplace violence" is brought up, the conversation seems to be exclusively aimed at violence perpetrated by people at lower levels of an organizational hierarchy toward people at higher levels of an organizational hierarchy (i.e., customers/patients/students/inmates being violent toward employees/ line staff being violent toward leaders/managers/supervisors). The discussion is rarely, if ever, focused on the reverse condition, such as when people of higher status in an organizational hierarchy are violent towards people at lower levels in the hierarchy in ways that are built into the organizational structure. This is what is known as *systemic violence*. Systemic violence is a type of workplace violence that is not talked about that may be a contributing factor to the type of workplace violence that is talked about. Something is considered systemic violence when the violence that occurs is perpetrated within the existing system. While systemic violence is neither as crude (or newsworthy, apparently) as workplace violence (using the standard definition), the victims are no less traumatized. For a firsthand account of systemic violence, I suggest Barbara Ehrenreich's excellent book *Nickel and Dimed: On (Not) Getting By in America*. See also *The Working Poor: Invisible in America* by David K. Shipler.

Furthermore, remember that people are always violent *in context*, which means that while people are always responsible for their individual choices, we need to consider the broader implications of the impact of systems and organizations on individuals. For a discussion of understanding people in broader contexts, I suggest Gordon Wheeler's excellent book *Beyond Individualism*, as well as Bob Lee's *The Voice of Shame*. For considerations of violence in a wider perspective, I suggest interested readers begin with my chapter on violence *Everyday Terrorism*, as well as Turpin and Kurtz's excellent book, *The Web of Violence*.

For an example of systemic violence going unrecognized, let us turn to the FBI, the experts in violence. In 2002, the FBI held a "Violence in the Workplace" conference that brought together a multi-disciplinary group of experts from such diverse fields as the military, mental health, victim services, academia, law enforcement, government, private industry, law and labor. As a result of this symposia, this learned and experienced group produced a monograph entitled "Workplace Violence: Issues in Response" (This monograph is available on-line through the FBI's website at: http://www.fbi.gov/ publications/violence.pdf.) This monograph defines workplace violence as "murder or other violent acts by a disturbed, aggrieved employee or ex-employee against co-workers or supervisors." (p.5). While these aggressive acts should be taken very seriously, there seems to be more to the story. The definition for the four types of workplace violence that the monograph details offers little room to describe systemic violence.

Without diminishing the important foundational work that this conference and resulting monograph accomplished, nor diminishing the truly devastating impact of workplace violence (as defined by the FBI), I argue that this definition of workplace violence is not broad enough. According to the definition offered by the FBI, violence apparently only goes up the hierarchical food chain and never down. While I applaud the FBI for taking a multidisciplinary perspective, there is no mention of etiological factors in the entire monograph, which seems to side-step some important questions: *Where is this violence coming from? What are the underlying factors that support this type of violence?* The Chinese have a saying to the effect that people resort to violence when their words fail. Could any of the "aggrieved" employees' words have failed? Did they have legitimate grievances that could not be addressed to their satisfaction within the "appropriate" (i.e., legitimate) channels of the organization? Not that holding a legitimate grievance excuses the use of violence, but if there are systemic processes in our organizations that are contributing to the violence, then these processes need to be addressed, if for no other reason than public health & safety concerns.

A significant leap of logic is not required to develop the hypothesis that people who are lower on the hierarchical food chain may chose to become violent *in response* to their treatment by people higher up in the hierarchy. Speak to anyone who has worked directly under a leader who abused his/her powers and listen to the physical, emotional and mental fallout. Now, multiply that experience by 5 or 10 or 20 years and consider the implications. A tremendous amount of research suggests that when people become powerless, violence quickly becomes an option. Michael Douglas' character in the movie *Falling Down* provides us with an interesting example of this scenario.

The situation around workplace violence today is reminiscent of how sexual abuse treatment came of age in this country. Initially (and appropriately), treatment providers focused on helping and supporting victims of sexual violence. Then treatment providers began to realize that if the problem was to be solved, then the treatment of the perpetrators must be considered. They realized that treating all the victims in the world would not stop the problem of sexual violence. Consequently, the field expanded into work with sexual perpetrators. In the same way, until we collectively begin to broaden our focus of workplace violence to include an examination of the structures within our organizations that perpetuate and support individual violence, we will never make in-roads into the problem of violence in the workplace.

Looking at the above material through the lens of Ken Wilber's work brings the problem into sharper focus. We can see how flatland perspectives (such as are currently being used by most organizations) potentially contribute to violence in the workplace because they isolate and alienate people. By attending to the external considerations, such as systems and external behaviors (Wilber's Upper Right and Lower Right Quadrants), organizations fail to recognize the interiors of people (Wilber's Upper Left and Lower Left Quadrants), which do not exist in flatland perspectives. Flatland perspectives (and the violence that ensues from them) produce people who are not only alienated and disengaged from what they are doing, but who are also unaware of the impact their behavior is having on people directly involved. Failing to recognize the repercussion of flatland paradigms on people's interiors—both collectively and individually—is not only a public health issue (as seen above), but, as you will discover in this book, causes a substantial drain on a company's bottom line.

The resulting consequences of systemic violence on both people and organizations is catastrophic, ranging anywhere from illness and increased stress on individuals (as discussed in Chapter One), through significantly reduced revenues due to employee disengagement (that will be discussed in Chapter Five), and acts of physical violence (shootings, stabbings, etc.). These acts of physical violence are perpetrated upon various (often innocent) people in the workplace by those individuals who, for a variety of reasons, choose violence as a problem solving method (a more detailed discussion of which is beyond the scope of this present work.)

Finally, I want to point out my awareness of the mixed implications of my language in this footnote, specifically regarding the use of the term systemic violence to describe the impact on the interiors of individuals. Wilber is quite explicit in his works, and he states that systemic perspectives are a continuation of a flatland perspective (because they only deal with exteriors), and thus are continuing the problem at hand. However, I do not believe that everyone who uses the term systemic is only referring to external dynamics. Peter Senge clearly referred to internal dynamics in his discussion of systems in *The Fifth Discipline*. However, helpful as I find Peter Senge's work, I differ with him when he writes about so-called "learning organizations." Organizations cannot learn, because there is no consciousness ("I") that exists at the organizational level. Organizations are groups of people, not separate entities. People within organizations can learn, and organizational cultures can support or interfere with people's learning, but organizations cannot learn on their own. This is not simply a semantic difference, but has significant practical implications.

In the clinical realm, the brilliant approach of the family systems approach in the field of family therapy is very much concerned with the interior dimensions of family systems. Take for example the fascinating efforts of German therapist Bert Hellinger. His study of constellations within a family is very much body-based and focused on the interior perspective of the family collective. For more on Hellinger's work, interested readers would do well to begin with Hellinger's book *Love's Hidden Symmetry: What Makes Love Work in Relationships*.

I use the term systemic throughout this book simply because I am not aware of language that encompasses and adequately describes the people's interior at the systemic level (which would be, I imagine, a language of *community*). I would be greatly indebted to any reader that might point me in the direction of such language.

33 *The Human Equation: Building Profits by Putting People First*, p. 149.

34 I deliberately placed the word *tough* in quotes to make the point that *toughness* seems in the corporate arena to mean *mean* and *cruel*. There is certainly a place for toughness in leadership, mentoring, and teaching in the sense of strictness, discipline and order. But that toughness must be leavened with equal parts of compassion and trust, or the "toughness" simply slides into semi- (if not outright) abusive behavior on the part of the leader or person in power. Some of my best teachers, coaches and mentors were the ones who could combine these qualities of toughness and compassion/trust.

It always strikes me as odd that the people who argue the most for a "tough" (in the semi-abusive/abusive sense) approach to (insert your favorite here: managing clients, raising children, leading employees) *are always the people in power* (i.e., parent, leader, boss, employer, care-giver, etc.). I have never heard a member of any of those less-powerful ranks of clients, children, and/or employees say, "Boy, what I need is some semi-abusive behavior to toughen me up!" " When I (somewhat provocatively and half-jokingly) suggest to a person in power that perhaps he or she could gain more in our coaching, consulting, or counseling session if I were to be "tough" (in the abusive sense) on them, my offer is declined every time! Leaders would do well to remember the "golden rule" that has countless variations throughout many cultures and times: "Do not do something to another person that you would not want done to you."

[35] For those readers who are unfamiliar with Aikido, please see the Introduction to this book for a brief explanation of the art. My thanks go out to Paul Linden, Ph.D. for teaching me—in a direct, physical way—the importance of harmony in Aikido. Paul currently holds a 5th degree black belt in Aikido and is the creator of *Being In Movement*®, a somatic education process that enables people to learn more about the body as self. Paul is a relatively unknown gem of a teacher, and I encourage anyone who has the opportunity to study with him to do so. Paul can be contacted via his website at: *www.being-in-movement.com*.

[36] In fact, true dialogue (of which open and active listening is a critical component) requires at least two different perspectives. In a 2003 lecture given by University of Dayton Chancellor Fr. James Heft, S.M. at the Australian Catholic University in Sydney, Fr. Heft offered this perspective on the importance of multiple perspectives in dialogue:

> Dialogue, about which so much is written today, is impossible and pointless unless there are at least two meanings: *dia-logos* (two-way communication). When dialogue is carried on as it should be, those who think differently are not 'diabolic', i.e., 'thrown apart' (*dia-bolos*, to be thrown apart), nor do they necessarily come together in agreement. But they do grow in real understanding of, and genuine respect for, each other.

[37] I encourage readers of my work to "listen" to my words in a *both/and* voice instead of an *either/or*. Other authors who have written about emotions in organizations are bringing valuable and important information to the field. At the same time, I believe there are vast areas in which our collective understanding about emotions in organizations can be expanded. This book was written toward that end. Based upon my experience in the corporate and non-profit worlds, there are times when my voice may differ from the "conventional wisdom" of other writers. I ask that the reader not interpret my critiques and differences as "*but...*" in the sense of a negative criticism of the existing literature on emotions and business, but rather to read my work in the "*yes, and...*" vein.

[38] Neurology is the study of how the brain works. Advances in neurological research are constantly confirming a simple, scientific fact. As leadership expert Daniel Goleman observes in *Emotional Intelligence*: "...feelings are indispensable to rational decisions; they point us in the proper direction, where dry logic can then be of best use." (p. 28). Suffice it to say that more and more research demonstrates that emotions play a crucial role in our ability to use logic in our workplace. This fact runs counter to the way science (and, subsequently, American culture) has viewed emotions for much of the 20th century. The neuropsychological aspects of emotions are covered so extensively in Goleman's *Emotional Intelligence*; Goleman, Boyatzis & McKee's *Primal Leadership*; as well as in Damasio's *The Feeling of what Happens*; and *Descartes Error*, that, rather than reiterate them in this present work, I refer interested readers to these works for further information about the neurological underpinnings of emotional/intellectual life.

[39] I define warrior in a broad, three-dimensional way, believing that both men and woman can be warriors, and that warriors are not only about violence. Mahatma Gandhi and Martin Luther King Jr. were modern-day warriors. In their book *The Warrior Within: Accessing the Knight in the Male Psyche*, Moore & Gillette speak about EarthKnight. This is the type of warriorship that I am talking about in this book. I refer interested readers to both Moore & Gillette's book as well as Richard Strozzi Heckler's *In Search of the Warrior Spirit* for more discussion on what being a warrior means.

[40] *In Search of the Warrior Spirit*, p. 91.

[41] Leaders would do well to remember that seeking excellence in work is vastly difference from seeking perfection. Perfection will never happen—and that's a *good* thing!. Leadership gurus Tom Peters and Dr. W. Edward Deming both agree that the highly touted goal of "zero defects" simply does not work. For more information on Tom Peter's view of zero defects, see his book *Re-Imagine!* For Deming's view, on p. 68 of *Deming: The Way We Knew Him*, author Frank Voehl recalls that Deming considers a zero-defects approach to be "a highway down the tubes." Consider also Voehl's discussion of the Japanese concept of *michi*, "...the footsteps that a person must follow to pursue cosmic oneness and peace with the universe" (p.81), in light of the present discussion of leadership. See also Dr. Deming's point #10 in "The Fourteen Points for the Transformation of Management" on p. 124 of Rafael Aguayo's *Dr. Deming: The American Who Taught the Japanese About Quality*. For an article comparing the perspectives of Deming and Peters, see *http://www.irmi.com/Expert/Articles/2005/Pryor01.aspx*.

[42] I wish to make the point clear that allowing oneself to make mistakes is **not the same** as granting oneself permission to engage in inappropriate, unethical and/or harmful behavior. That would be abusing the freedom cited earlier in this chapter, which Gandhi so eloquently described.

[43] For more information on the medical research, see *Descartes Error* and *The Feeling of What Happens* by Antonio Damasio, as well as "The Neuroanatomy of Leadership" in Part One of Goleman, Boyatzis & McKee's *Primal Leadership*.

[44] The mind-body problem has been bothering philosophers and intellectuals for centuries. Body and mind are, in some ways that seem inexplicable, one and the same. In other ways, they are radically different. Colleagues who practice massage tell me massage (and other forms of physical manipulation) commonly unearth intense, powerful memories and emotions in people. Many mental health professionals will tell you that working with people emotionally can result in significant physical changes. The fact –is that we simply do not understand how the brain and body work as one unit. As Ken Wilber argues rather persuasively, we can <u>never</u> know, in the sense of an intellectual knowing. (See the footnote that follows.) We use metaphors to describe ourselves, but metaphors never fully capture the entire essence of who we are. Our metaphors for understanding ourselves are constantly changing. When telephones were invented, they became the main metaphor for understanding how the brain works. With the advent of computers, that technology became the primary metaphor used to conceptualize the brain. Although the metaphor of computers and circuitry generally fits when describing the brain and body system, sometimes the analogy falls short. When we use a metaphor to describe airplanes as flying like birds, we do not mean that an airplane is exactly the same thing as a bird. Brains are more than computer circuits, and people are more than brains.

In a related but slightly separate point, I refer interested readers to the seminal work of Harvard professor Howard Gardner. Recognizing that individuals experience the world in at least eight different (and equally important) ways, Dr. Gardner championed the concept of *multiple intelligences,* of which bodily-kinesthetic is one of the ways. In the language of Dr. Gardner's framework, this present work seeks to increase the bodily-kinesthetic intelligence of leaders. I join others like Richard Strozzi-Heckler, James Kepner and Wendy Palmer in going beyond Dr. Gardner's position that bodily-kinesthetic intelligence is only important for certain careers, but that increased bodily-kinesthetic intelligence serves everyone, because everyone is embodied. I refer interested readers to Dr. Gardner's many works, especially *Intelligence Reframed: Multiple Intelligences for the 21st Century.*

[45] For further consideration of the mind-body problem, I refer the interested reader to Jim Kepner's *Body Process,* chapter 1-3, as well as Ken Wilber's chapter 14 of *Integral Psychology* (with special attention paid to footnote #15). In *Integral Psychology,* Wilber points out that the solution to the mind-body problem lies in the postrational levels of human development, and "...this nondual solution isn't something that can be fully grasped at the rational level." (p. 181). In the same work, Wilber also acknowledges that these postrational stages are "...generally suspect, ignored, or actively denied by most rational researchers." (p. 181). Given my limited understanding of Wilber, the salient points that I drew from chapter 14 include:

1. Wilber considers himself a pan-interiorist, stating that, "To say that the physical universe is a universe of all exteriors and no interiors is like saying that world has all ups and no downs—it makes no sense at all. Inside and outside arise together whenever they arise; and interiors go as far down as down has any meaning" (footnote #15, pp. 279).

2. Interiors and exteriors "develop and co-evolve" in a way that is correlated (footnote #15, pp. 280).

3. The mind-body problem cannot be solved rationally without falling into either a dualistic or scientific materialistic error.

4. The solution to the mind-body problem lies beyond words. As Wilber states, the solution "...is post-rational, and fully available to all who wish to move in that direction" (pp. 182).

[46] quoted in Stevens, 1987.

[47] This chapter describes simple and basic physical movement. As with any movement practice, it never hurts to discuss these practices with your doctor before starting. By "discipline," I do not mean "a method of punishment," but rather I follow the definition that Peter Senge offered in his book *The Fifth Discipline:* "...a body of theory and technique that must be studied and mastered to be put into practice." (p. 10). Aikido is a discipline, as is learning the culinary arts. Leadership is a discipline as well. While individual people contribute their own innate "gifts" that make leadership more or less easier for them, everyone who commits themselves to the discipline of leadership can learn to become a great leader.

[48] This quote was taken from p.232 in Scott Adams' book, *The Joy of Work: Dilbert's Guide to Finding Happiness at the Expense of Your Co-workers.* Besides containing outrageously hilarious comics and commentary, Mr. Adams' books often interweave serious, accurate,

and sophisticated observations about human behavior. I refer interested readers to Chapter 14 of *The Dilbert Future: Thriving on Stupidity in the 21ˢᵗ Century*. The chapter is entitled, *A New View of the Future*, where Mr. Adams explicitly turns "the humor mode off." In discussing the importance of "better perception instead of better vision," Mr. Adams notes, "One of our most fundamental beliefs is that the things we see with our eyes are a good approximation of reality." (p.227) He believes that we continue to hold onto major optical illusions, and he goes on to say,

"What are the odds that you live in exactly the window of human existence when all the major optical illusions have been discovered? Wouldn't that be an amazing coincidence, since every previous generation of human has believed they were born in that window of time? They were all wrong, but they all thought they were right, just like we do now." (p.228)

Given his depth of understanding of business, I'm amazed that Mr. Adams is not a multi-millionaire consultant at this point in his career. Apparently, poking fun at consultants by drawing cartoons is more lucrative and fulfilling for Mr. Adams than actually being one! (The only rational response one can give to Mr. Adam's choice is: "Hey, Scott! Can you teach me how to draw?!?")

[49] Thanks to Denise Tervo for teaching me this wonderful practice.

[50] Thanks for Paul Linden for teaching me this Love/Hate exercise.

[51] I came across the concept of the *tomato effect* in the book *Racketeering in Medicine: The Suppression of Alternatives*, page 102 by James Carter, M.D., Dr.P.H.

[52] This story can be found *ibid*, pps. 102-103.

[53] Found on-line at: http://www.ers.usda.gov/briefing/tomatoes/background.htm.

[54] Source: USDA website.

[55] Source: the respective drug companies' websites at: *www.zoloft.com* and *www.prozac.com*.

[56] See the article *"Name your Potion"* by Ali Ribis (2000) for more information about naming drugs. In regards to naming, legal drugs are no different from illegal street drugs. No matter who is doing the naming—whether a multi-billion dollar pharmaceutical company or a street dealer—both are after the same thing: creating a name that sells more of the drugs.

[57] See *Follow This Path* for a full description of the data. Highlights of their data pool include:

- 10 million customers and over 200,000 managers surveyed.
- 3 million employees interviewed between 1995 and 2001.
- All major industries, from fast-food chains to physicians groups were represented.
- A wide variety of job types included, as were all kinds of customers.
- This in-depth study crossed gender, race and ethnicity boundaries as it assembled data on various types of occupations, nationalities, age groups, levels of education and discretionary income and spending habits.

[58] *Follow this Path*, p. 145.

[59] *ibid*, p. 129. On a related but slightly separate note, in a 2003 lecture given by University of Dayton Chancellor Fr. James Heft, S.M. at the Australian Catholic University in Sydney, suggests using the word "engagement" in place of Harvard political theorist Michael Sandel's phrase "deliberative tolerance," which Sandel uses to describe, in Fr.

Heft's words, "an attitude of engagement rather than indifference." " This definition fits quite nicely into this present work. For a full transcription of Fr. Heft's lecture, see *http://dlibrary.acu.edu.au/research/theology/ejournal/aejt_2/James_Heft.htm*

[60] *Follow this Path*, p. 131.

[61] *ibid*, p. 133.

[62] The concept of Deep Knowledge is borrowed from a Taoist work written in medieval times entitled *The Book of Balance and Harmony*. Deep Knowledge, the Taoists wrote, "...is to be aware of disturbance before disturbance, to be aware of danger before danger, to be aware of destruction before destruction, to be aware of calamity before calamity...by deep knowledge of principle, one can change disturbance into order, change danger into safety, change destruction into survival, change calamity into fortune." (From *The Book of Harmony*, cited in Cleary's *Art of War*, p. 11).

[63] *Make Your Own Luck*, p. 169.

[64] I am using the term "worldview" in a similar sense to Peter Senge's "mental models" in *The Fifth Discipline* (see especially Chapter 10 in that work).

[65] For more information on the creation of organizational reality, see Chapter 2 entitled "Building A New Consciousness" in Nevis, Lancourt & Vassallo's excellent book *Intentional Revolutions*.

[66] Besides my own direct experience in coaching, consulting and clinical work, I have drawn the rules for emotional logic from a variety of sources, including both Jungian and Gestalt thought. Other thoughts I found to be of value included those of English writer Rupert Sheldrake, who (following many venerable traditions) proposed in *Seven Experiments that Could Change the World* that consciousness is not merely restricted to working through the brain, and that consciousness somehow has the ability to shape and impact natural laws. Further, in *The Nature of Things*, author Lyall Watson considers a concept that Nature can somehow take our "emotional fingerprints." There are probably many other sources for these ideas, as well, that I have either forgotten or have not been exposed to. The main point is this—that although speaking or writing about "enchantment" and other ways of thinking besides "logic" was typically seen as the realm of either children or the insane during the 20th century, more and more scientist-practitioners from physics, psychology, medicine and a host of other disciplines are increasingly coming to similar conclusions. In the words of Jungian Roger Brooke in his excellent book *Pathways into the Jungian World*: "[Jung] recollected what our culture has forgotten: a perceptual understanding that the world is a temple and the earth is consecrated ground." (p.14).

[67] For more on keeping the focus of change on oneself, I refer interested readers to Peter Block's excellent discussion in *The Answer to How is Yes*.

[68] For more on the importance of the poet at in the workplace, see David Whyte's two books, *The Heart Aroused* and *Crossing the Unknown Sea*.

[69] For more information on the underlying neurological issues, see Goleman, Boyatzis and McKee's *Primal Leadership*, chapters 2, 3 and 6; especially pps. 102 – 108. See also Damasio's *The Feeling of What Happens*.

[70] This was later confirmed by several of Marcia's direct reports.

[71] *Who Says Elephants Can't Dance?*, pps. 181- 182, italics in original, bold added for emphasis.

[72] *Make Your Own Luck*, p. 44.

[73] For more on the importance of interdependence to leaders, see Riane Eisler's discussion of the dominator model vs. the partnership model in her excellent book *The Chalice & The Blade*.

[74] *ibid.*, p. 45.

[75] The mainstream mental health profession views people through the *success/failure* position. For example, one of the failures of modern day psychotherapy, in developing relationships with managed care organizations, is the requirement for all clients/patients to have a formal medical diagnosis in order to meet "medical necessity," without which, mental health practitioners will not be reimbursed by insurance companies. This diagnostic imperative is often unnecessary. A person might be going through a divorce, the loss of a job, or the death of a child, but in order to receive mental health services through one's insurance benefits, one must be diagnosed as having a mental illness. Many mental health practitioners (the author included) are opposed to this type of diagnosis-on-demand, and have set up private practices outside of the managed care realm in order to avoid this success/failure mentality.

[76] *Primal Leadership*, p. 153.

[77] *ibid.*, p. 153, italics/bold added for emphasis.

[78] This example is used for illustrative purposes and is not meant in any way as a criticism of Goleman, Boyatzis, & McKee, all three of whom I hold in nothing but the highest regard. The success/failure trap, and the subsequent interpretive labeling that flows out of it is so rampant in our culture, that the authors of *Primal Leadership* cannot be blamed for falling into the trap. Anyone with any experience in the field of human performance and leadership (this author included) has fallen into this trap inadvertently. It is precisely because the success/failure trap is so rampant that awareness of the trap is crucial for leaders.

[79] My introduction to the Gestalt concept of creative adjustment came from my post-graduate training at the Gestalt Institute of Cleveland. Another idea that was central to my understanding of creative adjustment was Gestalt therapist Jim Kepner's concept of "right figure, wrong ground," which he writes about in page 224 of his book *Healing Tasks*. For more information about Gestalt, visit the Gestalt Institute of Cleveland's website at: www.gestaltcleveland.org.

[80] The Gestalt Cycle of Experience that I refer to throughout this book is a process model that I learned at the Gestalt Institute of Cleveland. Thanks to Edwin Nevis for clarifying several questions on the cycle for me. Edwin current teaches and trains out of the Gestalt International Study Center (GISC) at Cape Cod. The GISC website is: www.gisc.org.

[81] Additional information on the Cycle of Experience can be found on pps. 90-93 in Joseph Zinker's *Creative Process in Gestalt Therapy*.

[82] This is as important for leaders as well as consultants and coaches. For a relevant article, see Steven Berglas' article on *"The Very Real Dangers of Executive Coaching,"* which appeared in the June 2002 edition of the *Harvard Business Review*.

[83] For a variety of reasons, the numbers of sexually abused males is very likely drastically underreported. When considering sexual abuse, I prefer to keep in mind the 1:4 ratio for both genders. For more information on victimization issues in our culture, see my chapter on juvenile violence.

[84] Many people are sent to coaching or therapy because they are told that *they* are the problem. The person being sent to therapy and/or coaching is usually the one with less power in the relationship. For example, children have less power than their parents. Only parents bring their children in for therapy—children and teens rarely ask for therapy on their own. When I ask parents what the problem is, Rarely ever have I heard a parent say: "I think the problem is with my parenting style." " More typically, the blame game begins. The parent says, "The problem with Johnny is that he doesn't listen and doesn't know how to show respect and I want you to *change* him!"

When I talk with parents who want me to "fix" Johnny in therapy, I explain to them that their presence is required in the sessions. *That* news usually raises a few eyebrows. I find myself imagining that the parents had been counting on the free hour they were going to enjoy while Johnny was being "fixed" by this goof-ball therapist—almost the same as dropping your car off for an oil change and going shopping.

In the same vein, when I am called in to work with an organization, I typically meet with the executive who is requesting the consultation or coaching. Do you think he says, "Tim, I think there is something wrong with my management style?" " Never! What he usually says is, "The problem with my managers (or line staff or contract people)....I want you to *fix* them!"

If the leaders in power are not willing to change, then there is usually very little chance that the manager or line staff (or whomever who holds little power) is going to change. So, if the leaders buy into coaching or consultation process, they begin the process—which involves change, which involves conflict, which can be, at times, very painful and difficult, and which ultimately can be very rewarding.

[85] I reference systems thinking here with the full awareness that Ken Wilber describes systems thinking as part of flatland because (at least as I understand Wilber) systemic processes are based on exteriors and leave out the interiors. While I agree with Wilber on this point completely, I write about systemic processes (understanding that they are exteriors) in this present work simply because leaders have to start somewhere. This is the same tack that is taken by Peter Senge in his best-selling book, *The Fifth Discipline*, the fifth discipline being systemic thinking.

Assuming that developmental understanding flows from exterior awareness to interior awareness, then it logically follows that leaders need to develop an awareness of systems (Wilber's Right Hand Quadrants) in order to develop an appreciation, awareness and sensitivity for the interior perspectives (Wilber's Left Hand Quadrants) of those same systems. In my experience, many leaders simply fail to appreciate or even recognize the interactions of systems. One cannot appreciate the interior of a holon (a whole that is part of another whole) until one recognizes the existence—the exterior—of that holon. (If I'm correct on this point, I'm certain that Wilber has elucidated the point more clearly than I. Any knowledgeable reader who can point me to the proper Wilber citation would be deeply appreciated.)

[86] The paradoxical theory of change comes out of the Gestalt human potential movement. For more on the paradoxical theory of change, see Beisser's 1970 article *The Paradoxical Theory of Change*, as well as Sylvia Crocker's excellent book, *A Well-Lived Life: Essays in Gestalt Therapy*.

[87] *Primal Leadership*, page 99.

88 The concepts of *figure* and *ground* are taken from Gestalt psychology.

89 The concepts of figure and ground also explain how well-intentioned people of equal intelligence and insight can arrive at vastly different solutions to problems, as you will see further on in this book.

90 For a slightly different (but related) perspective on individual change, see Kegan and Lahey's excellent article, *The Real Reason People Won't Change.*

91 For a further explanation of Scientific Management and other management processes, I suggest reading Brindle and Stearns' (2001) excellent book: *Facing Up to Management Faddism: A New Look at an Old Force.*

92 ...and a member of the human race. For a further discussion of anxiety and mistakes, stumblings and miscalculations as indications of membership in humanity, see Koestenbaum & Block (2001).

93 Several schools of psychological thought—most notably Jungian and Gestalt—have identified what I will refer to here as *polarities.* As used here, the concept of polarities also draws somewhat from Hegel's concepts of *thesis, antithesis* & *synthesis.*

94 *Bulfinch's Mythology* p. 898.

95 The fact that the bull is the symbol of a prosperous stock market is not without irony in light of this myth.

96 For more on tyrants in organizations, see Tom Peter's book *Re-Imagine!*, particularly Tom's foreword.

97 The case for seeking to master hard skills should be obvious to most leaders. For additional reasons (beyond this book) about why soft skills are important in a business environment, I refer interested readers to Daniel Goleman's book *Working with Emotional Intelligence*, and particularly Chapter 3, "*The Hard Case for Soft Skills*".

98 To be maintained, employees' basic emotional engagement levels must be supported and monitored through dialogue and relationship. To do otherwise violates the spirit of emotional engagement. For more on the importance of dialogue in the business setting, I refer interested readers to Peter Block's wonderful book *The Answer to How is Yes.*

99 *Primal Leadership*, pps. 19-20.

100 ibid., p. 20.

101 *Aikido and the Harmony of Nature*, p.68

102 In their book *The Warrior Within*, Robert Moore and Douglas Gillette call for men to become EarthKnights and put forth an "EarthKnight Manifesto," which echoes many of the qualities and principles found in this present work.

103 For the purposes of this book, I will assume that the reader has a basic familiarity with the story of *A Christmas Carol.* For those unfamiliar with the story, I suggest a quick trip to a nearby bookstore, library or video store. Any version will do. The book is not copyrighted and the text remains in the public domain. Interested readers can download an electronic version of the book at Project Gutenberg's website, *www.gutenberg.org.* My favorite movie version has George C. Scott in the role of Scrooge. For those leaders with children (or the young at heart), the movie *A Muppet's Christmas Carol* is quite enjoyable for all ages, while staying fairly close to the story. In fact, inspiration for this section struck me while I was watching the Muppet's version with my wife and children.

104 For further understanding of the archetypal journey of transformation, interested readers are referred to Joseph Campbell's 1949 classic *The Hero with a Thousand Faces*, in

which Campbell outlines "The Hero's Journey", which is the transformational journey discussed in process language. Campbell identified the steps of the Hero's Journey as *Departure, Initiation,* and *Return.* Although outside the scope of this present work, a fascinating written piece of work lies in describing Scrooge's transformation through the lens of Campbell's Hero's Journey.

[105] Kubler-Ross identified the stages as: (1) Denial & Isolation; (2) Anger; (3) Bargaining; (4) Depression; and (5) Acceptance.

[106] Leaders sometimes erroneously use "Science" and "Research" as a subtle way of pressuring people to accept whatever emotional worldview the leader is holding at the time. I capitalize "Science" and "Research" to identify them as scientific materialistic worldviews rather than truly open-minded science and research. I have noticed that leaders who use scientific materialism to defend their pet world-views (usually without being aware that they are doing so) speak of "Science" and "Research" less as areas of exploration and learning and more like twin gods whose capitalized names should be spoken with reverence. But true science and research—by definition—never have the final word on a subject. Leaders—who should be educated consumers of science and research—should be aware that both fields are frequently subject to outside influences. For example, a recent article in *USA Today* reported a study published in the *Journal of the American Medical Association* which identified that about one-fourth of biomedical researchers have financial ties to companies whose products they are studying, while about two-thirds of schools have financial ties to start-ups investigating new drugs. Research led by Yale University professor Cary Gross showed that industry funding increases the likelihood that a study result will be 3.6 times more favorable to the sponsor. The article continues with the observation of a watchdog organization: "There is a lot of idealism about how science is isolated and objective," says bioethicist Virginia Ashby Sharpe of the Center for Science in the Public Interest. "Unfortunately, that's not the case. Money can absolutely influence scientists." " The USA Today article can be found on-line at: *http://www.usatoday.com/news/education/2003-01-22-reearch-funds_x.htm.* The website for the *Center for Science in the Public Interest* is: *http://www.cspinet.org/.* For more on Scientific Materialism see Ken Wilber's *Integral Psychology,* esp. pp. 50-65, noting that Wilber describes the currently dominant scientific materialistic worldview (which he terms "flatland"—see endnotes #7-12, above) with words such as "chilling" and "horrifying." See also Chapter 12, "The Collapse of Kosmos," in Wilber's *Sex, Ecology & Spirituality.*

[107] Dickens, Charles. *A Christmas Carol.* Retrieved 19 June 2005, from the World Wide Web. http://www.online-literature.com/dickens/christmascarol/1/.

[108] Ibid.

[109] Dickens, Charles. *A Christmas Carol.* Retrieved 19 June 2005, from the World Wide Web. http://www.online-literature.com/dickens/christmascarol/2/.

[110] Ibid.

[111] Ibid.

[112] The wise Lao Tzu has this to say about the process of moving backwards in order to move forward:

The generals have a saying: "Rather than make the first move it is better to wait and see. Rather than advance one inch it is better to retreat a yard. This is called going forward without advancing, pushing back without using weapons. (Tao Te Ching, Chapter 69)

[113] Goleman, Boyatzis, & McKee discuss many paradoxes throughout *Primal Leadership*.

[114] Dickens, Charles. *A Christmas Carol*. Retrieved 19 June 2005, from the World Wide Web. http://www.online-literature.com/dickens/christmascarol/3/.

[115] Ibid.

[116] For more on this concept, see Peter Block's excellent discussions of freedom in his book *The Answer to How is Yes*.

[117] Dickens, Charles. *A Christmas Carol*. Retrieved 19 June 2005, from the World Wide Web. http://www.online-literature.com/dickens/christmascarol/4/.

[118] Ibid.

[119] Dickens, Charles. *A Christmas Carol*. Retrieved 19 June 2005, from the World Wide Web. http://www.online-literature.com/dickens/christmascarol/5/.

[120] We can speak in psychological terms of repression and trauma and the like, but sometimes jargon has a way of distancing us from reality in ways that are not helpful.

[121] For more discussion on the non-dual nature of yin and yang, see Richard Wilhelm's discussion of Tao, *yin* and *yang* on page 12 of *The Secret of the Golden Flower: A Chinese Book of Life*, translated by Richard Wilhelm with a commentary by C.G. Jung.

[122] Such is our paucity of understanding yin power that we do not even have language to discuss power in terms of polarity. That is to say, when one speaks of power in organizations, the default assumption is that one is talking about power in its yang form. The absence of language around phenomena powerfully impacts how we construct reality.

[123] I am constantly amazed at how similar the process of juvenile aggression mirrors so many other aspects in our culture. We adults seem to handle situations in a similar process to our teens, albeit in a more sophisticated fashion. But whether adult or teen, the negative side effects of our over-reliance on yang style problem solving methods remain the same. For more on the cultural underpinnings of juvenile violence in America (which has a great deal of similarity with corporate culture), see my chapter on juvenile violence, *Everyday Terrorism: The Long Shadow of Our Hidden Dragon*.

[124] This "sign of weakness" is especially true with males in our culture. If men back down, not only is their behavior called into question, but so is the very essence of their masculinity. For many in our culture, men who back down are no longer seen as men. This inability to value and respect the power of yin is having a significant impact on all of us—children, adolescents and adults, as well as on our domestic and foreign policies.

[125] For more on the Emotional Economy, see Silverstein & Fiske's important work in their book *Trading Up: The New American Luxury*.

[126] However, keep in mind the importance of distinguishing the difference between keeping employees informed with information that is relevant to their jobs, and flooding them with information that serves no purpose. I have coached countless individuals who report being flooded (and feeling overwhelmed) by the amount of extraneous information provided by their organizations. Wise leaders share information effectively.

[127] The management theory of Action Science carries similar concepts, entitled *espoused theory* and *theory-in-use*. For more on Action Science, see McGonagill in Fitzgerald & Berger, 2002. For a similar discussion, see also Jeffrey Pfeiffer's excellent book *The*

Knowing-Doing Gap: How Smart Companies Turn Knowledge into Action, especially Chapter 1, "*Knowing "What" to Do is Not Enough.*"

[128] *The E-myth Revisited,* p. 192, italics in original.

[129] Whenever I hear presenters brag about how much they enjoy conflict, I'm always half tempted to rise out of my seat and start shouting and throwing chairs. I have always been too afraid to do this, but I am always curious to see how much the presenter walks his talk when faced with escalating conflict. After years of working closely with a broad range of people, my experience is that there is something deeply innate within us that invites us to move away from conflict (most likely as a mechanism for survival). To be successful, people need to learn to modulate this desire to move away from conflict, but the impulse is always there. Consequently, I tend to distrust people who claim not to experience this desire to move away from conflict.

[130] From *A Path with a Heart,* p. 73.

[131] I drew this exercise from a similar exercise in John Daido Loori's book, *The Zen of Creativity.* Another helpful book is *Coming to Our Senses: Healing Ourselves and the World Through Mindfulness,* by Jon Kabat-Zinn. I also recommend the excellent mindfulness practices that Wendy Palmer suggests in her book *The Intuitive Body.* For a Gen-X account of mindfulness practice, Brad Warner's *Hardcore Zen* is a great place to start. A word for newcomers to mindfulness practice: Although the concept of mindfulness sounds exciting, the day-to-day practice of mindfulness is, in fact, rather boring. But the practice works. In fact, Peter Senge states that the idea for his best-selling book *The Fifth Discipline* came to him suddenly when he was practicing mindfulness. So, keep plugging away, and let me know how it works for you.

[132] If there isn't any truth to the statement that the person bringing you the problem is neither competent nor capable, then you have an entirely different, deeper set of leadership problems that need to be addressed.

[133] Avoiding personal responsibility goes hand-in-hand with avoiding feelings of guilt. For a fascinating perspective on guilt in relation to personal responsibility, I encourage interested readers to read Hellinger's book *Love's Hidden Symmetry.*

[134] See Bill Moyer's interviews with Joseph Campbell in *The Power of Myth,* p. 151.

[135] *Creative Mythology,* p. 540, italics in original.

[136] Paraphrased from *The Power of Myth,* p. 151.

[137] This quote is often wrongly attributed to Nelson Mandela. It was actually written by Marianne Williamson in her book, *A Return to Love.* Thanks to Wendy Palmer for setting me straight on this quote.

[138] *Lessons from the Top,* p. 188

[139] *The Eye of Spirit,* pps.15-16, italics in original.

[140] *How to Argue and Win Every Time,* p. 113, italics in original. I suggest this book as a "must-read" for anyone interested in either stories and/or public speaking (and as a mission-critical read for leaders).

[141] I tell stories from my experiences in consulting, coaching and psychotherapy. I am assuming that the majority of readers will be unfamiliar with the practitioner's perspective of psychotherapy. I use the examples from my psychotherapy practice because, when I am first learning something, I find that hearing about a process in an unfamiliar area can help me better digest the learning I want to accomplish.

[142] Fr. Heft spoke these words at the December 8th, 2004 celebration of Christmas on Campus at the University of Dayton. Christmas on Campus is a celebration of the Catholic feast of the Immaculate Conception that is steeped in the wonderful hospitality endemic to the Society of Mary (the Catholic religious order that founded and runs the University) and to the University. If you've never had the opportunity to participate in this event, I recommend that you do if at all possible. The full text of Fr. Heft's speech can be found at: *http://alumni.udayton.edu/NP_Story.asp?storyID=1887.*

INDEX

QUICK ORDER FORM

To order this book on-line (or to learn about our e-book and audio versions of this book) please visit us on-line at *www.blackbeltconsultants.com*

This book is available at quantity discounts for orders of 10 or more copies for individuals, corporations, institutions and organizations. Sections of this book can be customized into Specialized Booklets and Promotional Material for your corporation, organization, team, and institution. For **Quotes on larger Quantities or for Special Sales orders**, please contact Patrick at Patrick@blackbeltconsultants.com or by calling (440) 944-4746.

****

Name: _____

Address: _____

E-mail: _____

Phone Number: (   ) _____ - _____ (home)

Please send me (price subject to change):
_____ copies of this book **in paperback** @ $15.95 each.   = $_____ USD
_____ copies of this book **in hardback** @ $24.95 each.   = $_____ USD

                                        + shipping/tax*   = $_____ USD

       TOTAL AMOUNT DUE   = $_____ **USD**

SHIPPING U.S.: $5.00 for first copy + $2.00 for each additional book. International: Call/email for quote.

*Sales Tax: Ohio residents only, please add 7% for sales tax.

Payment
[ ] Check enclosed - made payable to "The Black Belt Consulting Group"
[ ] Please charge my credit card: MasterCard [ ] or Visa [ ]

Name on Card: _____
Card Number:_____
Expiration Date:_____
Security Code:_____ (3 digits from back of card)

Signature (required for processing):_____

Please send completed form with payment to:
The Black Belt Consulting Group
P. O. Box 20
Cleveland, OH 44092

Printed in the United States
38061LVS00005B/259-276

9 780976 862710